EASY HITS PIANO EDITION

Plus Uke & Guitar Chords

Alfred's *Easy*

Best-Loved CHILDREN'S SONGS

MP3 DOWNLOADS

To demonstrate what the songs sound like, professional MP3 recordings of every song can be downloaded from **Alfred.com/EasyChildrensSongs.** The MP3s can be saved one by one as needed, or downloaded in full as a .zip file.

Produced by
Alfred Music
P.O. Box 10003
Van Nuys, CA 91410-0003
alfred.com

Printed in USA.

ISBN-10: 1-4706-3765-0
ISBN-13: 978-1-4706-3765-1

Besides noted exceptions, cover and inside images sourced from Getty Images, Freepik.com, and Vecteezy.com • Images sourced from Wikimedia Commons: pg. 12 top left (by Dave Menke), pg. 12 top right (by Carl Chapman), pg. 46, pg. 54 (by L. Leslie Brooke), pg. 92 (by Paul Downey), pg. 93 (by William Wallace Denslow), pg. 94, pg. 126 (by Eugène Joseph Verboeckhoven), and pg. 180 (by Carl Massmann) • pg. 158 image sourced from the Library of Congress, LC-DIG-ppmsc-05241

All songs arranged by Bill Galliford and Ethan Neuburg • Recordings by Bill Galliford, Ethan Neuburg, Jack Allen, and Aaron Stang • Vocals by Alaina Lorenzo and Joy Galliford; children's vocals courtesy of South Florida Music.

Facts in "About the Songs" section were compiled from various online sources, including Wikipedia.org.

Contents

Genre Index

Musical Round Songs

Nursery Rhymes

Religious Songs

Rocking Songs

Silly Songs

Spirituals

Transportation Songs

About the Songs

"A-Hunting We Will Go" is a British folk song written by Thomas Arne for a 1777 production of *The Beggar's Opera* (the source for Bertolt Brecht and Kurt Weill's *The Threepenny* Opera). It was originally sung by the character Macheath (also known as Mack the Knife), an infamous highwayman/robber. The simple rhyme, tune, and lyrics have since made it a popular children's song.

"All the Pretty Little Horses" is an American lullaby. It began as a quiet song that African slaves would sing to their own babies as they left to go take care of their masters' children. The original lyrics contained the following disturbing lines:

> Way down yonder, down in the meadow,
> Sweet little baby crying "mama,"
> The birds and the butterflies peckin' at his eyes.
> Sweet little baby crying, "mama."

"All Through the Night" is a very old Welsh folk song ("Ar Hyd y Nos"). The well-known English lyrics presented here were written by Harold Boulton in 1884. Starting from the original somber Welsh theme of a dim starlight that softens the affliction of old age, Boulton converted the tune to a gentle lullaby of comfort sung to a young child laying in bed.

"Alouette," the unofficial song of French Canada, was probably created by French fur traders in colonial Canada. Most English speakers are probably unaware that *alouette* is French for "lark," a favorite food of the fur traders; the lyrics of the song detail plucking the various parts of a bird in preparation for cooking. Like "Frère Jacques" and "Row, Row, Row Your Boat," "Alouette" is often sung as a round.

"The Alphabet Song" is familiar to generations of English speakers as the mnemonic device by which they memorized the alphabet. The melody of "The Alphabet Song" is the same as "Twinkle, Twinkle, Little Star" and "Baa, Baa, Black Sheep." The tune can be traced to a French nursery rhyme that was famously incorporated by W.A Mozart in his *Twelve Variations on "Ah vous dirai-je, Maman"*, K. 265/300e (ca. 1781). In 1835, American music publisher Charles Bradlee copyrighted "The Alphabet Song" lyrics.

"The Animal Fair" is a nonsensical 19th-century tune silly enough to entertain both children and adults for more than a century.

"Apples and Bananas" is an American folk song. The song is basically a game in which you repeat the same lines while changing vowel sounds in each successive verse. Boasting recordings by both Barney (the purple dinosaur) and Raffi (the Canadian singer/songwriter), the tune is especially popular with toddlers, since apples and bananas tend to be their most favorite fruits.

"Baa, Baa, Black Sheep" is an English nursery rhyme. Its melody is derived from the same 18th-century French tune as "The Alphabet Song" and "Twinkle, Twinkle, Little Star." The lyrics could refer to high taxation on wool, which began in England in the 13th century and persisted for hundreds of years. One for the master (King Edward I) / One for the Dame (The Church) / And one for the little boy who lives down the lane (the citizens).

"The Bear Went Over the Mountain" is an American folk song that uses the melody of "For He's a Jolly Good Fellow." The idea of a bear climbing over a mountain just "to see what he could see" might be based on German folklore similar to our own Groundhog Day, or may be a metaphor for the search for something different or exciting when, as the saying goes, "wherever you go, there you are."

"Billy Boy" is thought to be from 19th century England and was originally "Willie Lad" or "Charming William." The song was often sung as a shanty.

"Bingo" is a spelling song attributed to a London actor named William Swords, with the song first appearing in print around 1780. There have been many variations in the name of the animal and its owner's profession, but the fun inherent in spelling and clapping means the song is always associated with children's games.

"Bobby Shafto" is an early 19th-century English folk song. It is purportedly based on Robert Shafto, an 18th-century British member of parliament.

"Boys and Girls Come Out to Play" was first published in England in 1708. With the lyrics "the moon does shine as bright as day," the song refers to a time when children were expected to work most of the day (as were adults) and playtime was reserved for after supper.

"Brahms' Lullaby (Lullaby and Goodnight)" The melody familiar to most as "Brahms' Lullaby" (a.k.a. "The Cradle Song") is actually titled *"Wiegenlied: Guten Abend, Gute Nacht."* Johannes Brahms dedicated this lovely song to his friend (and lifelong love) Bertha Faber on the birth of her second child. Between the notes of the melody is another melody, this one from a German love song (*"S' Is Anderscht"*) that Bertha used to sing to Johannes on romantic walks ten years prior. In appreciation, Bertha named her second child Johannes.

"Brush Your Teeth" is a song that gets the seal of approval from the American Dental Association.

"Cockles and Mussels (Molly Malone)" is a sad tale of a sweet fishmonger in Dublin who succumbed to a fever while plying her wares from a wheelbarrow. Contrary to popular legend, Molly Malone is a fictitious character, and the song was a mid-19th century music-hall creation.

"Come Little Leaves" is a children's song by American poet George Cooper and composer Thomas J. Crawford.

"Deck the Hall" is a traditional Welsh New Year's Eve carol dating back to the 16th century. Thomas Oliphant wrote the English lyrics, more an interpretation than a translation of the original Welsh words by poet John Jones (a.k.a. Talhaiarn). The song did not start being called by the name "Deck the Hall" until about the 1930s.

"Did You Ever See a Lassie?" was first published in the U.S. in the late 19th century. Its exact origins are unknown, but, from the use of "laddie" and "lassie," most assume its author was of Scottish origin.

"Do Your Ears Hang Low" is an American adaptation of the early 19th-century folk tune "Turkey in the Straw." The song's melody is often played over the loudspeakers of ice cream trucks as they drift through residential neighborhoods on summer days.

"Down by the Bay" features the Greek folk-song melody *"Yalo Yalo"* punctuated by the refrain of "my mother will say …" followed by rhyming nonsense lyrics that children love.

"Down in My Heart (I've Got the Joy)" was composed by 19th-century American minister George W. Cooke. With its call-and-response lyrics, it has become a very popular gospel standard.

"Eency Weency Spider" is a classic children's song, made unique by the specificity of the hand gestures that usually accompany its performance. Early instances of the song include a 1910 appearance in the book *Camp and Camino in Lower California*, but there it was called the "Spider Song." Like many songs from the folk tradition, variations in the lyrics and title abound, but when you hear the melody, it's unmistakably "Eency Weency Spider."

"The Farmer in the Dell" is a late 19th-century American adaptation of a German folk song from earlier in the century. It is often performed as part of a game where children standing in a circle are designated as characters from the lyrics. With each successive verse, one more child leaves the circle to join "the farmer" in the center until "the cheese stands alone."

"Father's Whiskers" is often attributed to Englishman Frank Wood from the early 1900s. But this silly song with nonsensical lyrics likely predates Wood's performance and copyright claim.

"Five Little Monkeys" is a children's counting song used to help children learn numbers 1 through 5.

"Frère Jacques/Are You Sleeping" has an unknown origin, but this French round was first published in the late 18th century. It has subsequently been translated into many languages (including the English version "Brother John") and, surprisingly, The Beatles sing "Frère Jacques" as the background vocal part in the third verse of "Paperback Writer."

"Frog Went A-Courtin'" originated in Scotland more than 450 years ago. The English version of the song has developed at least 150 variations on the verses, but almost always retains some original nonsense lyrics in the chorus. "Frog Went A-Courtin'" has become a folk music standard with recordings by everyone from Burl Ives to Bruce Springsteen.

"Go In and Out the Window" is an English nursery rhyme that is often performed as part of a children's game.

"Goodnight, Ladies" has been attributed to American composer Edwin Pearce Christy, who published the first part of the song in 1847 as "Farewell, Ladies." The chorus ("Merrily we roll along…") is sung to the melody of "Mary Had a Little Lamb."

"The Grande Olde Duke of York" is an English nursery rhyme that refers to either Richard of York from the War of the Roses (15th century) or Frederick, Duke of York (late 18th century). Both dukes led unsuccessful campaigns in battle. "The Grande Olde Duke of York" is customarily performed as an action song, with children moving "up," "down," and "half-way up" along with the lyrics.

"Happy Wanderer" This sprightly song's lyrics were written in the 19th century by one Florenz Friedrich Sigismund, and its tune was written after World War II by Friedrich-Wilhelm Möller. The original composition is German, but funny enough, the specific pronunciation of the refrain *"Val-da-ri, val-da-ra"* is actually French. The pronunciation is derived from the woman who translated the song into English, Antonia Ridge, who first heard the French translation and liked the sound of the soft "f" better.

"Head, Shoulders, Knees, and Toes" first appeared in the 1950s, and often is used as a song that children can exercise to while singing. At a galloping tempo, kids touch the body part named in the song as each lyric is sung. For variety on subsequent repetitions, children are often called on to actually leave out a lyric—for example, "________ , shoulders, knees, and toes"—while still touching their heads, and so on.

"Here We Go Looby-Loo" is yet another singing game that was first printed at the end of the 19th century in England. Some sources actually call it an early version of "The Hokey Pokey."

The song was also popularized by a 1950s British television children's show called *Andy Pandy*, which featured a character named Looby Loo whose signature song was the tune included in this book. *Andy Pandy* may be familiar to some modern readers, as it was remade in the '70s and again in the first decade of the 2000s.

"Here We Go 'Round the Mulberry Bush," like many such songs, emerged from the folk tradition; it was first noted in the middle of the 1800s by English nursery-rhyme and fairy-tale collector James Orchard Halliwell. The song goes along with a simple game in which children hold hands and spin in a circle, singing each verse and alternately dispersing to perform whatever the lyrics indicate.

A similar song called "Stop Beatin' Round the Mulberry Bush" became popular in the '30s through renditions by Count Basie and others, and later again in the 1950s when Bill Haley & His Comets did a recording.

"He's Got the Whole World (in His Hands)" is a spiritual tune that has been sung by such varied artists as jazz/blues singer Nina Simone, pop crooner Andy Williams, rock band The Sisters of Mercy, and more. But it was actually English singer Laurie London who took it to No. 1 on the Most Played by Jockeys U.S. pop chart, making it the only gospel tune to climb such heights in the States. Its simple and repetitive refrain makes it perfect for a children's sing-along.

"Hey Diddle Diddle" This very common English nursery rhyme first appeared as the version we all know in 1765, printed in *Mother Goose's Melody*. But as with many songs in the folk tradition, there's evidence the poem existed as far back as 1569, when playwright Thomas Preston referred to it in one of his works with the lines, "They be at hand Sir with stick and fiddle; / They can play a new dance called hey-didle-didle" (quote spelled as found).

There are many, many theories about the meaning behind the simple tune: one that it involves a love triangle with Queen Elizabeth I, one that it came from ancient Greece and is actually a mis-translation, and one that it's a poem about constellations. But most scholars think it's just a silly tune.

"Hickory Dickory Dock" became solidified in public consciousness with its publication under the Mother Goose banner, specifically in *Mother Goose's Melody*. Mother Goose herself is something of a mysterious figure who may not be rooted in actual history; there have been rumors that the concept is based on a woman who lived in Boston in the late

1600s, but the fact that there are earlier French references to Mother Goose render the point moot.

Whether she was real or not, the Mother Goose umbrella gave us *Sleeping Beauty*, *Little Red Riding Hood*, *Cinderella*, and, of course, "Hickory Dickory Dock."

"Home on the Range" President Franklin D. Roosevelt apparently called this his favorite song after being elected in the early 1930s, at that time making this oral-tradition tune even more popular than before. But its murky past inspired the nation to search for the song's origin. By now, most scholars agree that it's based on a poem called "My Western Home," by Dr. Brewster M. Higley—it first appeared in print in 1873, with its music written later. Here are a few lines from the original:

> I love the wild flowers in this bright land of ours,
> I love the wild curlew's shrill scream;
> The buffs and white rocks, and antelope flocks,
> That graze on the mountains so green.
> A home! A home!

"Hot Cross Buns" is a nursery rhyme about an English spiced bun that Christians traditionally eat on Good Friday in some parts of the U.S., but also in Australia, Britain, Canada, and beyond. An "X," which has some significance related to Jesus on the cross, usually appears on top of the treat.

As a fun fact, the tune to "Hot Cross Buns" is usually the first children are taught when learning to play the recorder.

"Humpty Dumpty" This classic rhyme actually used to be presented as a riddle for children. What type of object might be difficult to put together again once it breaks? An egg, of course.

Though nowhere in the text is the word "egg" used, most renderings of Humpty Dumpty show him as one. The first time he appeared as an egg in print was in 1872, in Lewis Carroll's *Through the Looking Glass*, and eventually, through the sands of time, we altogether lost the "riddle" part of the rhyme.

"Hush, Little Baby" is a peculiar song, but in relation to soothing a crying baby, its heart and logic are sound. The lyrics describe a surrealistic parade of presents—from baubles, to animals, to expensive diamond rings—meant to calm down a restless child. In the end, if none of these gifts accomplish their mission, the babe will "still be the sweetest little baby in town."

"I Have a Little Dreidel" is a song about making a dreidel to amuse oneself with. In the Jewish tradition, a dreidel is a wooden top that's usually played with during Hanukkah. There is some debate over whether it was Samuel E. Goldfarb or Mikhl Gelbart who wrote the melody to the tune—each had a hand in crafting the English and Yiddish versions, respectively—since both language renditions use the same music.

"If You're Happy (and You Know It)" is a jovial tune, complete with hand claps, about—you guessed it—being happy. Not much is known about the origins of the song, but we do know it has international appeal, boasting a Japanese version ("*Shiawase Nara Te o Tatako*") and remarkable similarity to parts of the tune "*Molodejnaya*" from the 1938 Soviet film *Volga-Volga*.

"I'm a Little Teapot (and You Know It)" This song dating from the 1930s encourages children to perform moves to emulate the look and motions of a teapot, and is a fun tune to dance and sing in a group setting. One of the writers of the song, Clarence Kelley, actually owned a dance studio for children, where he taught a tap dance called "Waltz Clog." It turns out the dance was too hard for the kids he was teaching. Instead, he taught them "I'm a Little Teapot," with its rudimentary and easy-to-execute dance moves. The rest is history.

"I'm a Nut," also known by some as "Acorn Brown," is a tongue-in-cheek song that is sure to amuse kids everywhere. The speaker describes how he or she is literally an acorn, but also explores the other meaning of being a nut—being a little wacky. We hear about this person (or acorn) calling himself up on a date, going out to the movies, and so on. For added fun, after every iteration of the refrain ("I'm a Nut"), singers can use their tongues on the roof of their mouths to make two consecutive clicking sounds: *click click!*

"I'm H-A-P-P-Y!" This song about feeling good is not as famous as "If You're Happy (and You Know It)," but it can still be a lot of fun to perform with kids. To change up the repetition of "H-A-P-P-Y," on subsequent repetitions children can drop a letter: I'm _-A-P-P-Y, I'm H-_-P-P-Y, and so on.

"It's Raining, It's Pouring" sounds a lot like the melody from "A-Tisket, A-Tasket," and since both songs were floating around in the ether and in the public record within the same time period (early 1900s for "It's Raining," and late 1800s for "A-Tisket"), it's unclear which came first. "It's Raining, It's Pouring" did make an appearance in a songbook by composer Charles Ives in the earlier part of the 20th century, and was also copyrighted by Freda Selicoff in the '40s, though that may have been a variation of the tune.

"I've Been Working on the Railroad," now considered classic Americana, was first published in 1894. This song has a very rich history, some of it dark but altogether true. When originally published, the song had a verse like the modern version, except in minstrel dialogue. The current version contains three distinct sections: the railroad part, the "Dinah" part, and the "fee, fie, fiddly-i-o" part. Scholars believe the "Dinah" part was from a song published earlier in the 1800s, a tune called "Old Joe, or Somebody in the House with Dinah."

Finally, "I've Been Working on the Railroad" is actually a popular nursery rhyme in Japan. The story is the same in the Japanese rendition of the song, but the name has a slightly different meaning: "The railroad continues forever."

"Jack and Jill" is often related to France's Louis XVI and Marie Antoinette, who were executed in 1793. But this English poem dates from at least 28 years prior to that event. The words may refer to King Charles I reducing the volume on "jacks" (half pints) and "gills" (quarter pints) after Parliament rejected a suggestion to reform taxes on liquids. The village of Kilmersdon in north Somerset lays claim to the nursery rhyme's origin and has gone so far as to set six marker stones along the path where they say a 17th-century couple named Jack and Jill went up the hill for romantic liaisons (the surname Gilson—Jill's son—is still common in the village). Still another theory says "Jack and Jill" derives from a Scandinavian story of children named Hjuki and Bil.

"Jingle Bells" was originally published under the title "One Horse Open Sleigh" in 1857. James Pierpont (uncle of 19th-century financier J.P. Morgan) wrote the song at Simpson's Tavern in Medford, Massachusetts. The rollicking tune was inspired by Medford's annual one-horse open-sleigh races. "Jingle Bells" did not become popular until the 20th century, especially after Bing Crosby and the Andrews Sisters recorded it in 1943. It has since usually been associated with Christmas, although the lyrics make no mention of the holiday.

"John Jacob Jingleheimer Schmidt" probably originates in the United States and likely was intended to mock the names of German immigrants to America in the 19th and early 20th century. The nursery rhyme has outlived any negative connotation and today thrives as a lively sing-along for children. The verse is usually repeated over and over with a variety of tempos and dynamics.

"Kumbaya" is a corruption of the phrase "come by here" in the Gullah language. This quiet prayer was first recorded in 1927 by Robert Winslow Gordon in South Carolina. Since its adoption by the folk movement of the 1950s and the Civil Rights movement of the 1960s, the song has become associated with both pacifism and any gathering around a campfire.

"Lavender's Blue" is a traditional 17th-century English folk song that became a nursery rhyme by 1805. Burl Ives recorded a dilly of a version for the 1948 Disney film *So Dear to My Heart*. This rendition was later nominated for an Academy Award.

"Limericks" is a nursery rhyme that uses the humorous five-line poetic style popularized in the 19th century by Edward Lear. A series of unrelated stanzas are presented here—singers should feel free to create their own.

"Little Bo Peep" is an old English nursery rhyme that was set to music in 1870 by James William Elliott. The moral of the story is don't fall asleep on the job, or be prepared to accept the consequences.

"Little Boy Blue" is sometimes thought to refer to boastful 16th-century English scholar Cardinal Thomas Wolsey ("come blow your horn"), but it more likely is a simple paean to a peaceful country life that children of the time would find either familiar or appealing.

"Little Jack Horner" is actually Thomas Horner, a 16th-century English steward to the Abbot of Glastonbury. "Jack" is a common nickname for a knave (an unscrupulous man) and, naturally, Thomas Horner pulled a prank that earned him infamous immortality in this 18th-century nursery rhyme. King Henry VIII was confiscating church properties and the abbot dispatched Horner to bribe the king with the title deeds to some lesser properties in hopes the abbot could retain his monastery. Before reaching London, Horner took the deed for Mells Manor for himself. This "plum" piece of property remained with the Horner family until the 20th century.

"London Bridge Is Falling Down" is an English nursery rhyme that is often sung as part of a children's arch game in which two children hold hands and make an arch with their arms, beneath which the other children pass in single file until the song's conclusion, when the arch is brought down to capture one child. The original stone London Bridge lasted for more than 600 years but it did suffer a number of collapses. "My fair lady" may refer to Queen Eleanor of Castile, who was accused of misappropriating repair funds that resulted in a bridge collapse in 1281.

"Mary Had a Little Lamb" is a 19th-century American nursery rhyme. Sarah Josepha Hale wrote the poem about a real incident in which a young girl named Mary Sawyer brought her pet lamb to school. In the 1830s, American composer Lowell Mason ("Nearer My God to Thee") set Hale's poem to the tune children have been singing ever since. Interestingly, Paul McCartney recorded an original version of the rhyme, which actually became a hit record in the early 1970s.

"Michael Finnegan" may have actually begun as a ditty about a real British WWI soldier. The song caught on and continued to develop additional verses. It's a great example of a "repetition" song. In this style the body of the verse remains the same but the end of it keeps changing with each repetition.

"Michael, Row the Boat Ashore" is another traditional folk song that dates back to slave songs from 1800s. In the original lyric, the "river" is the River Jordan and "Michael" is the Archangel Michael. Versions by Pete Seeger and other folk artists were adopted by the Civil Rights movement and the lyrics tend to imply we are rowing towards our goal of freedom and equality.

"The More We Get Together" is a traditional children's rhyme that dates back to the 1800s. The lyric promotes friendship and cooperation: "The more we get together the happier we'll be." The tune is the same as the one in "Did You Ever See a Lassie."

"The Muffin Man" is a nursery rhyme dating back to England in the 1800s when muffins became an extremely popular and inexpensive British treat for children. The lyric was used to great effect in a scene in the movie *Shrek*.

"My Bonnie Lies Over the Ocean" is a hugely popular Scottish folk song. There was even an early 1960s hit version of the song in Germany recorded by Tony Sheridan and "The Beat Brothers." The Beat Brothers was a pseudonym for a young, pre-breakout Beatles. Their version of the song begins as a ballad in the style of Elvis Presley's gospel hits with the Jordanaires, and then transitions to a Chuck Berry-style rock 'n' roll beat.

In October of 1961, a young man visited the NEMS record store in Liverpool requesting the Tony Sheridan recording. The store's manager, Brian Epstein, had never heard of either the record or the performers, but promised to try to get it in the store. A little investigating revealed that "The Beat Brothers" were in fact a local group curiously called The Beatles who frequently played lunchtime sessions at a nearby cellar club—the Cavern. Epstein and his assistant walked to the club, saw the band, and signed the band to a management agreement. The rest is history.

"Oats, Peas, Beans and Barley Grow" is often sung as "Oats, Beans and Barley Grow." This is a traditional game or activity song in which children stand in a circle and act out the lyrics. Alternatively, they can stand in two facing lines, and the two kids at the front of each line join hands and skip down the lines to the end.

"Oh Dear, What Can the Matter Be?" originated in England in the 1770s. It is also known as "Johnny's So Long at the Fair." As with most nursery rhymes and folk tunes, there are many, many lyric variations.

"Oh Where, Oh Where Has My Little Dog Gone?" is a sad tune written by American Septimus Winner in 1864, originally with the title "Der Deitcher's Dog" and meant to be sung in English with a German dialect. Using the pseudonym Alice Hawthorne, Winner also wrote "Ten Little Indians," as well as the songs "Listen to the Mockingbird" and "Whispering Hope."

"The Old Gray Mare" is an American folk song written by Thomas Francis McNulty in the 19th century. It is nominally about horses, but the song is often is used to refer to anything or anyone past their prime.

"Old MacDonald Had a Farm" was originally published in 1917 as "Old MacDougal." The refrain of "moo moo here …" was borrowed from an earlier song titled "The Farmyard" (ca. 1908). The names of the animals mentioned in the lyrics, along with the sounds they produce, accumulate throughout the song, requiring children to exercise their memory muscles.

"On the Bridge of Avignon" is a very old French song (dating back to the 15th century) about an even older bridge. The remnants of the 12th-century bridge still partially span the Rhône river, but very few people now dance on it as the song has encouraged children to do for 600 years.

"On Top of Old Smokey" is a traditional American folk ballad redolent of the Scottish and Irish immigrants who settled in the Appalachian Mountains. The song has widely been parodied by generations of children with titles such as "On Top of Spaghetti."

"Over the River and Through the Woods" has lyrics taken from an 1844 poem by journalist and human rights advocate Lydia Maria Child, titled "The New-England Boy's Song About Thanksgiving." For those who wonder about a sleigh ride through snow in November, in the mid-19th century New England was still in the "Little Ice Age" and experiencing colder than normal weather. It is unsure when the poem was set to the tune that's been taught to children for generations.

"Pat-a-Cake" is an English rhyme that's been known since the late 17th century—even earlier than Mother Goose. The song is usually accompanied by a clapping game.

"Peas Pudding" The source for this song is not known, but the nursery rhyme probably dates to 17th-century England, where peas porridge was a form of sustenance in peasants' cottages. Like "Pat-a-Cake" this activity tune is often sung as part of a clapping game with children.

"Polly, Put the Kettle On" is an English nursery rhyme from the late 18th century. The melody is from the Scottish song "Jenny's Bawbee," but, curiously, the original title with these lyrics was "Molly, Put the Kettle On." In 1840, Charles Dickens changed the name to "Polly" for his novel *Barnaby Rudge: A Tale of the Riots of Eighty*, and we have been singing it that way ever since.

By the way, "Suckey" (from the lyrics) was a common nickname for Susan.

"Polly Wolly Doodle" likely has origins in slave songs, but may have been written by Daniel Decatur Emmett, an entertainer in the minstrel tradition who also wrote "Dixie." The song was delightfully performed by Shirley Temple in the 1935 film *The Littlest Rebel*.

"Pop! Goes the Weasel" is a mid-19th century British song that seems to have nonsense lyrics that have been subject to various interpretations. Some say "pop" is Cockney slang for pawning a piece of merchandise and "weasel" is slang for a jacket or coat. Poor Londoners would wear their best jacket to church on Sunday and pawn it on Monday. Another version says the "weasel" was part of the apparatus on a spinner's wheel that would "pop" when a measure of yarn had been used. Lost in thought during the drudgery of their factory work, textile workers in Britain's sweatshops would have their reveries disturbed by the "pop" of the "weasel." Related to this notion, "Pop! Goes the Weasel" has been used for more than a century as the song for jack-in-the-box toys.

"Raisins and Almonds" is a gentle Yiddish lullaby composed in 1880 by Avrohom Goldfaden. Goldfaden adapted much of the song's melody and words from a Yiddish folk song titled "*Unter Dem Kinds Vigele*." The source song is sung by a mother to her son predicting an auspicious future "trading in raisins and almonds."

"Rig-a-Jig-Jig" is a good exercise for memory—each succeeding verse has children replacing the characters in question, from "A girl who can twirl" to "A man in a kilt" to "Twins who can dance," and so on. The song is further engaging in that children can act out the lyrics' described activities.

"Ring Around the Rosie" first appeared in its current form in the late 1800s, though versions of it date back another hundred years. Both a nursery rhyme and a playground game, the song may have darker origins; it's rumored to be about the black plague, though such claims are unsubstantiated.

"Rock-a-Bye Baby" dates back to the 1600s. One theory on its origin is that it's one of the first poems written in America, describing the way some Native American women rocked their babies in cradles that could hang down from the branches of trees. Whether that's true or not, modern audiences sometimes note that the lyrics, "down will come baby, cradle and all" are disturbing for something that's considered a gentle lullaby.

"Roll Over (Six in the Bed)" is a counting song that became especially popular after its use on the *Barney & Friends* children's television show. It's also known as simply "Six in the Bed," and even "Ten in the Bed."

The tune is a counting song that allows children to learn to count backwards from the starting number. Children often sing the song while also performing the "roll over" action as it comes up in the lyrics.

"Row, Row, Row Your Boat" dates back to the 1800s. It's a simple song with a positive life message for children—a quick Google search will yield several interpretations of the song as a great philosophy for life: put one foot in front of the other, and travel "merrily." The tune can also be an activity song, with children seated, facing each other, and holding hands as they rock to the motion of an imaginary sea and row.

"Sailing, Sailing" was written in 1880, and is a straightforward sailing song that expresses joy and love of the sea.

"She'll Be Coming 'Round the Mountain" is derived from the gospel song "When the Chariot Comes." In the first publishing of "She'll Be Coming 'Round the Mountain," it was suggested that the song is a protest song and that "she" in the tune is a reference to Mary "Mother" Jones, a labor organizer who travelled to the Appalachian Mountains to organize workers' unions.

"Shoo Fly," first appearing around the time of the Civil War, unfortunately has a racist origin. But the lyrics have evolved over the years and it's now seen as a fun, silly song for kids.

"Shortnin' Bread" has a checkered history—in some versions it was sung by slaves in the south, but other renditions were highly offensive and racist. Today, the lyrics simply rejoice in the flavor and healing powers of a delicious bread recipe.

"Sing a Song of Sixpence" is a rhyme that dates all the way back to the 16th century, with many theories as to its origin and meaning. It's possible that early minstrels would make up songs to sing in the royal courts for tips, amounting to a sixpence. There are also early references to royal bakers creating pies with live birds in them for special events. When the pie were sliced—hopefully very carefully—the birds would fly out.

"Six Little Ducks" is another great "nonsense" song that is also a fun children's game. To perform the activity, children stand in a line, and the child in front places her hands over her face, imitating the look of a duck's bill. The child in the back places his hands behind himself, like a duck's wings. Together, as one big duck, the children march and dance around the room while singing the song.

"Skip to My Lou" is from the 1800s, and children often skip, march, clap, or even dance as they sing the lyrics.

"Take Me Out to the Ball Game" was composed in 1908 by the popular Vaudeville team of Norworth and Tilzer. The song was first performed at a major league game in the 1930s and has since become a standard feature during the "7th Inning Stretch" for all major league baseball games.

"There's a Hole in My Bucket" dates back to when children would haul water home from a well or stream. The predicament for poor Henry is that his bucket has a hole in it.

"This Is the Way the Ladies Ride" is an activity song loved by toddlers. Sit the child on your knee and follow the instructions in the song as you bounce, weave, and dip the toddler on your knees.

"This Little Light of Mine" is a children's gospel song dating back to 1920. The basic message of the song, that each of us can let our individual "light" serve as a beacon to others, has been adopted by various social causes through the years, including the Civil Rights movement.

"This Old Man" is an extremely fun song to sing but actually has some dark origins. Its roots are as an Irish protest song about the often brutal treatment they received by their English occupiers.

"This Train Is A-Comin'" is a classic spiritual. On the surface it works wonderfully as a children's song about trains, but the underlying and original meaning is more likely about attaining spiritual glory by "getting on board" with the teachings of the church.

"Three Blind Mice" dates back to the England in the early 1600s, and it's believed it was a political allegory. The three blind mice are actually three people accused of unsuccessfully plotting against Queen Mary, who's represented in the tune by the "farmer's wife."

"Three Little Kittens" is attributed to a poem by Eliza Lee Cabot Follen published in 1833. She probably refined the poem from a previously existing rhyme.

"A-Tisket, A-Tasket" is a rhyme that became a popular children's game in the late 1800s. Children would sing the song while dancing in a circle, and one child would dance outside of the circle and drop a handkerchief. The closest person would then grab the handkerchief and become the dropper. The nursery rhyme became the foundation of a popular song by Ella Fitzgerald in the 1930s.

"To Market, to Market" is a children's nursery rhyme dating back to England in the early 1600s. The simple lyric is about a journey to and from the market to buy food.

"The Twelve Days of Christmas" began as a rhyme and was set to the tune we know today around 1900. The rhyme was originally intended as a children's game with the challenge being to remember the ever-increasing lines of the rhyme. The twelve days begin with Christmas day, though in some countries they may be considered to begin on the day after.

"Twinkle, Twinkle, Little Star" has a melody that first appeared in France in the song *"Ah vous dirai-je, Maman,"* meaning, "Shall I Tell You, Mommy." This same tune was used for "Baa, Baa, Black Sheep" and "The Alphabet Song," both also featured in this book. The lyrics for "Twinkle, Twinkle" were taken from an English poem by Jane Taylor, written in the early 1800s.

"Waltzing Matilda" is a very popular Australian song, sort of like their version of "Yankee Doodle." The song uses Australian slang such as "jumbuck" (sheep) and "billabong" (stream).

"We Wish You a Merry Christmas" dates back to 16th-century England, when poor Wessex carolers would stand on wealthy persons' doorsteps in the freezing cold demanding handouts of figgy pudding—the traditional dessert at the end of an English Christmas meal in the 1500s. The lyric line " … and a Happy New Year" was likely added later, as the New Year did not commence on January 1st until the Gregorian calendar was adopted (1752 in England). Prior to that, the Feast of the Annunciation on March 25th was celebrated as the beginning of the New Year.

"The Wheels on the Bus" originated in the United Kingdom. The repetitive nature of the lyrics and melody make it very popular and fun to sing with children.

"When Johnny Comes Marching Home" is a Civil War-era song. Its lyrics gave hope to families on both sides of the conflict that their sons and husbands would return home safe and triumphant. As is common with children's songs, the melody had already been used in other songs before these lyrics were set to it.

"Yankee Doodle" is a Revolutionary War-era song, popular with both British and American troops. "Yankee" refers to American settlers. "Doodle" was a derogatory term implying someone who was not very smart. The lyrics were meant to imply that silly Americans would stick feathers in their coonskin caps and think themselves equal to British aristocrats. However, even though the song was poking fun at the revolutionaries, they adopted the song as their own.

A-Hunting We Will Go

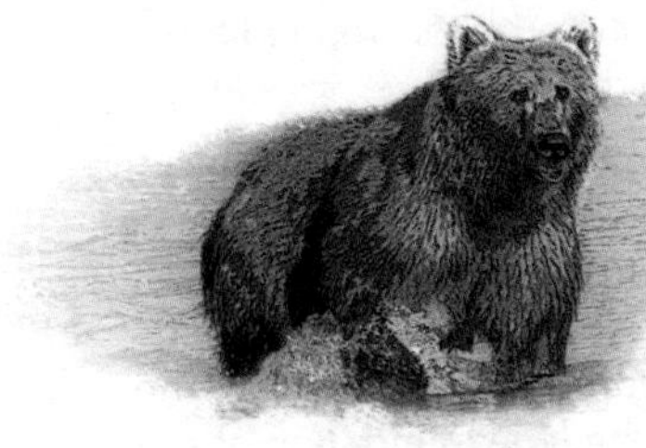

F
B♭m
C7
Dm7
Gm7

By Thomas Arne

Moderately (♩. = 92)

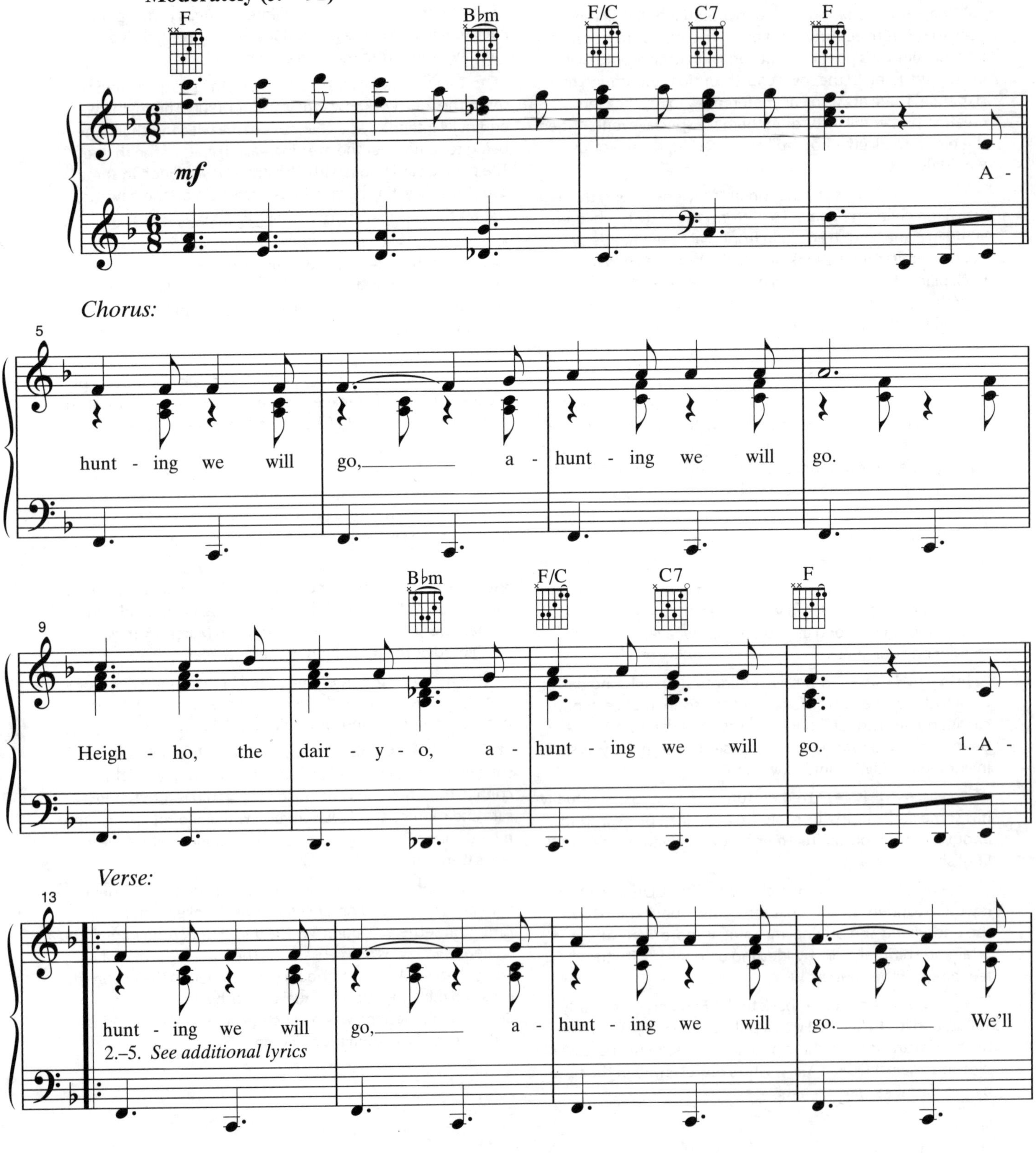
F
B♭m
F/C
C7
F
mf
A -
Chorus:
hunt - ing we will go, a - hunt - ing we will go.
B♭m
F/C
C7
F
Heigh - ho, the dair - y - o, a - hunt - ing we will go. 1. A -
Verse:
hunt - ing we will go, a - hunt - ing we will go. We'll
2.–5. See additional lyrics

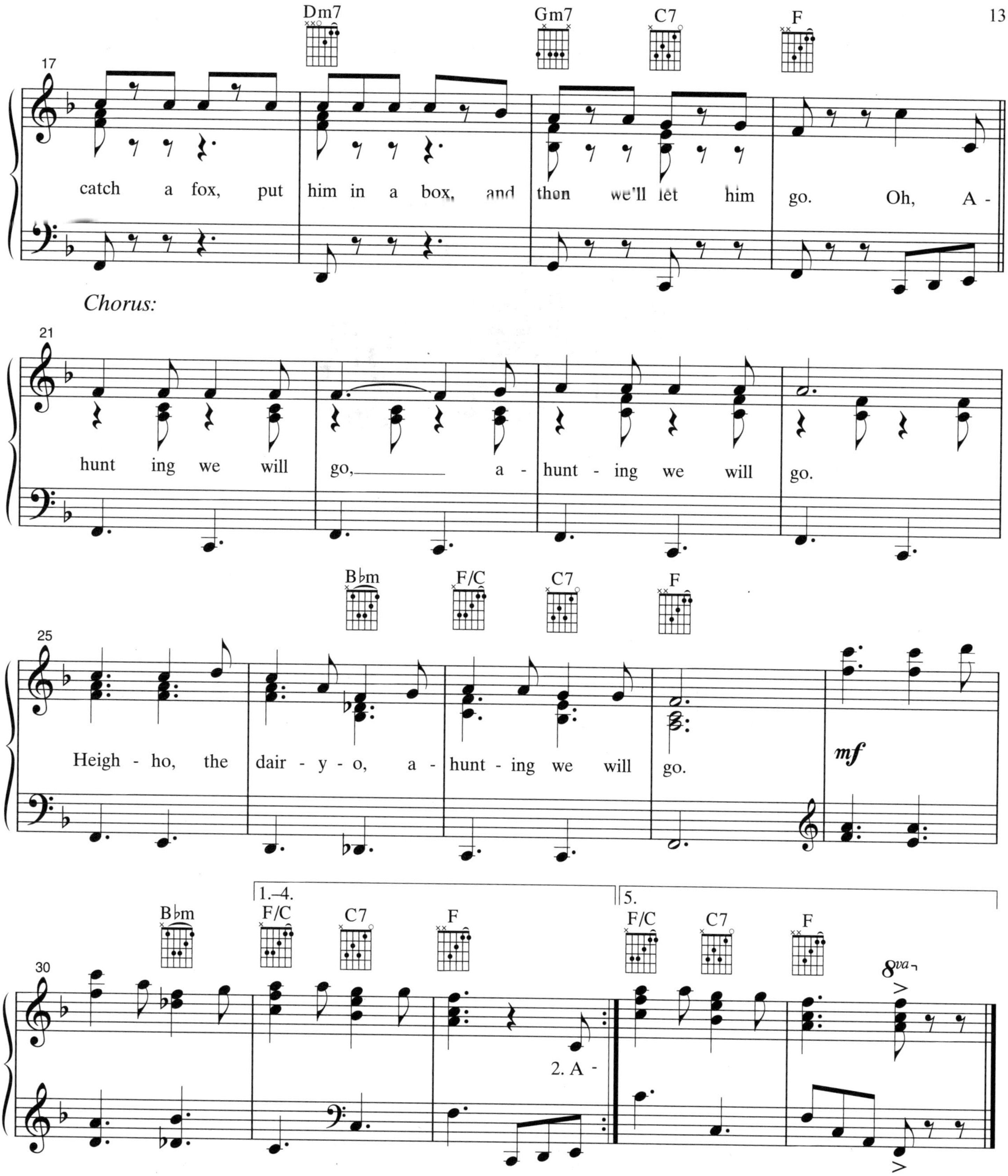
Dm7
Gm7
C7
F
17
catch a fox, put him in a box, and then we'll let him go. Oh, A -
Chorus:
21
hunt ing we will go, a - hunt - ing we will go.
B♭m
F/C
C7
F
25
Heigh - ho, the dair - y - o, a - hunt - ing we will go.
mf
1.–4.
5.
B♭m
F/C
C7
F
F/C
C7
F
30
2. A -
8va

Verse 2:
A-hunting we will go, a hunting we will go.
We'll catch a fish, put him on a dish,
And then we'll let him go!
(To Chorus:)

Verse 3:
A-hunting we will go, a hunting we will go.
We'll catch a bear and cut his hair,
And then we'll let him go!
(To Chorus:)

Verse 4:
A-hunting we will go, a hunting we will go.
We'll catch a pig and dance a little jig,
And then we'll let him go!
(To Chorus:)

Verse 5:
A-hunting we will go, a hunting we will go.
We'll catch a giraffe and make him laugh,
And then we'll let him go!
(To Chorus:)

All the Pretty Little Horses

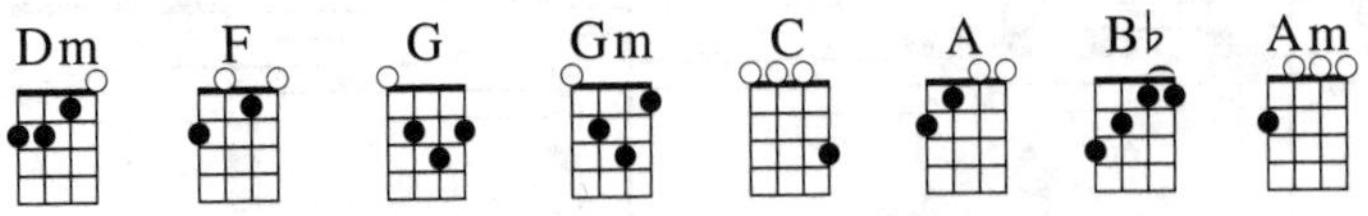
Dm
F
G
Gm
C
A
B♭
Am

Moderately slow lullaby (♩ = 92)

Traditional

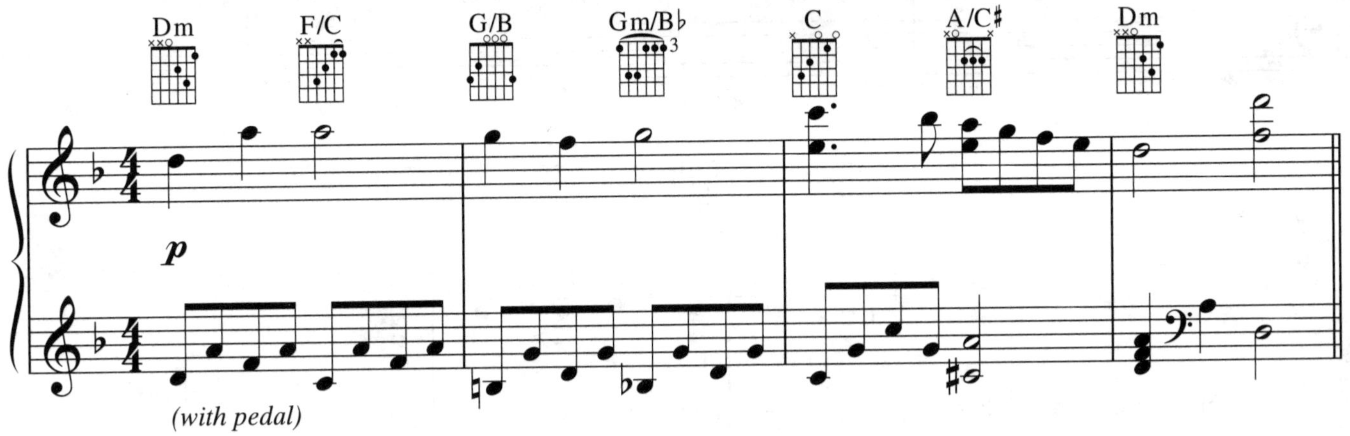
Dm
F/C
G/B
Gm/B♭
C
A/C♯
Dm
p
(with pedal)

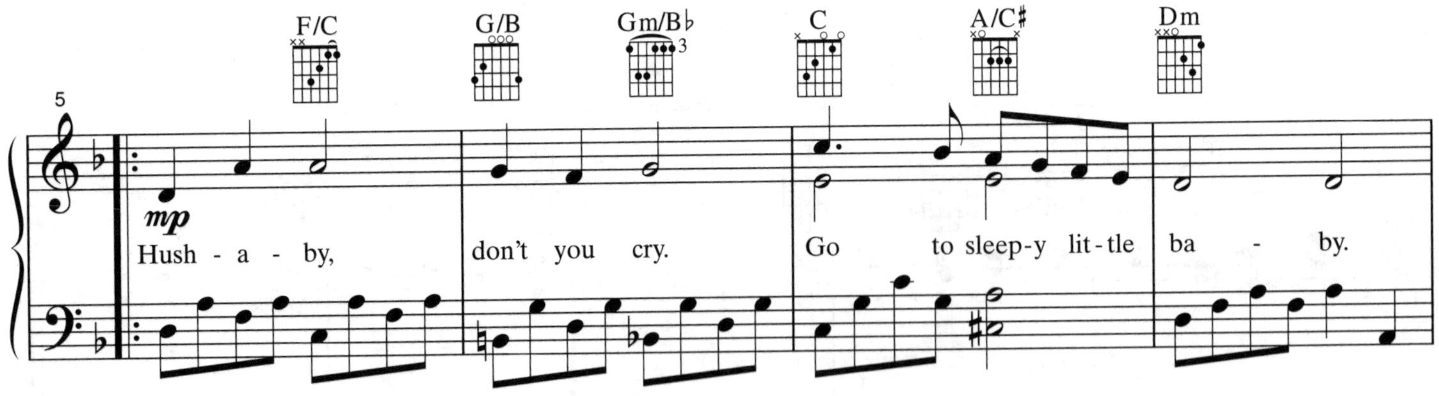
5
F/C
G/B
Gm/B♭
C
A/C♯
Dm
mp
Hush - a - by, don't you cry. Go to sleep-y lit-tle ba - by.

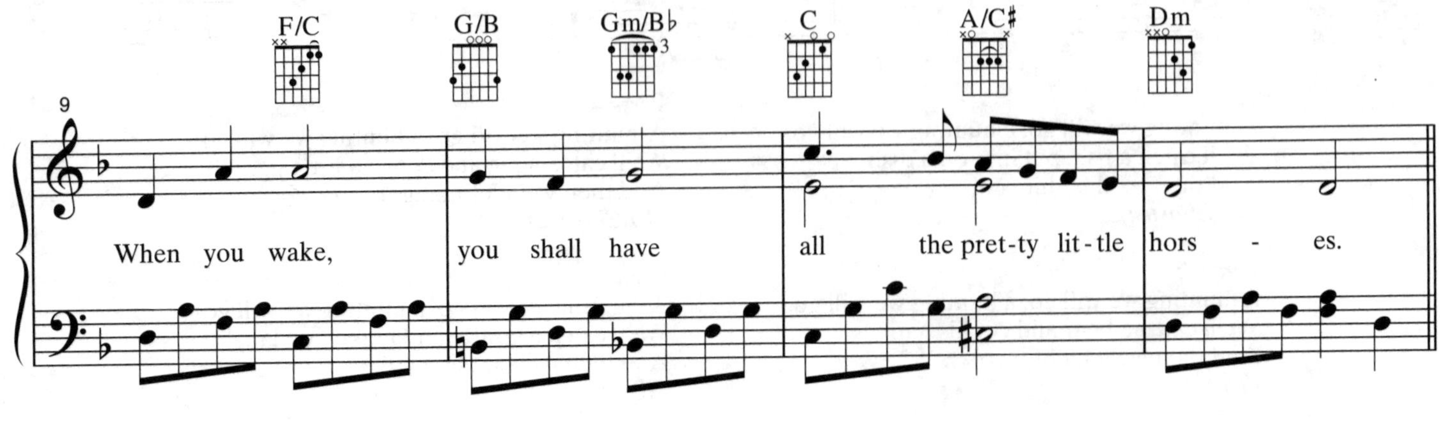
9
F/C
G/B
Gm/B♭
C
A/C♯
Dm
When you wake, you shall have all the pret-ty lit-tle hors - es.

F Bb Am7 A7 Dm
13
mf
Blacks and bays, dap-ples and grays, coach and six-a lit-tle hors - es.
F/C G/B Gm/Bb 3 C A/C#
17
mp
Hush - a - by, don't you cry. Go to sleep-y lit-tle
Dm F/C G/B Gm/Bb 3
20
ba - by.
p
1. 2.
C A/C# Dm C A/C# Dm
23
rit. e dim.
pp

All Through the Night

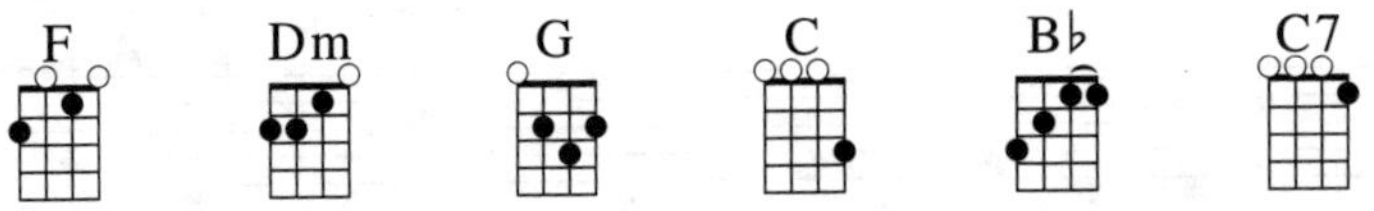
F
Dm
G
C
B♭
C7

Lyrics by
Harold Boulton

Traditional

Tenderly (♩ = 86)
F
Dm
G/B
C
B♭
C
F
mp
(with pedal)
5
B♭
G
C
B♭
C7
F
Sleep, my child, and peace at-tend thee all through the night.
While the moon her watch is keep - ing all through the night,
9
B♭
G
C
B♭
C7
F
Guar - dian an - gels God will send thee all through the night.
white the wea - ry world is sleep - ing all through the night.

B♭/F F B♭/F C/E B♭/F C/E B♭/F F B♭/F F G7
Soft the drow - sy hours are creep - ing, hill and vale in
O'er thy spir - it gent - ly steal - ing, vi - sions of de -
F/C C7 F B♭ G C
slum - ber steep - ing. I my lov - ing vig - il keep - ing
light re - veal - ing, breathed a pure and ho - ly fell - ing
rit. e dim.
mp a tempo
1.
B♭ C7 F B♭ C F
8va
all through the night.
2.
B♭ C7 F B♭ C F
8va
all through the night.
rit. e dim.
p

Alouette

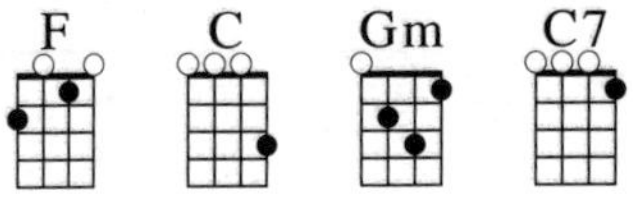
F
C
Gm
C7

Moderately bright march (♩ = 132)

Traditional

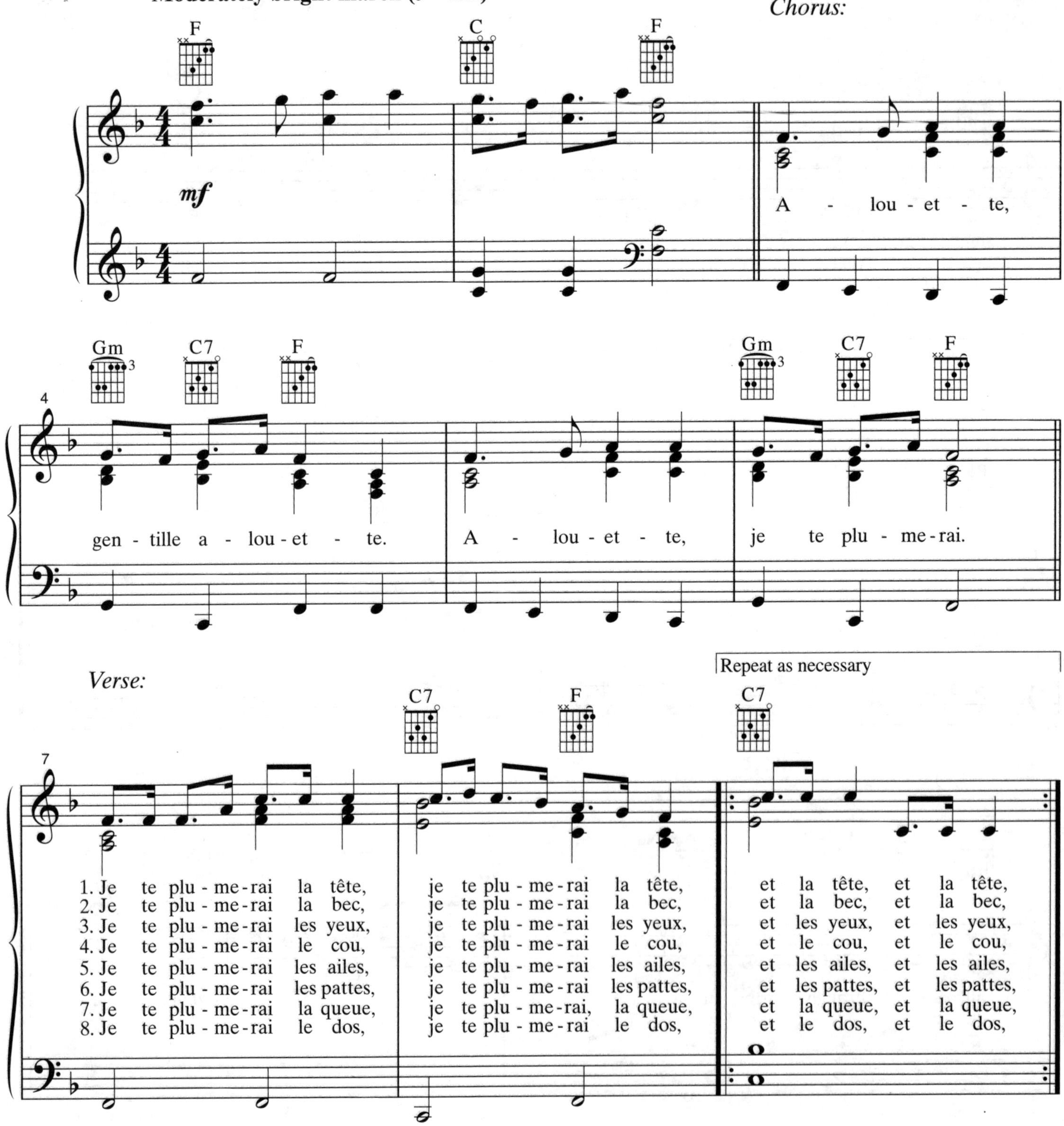
Chorus:
F C F
mf
A - lou - et - te,
Gm C7 F
gen - tille a - lou - et - te.
A - lou - et - te,
Gm C7 F
je te plu - me - rai.
Verse:
Repeat as necessary
C7 F C7
1. Je te plu - me - rai la tête, je te plu - me - rai la tête, et la tête, et la tête,
2. Je te plu - me - rai la bec, je te plu - me - rai la bec, et la bec, et la bec,
3. Je te plu - me - rai les yeux, je te plu - me - rai les yeux, et les yeux, et les yeux,
4. Je te plu - me - rai le cou, je te plu - me - rai le cou, et le cou, et le cou,
5. Je te plu - me - rai les ailes, je te plu - me - rai les ailes, et les ailes, et les ailes,
6. Je te plu - me - rai les pattes, je te plu - me - rai les pattes, et les pattes, et les pattes,
7. Je te plu - me - rai la queue, je te plu - me - rai, la queue, et la queue, et la queue,
8. Je te plu - me - rai le dos, je te plu - me - rai le dos, et le dos, et le dos,

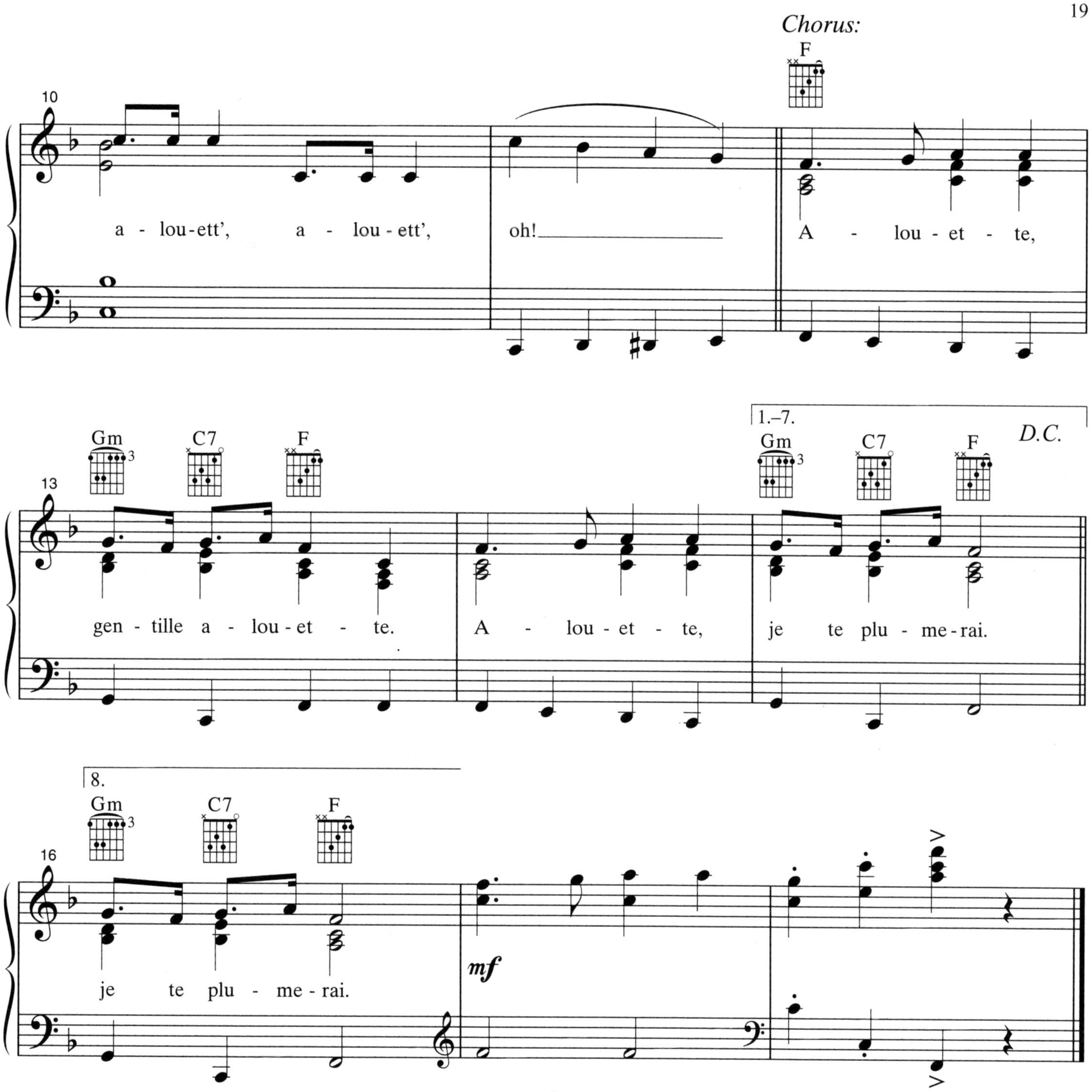
Chorus:
F
10
a - lou-ett', a - lou-ett', oh!
A - lou - et - te,
Gm C7 F
13
gen - tille a - lou - et - te.
A - lou - et - te,
1.–7.
Gm C7 F
D.C.
je te plu - me - rai.
8.
Gm C7 F
16
je te plu - me - rai.
mf

THE ALPHABET SONG

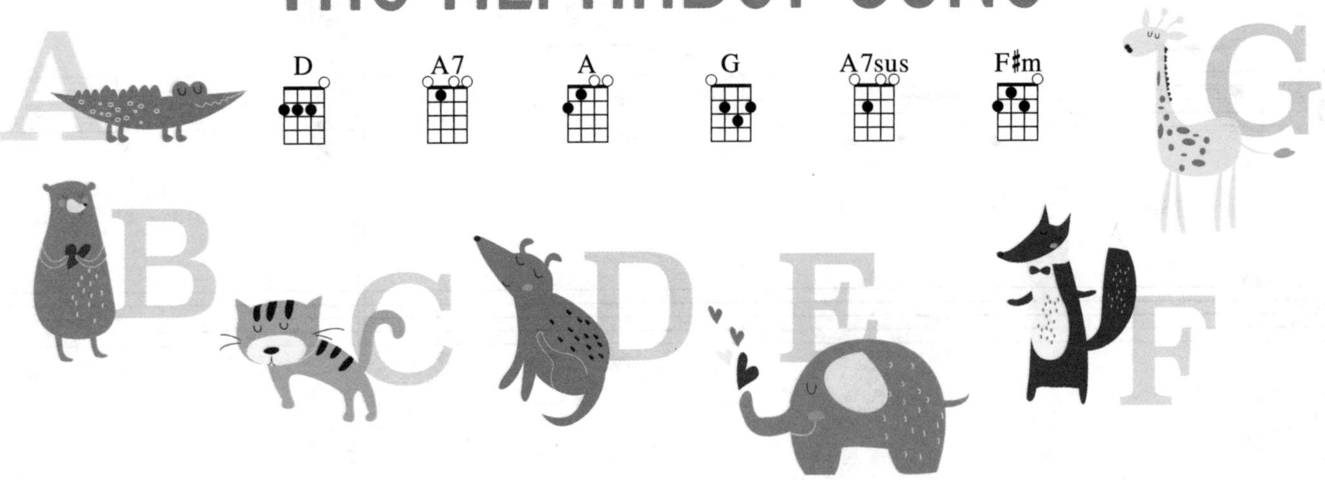
D
A7
A
G
A7sus
F♯m

Moderately, but gently (♩ = 102)

Traditional

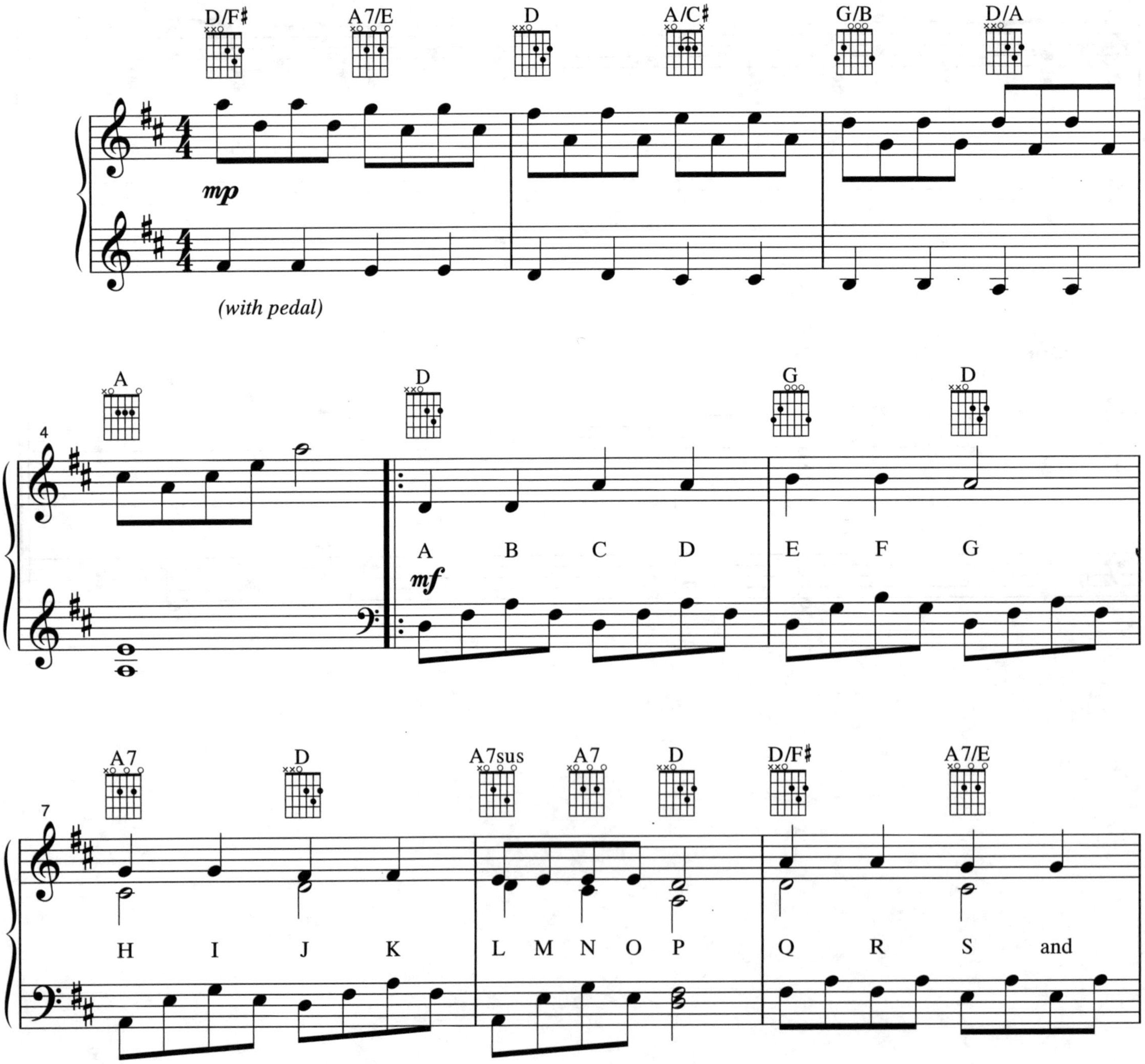
D/F♯
A7/E
D
A/C♯
G/B
D/A
mp
(with pedal)
A
D
G
D
A B C D
E F G
mf
A7
D
A7sus
A7
D
D/F♯
A7/E
H I J K
L M N O P
Q R S and

D A/C♯ D/F♯ A7/E D A7sus A7
10
T U V dou - ble U X and Y and Z.
(W)
D F♯m G D A7 D
13
Now I know my A B Cs, next time won't you
1.
A7sus A7 D A7 D A7 D
16
sing with me?
mp
2.
A7sus A7 D A7 D A7 D
19
sing with me?
mp
rit. e dim.
p

The Animal Fair

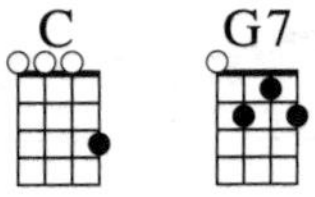
C
G7

Moderately bright march (♩. = 84)

Traditional

C
mf

5
I

9
G7
went to the an - i - mal fair. The birds and the beasts were there. The

13
C
big ba - boon by the light of the moon was comb-ing his au - burn hair. you

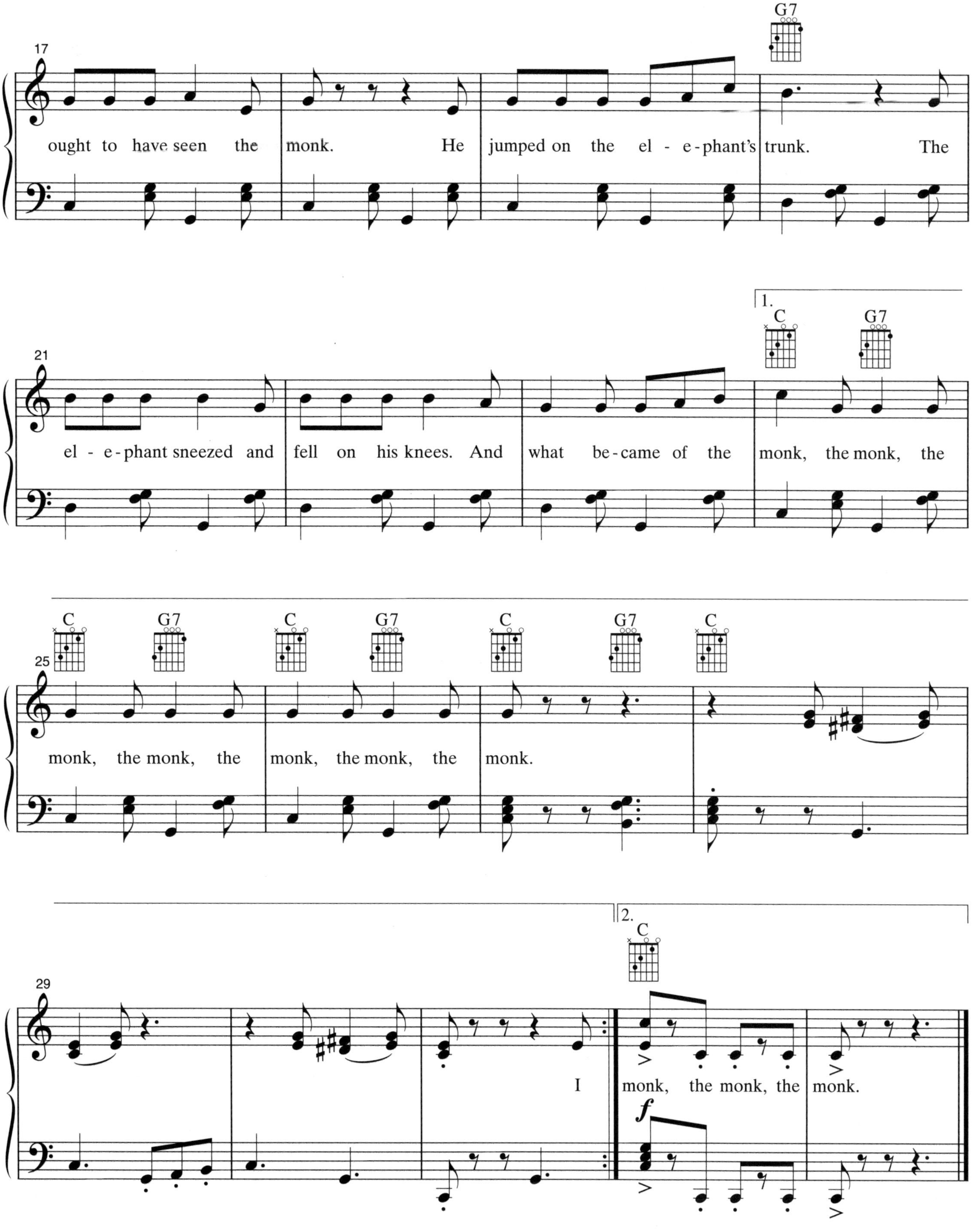
G7
17
ought to have seen the monk. He jumped on the el - e-phant's trunk. The
1.
C G7
21
el - e-phant sneezed and fell on his knees. And what be-came of the monk, the monk, the
C G7 C G7 C G7 C
25
monk, the monk, the monk, the monk, the monk.
2.
C
29
I monk, the monk, the monk.
f

Apples and Bananas

G7 G D7 C D F F♯ G6
2fr.
Moderately (♩ = 116) (♫ = ♩♪ triplet)
Traditional
G7
mf
G
1. I like to eat, eat, eat ap - ples and ba - na - nas.
ite, ite, ite i - ples and bi - ni - nis.
oot, oot, oot oo - ples and boo - noo - noos.
D7
I like to eat, eat, eat ap - ples and ba - na - nas.
I like to ite, ite, ite i - ples and bi - ni - nis.
I like to oot, oot, oot oo - ples and boo - noo - noos.
G
I like to
I like to
I like to

D7
ate, ate, ate ay - ples and ba - nay - nays.
ote, ote, ote oh - ples and bo - no - nos.
eat, eat, eat ap - ples and ba - na - nas.
I like to ate, ate, ate ay - ples and ba -
I like to ote, ote, ote oh - ples and bo -
I like to eat, eat, eat ap - ples and ba -
G
1.2.
C
nay - nays.
no - nos.
na - nas.
D
G
F
F♯
G
3.
G6
2. I like to
3. I like to

Baa, Baa, Black Sheep

C F Gsus G Dm G7 Dm7 F♯dim7 G7sus

Moderately (♩ = 108)

Traditional

C/E F(9) Gsus G C C/E
mp
Baa, baa, black sheep,
(with pedal)
F C/E F C Dm G7 C C/E Dm7
have you an-y wool? Yes, sir, yes, sir, three bags full. One for the mas - ter,
C G7 C/E F F♯dim7 Gsus G7
one for the dame, one for the lit - tle boy who lives down the lane.

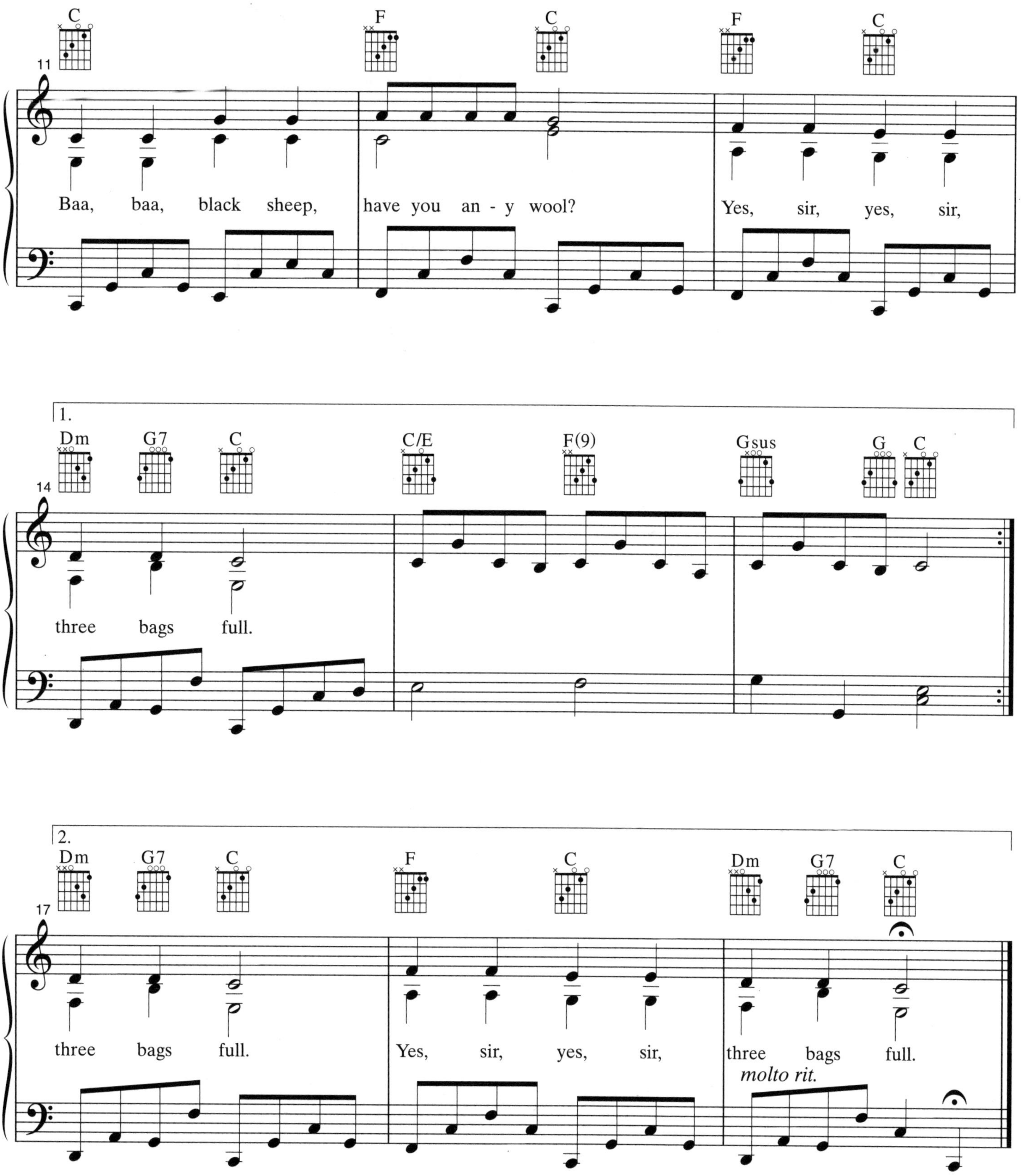

11
C F C F C
Baa, baa, black sheep, have you an - y wool? Yes, sir, yes, sir,
1.
14
Dm G7 C C/E F(9) Gsus G C
three bags full.
2.
17
Dm G7 C F C Dm G7 C
three bags full. Yes, sir, yes, sir, three bags full.
molto rit.

The Bear Went Over the Mountain

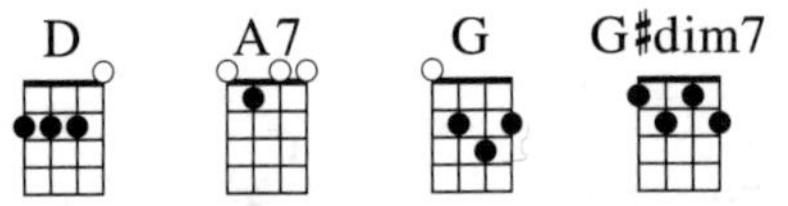
D
A7
G
G♯dim7

Moderately bright (♩. = 88)

Traditional

D A7 D A7 D
mf
1. The
G D A D
bear went o - ver the moun - tain, the bear went o - ver the moun - tain, the
bear wemt o - ver the riv - er, the bear went o - ver the riv - er, the
G G♯dim7 D/A A7
bear went o - ver the moun - tain to see what he could
bear went o - ver the riv - er to see what he could
D G D
see. To see what he could see, to
see. And all that he could see, and

15
G D
see what he could see was the oth - er side of the
all the he could see was the oth - er side of the
18
G D A D
moun - tain, the oth - er side of the moun - tain, the
riv - er, the oth - er side of the riv - er, the
21
G G♯dim7 D/A A7
oth - er side of the moun - tian, was all that he could
oth - er side of the. riv - er was all that he could
1. 2.
24
D A7 D D
see. 2. The see.

BINGO

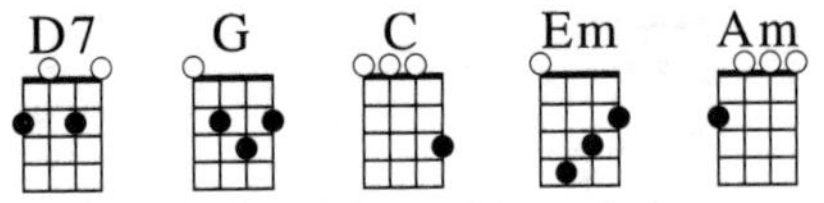
D7
G
C
Em
Am

Moderately bright (♩ = 152)

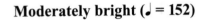

Traditional

D7
G
C
G
mf
1. There
was a farm - er had a dog, and
was a farm - er had a dog, and
3.4.5.6. *See additional lyrics*
D7
G
C
Bin - go was his name - o.
Bin - go was his name - o.
B I N G O,
(Clap) I N G O,
D7
G
Em
Am
B I N G O,
(Clap) I N G O,
B I N G O, and
(Clap) I N G O, and

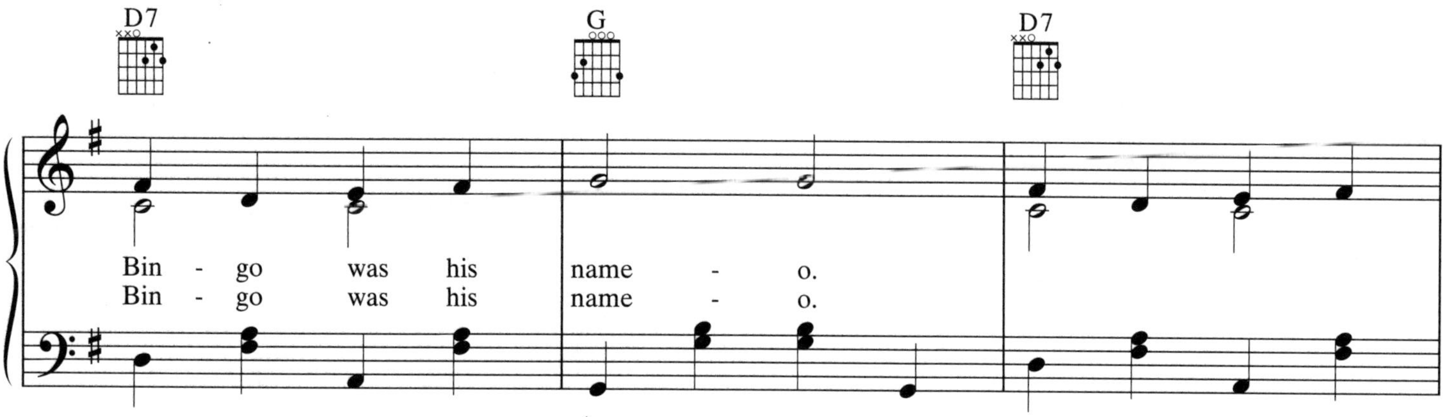
D7
G
D7
Bin - go was his name - o.
Bin - go was his name - o.

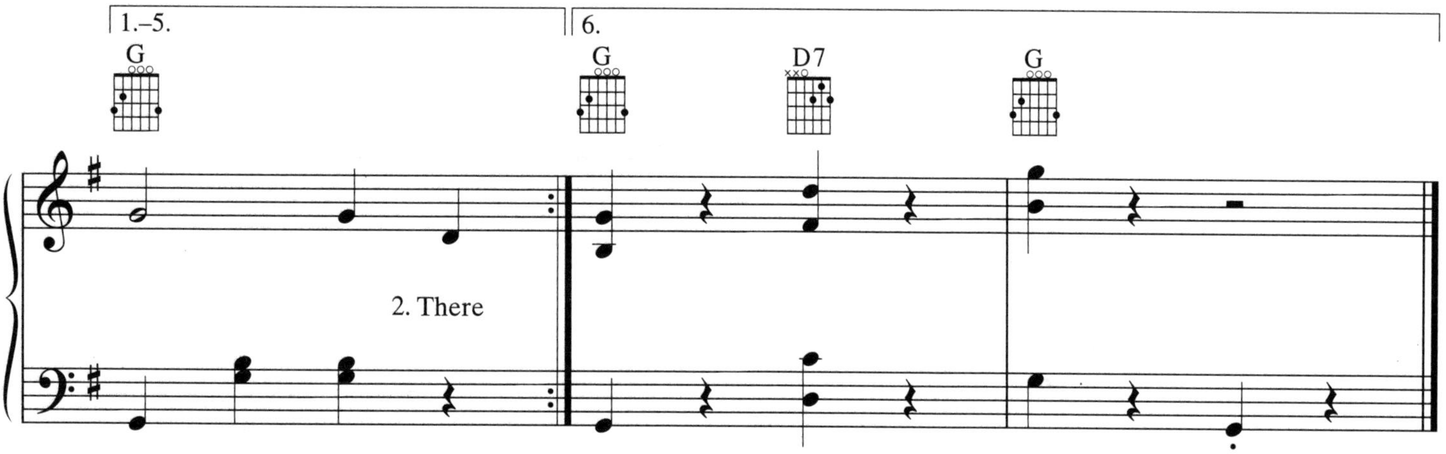
1.–5.
6.
G
G
D7
G
2. There

Verse 3:
There was a farmer had a dog
And Bingo was his name-o.
(Clap, clap) N G O,
(Clap, clap) N G O,
(Clap, clap) N G O,
And Bingo was his name-o.

Verse 4:
There was a farmer had a dog
And Bingo was his name-o.
(Clap, clap, clap) G O,
(Clap, clap, clap) G O,
(Clap, clap, clap) G O,
And Bingo was his name-o.

Verse 5:
There was a farmer had a dog
And Bingo was his name-o.
(Clap, clap, clap, clap) O,
(Clap, clap, clap, clap) O,
(Clap, clap, clap, clap) O,
And Bingo was his name-o.

Verse 6:
There was a farmer had a dog
And Bingo was his name-o.
(Clap, clap, clap, clap, clap),
(Clap, clap, clap, clap, clap),
(Clap, clap, clap, clap, clap),
And Bingo was his name-o.

Bobby Shafto

F
Gm7
C7
B♭

Moderately bright (𝅗𝅥 = 86)

Traditional

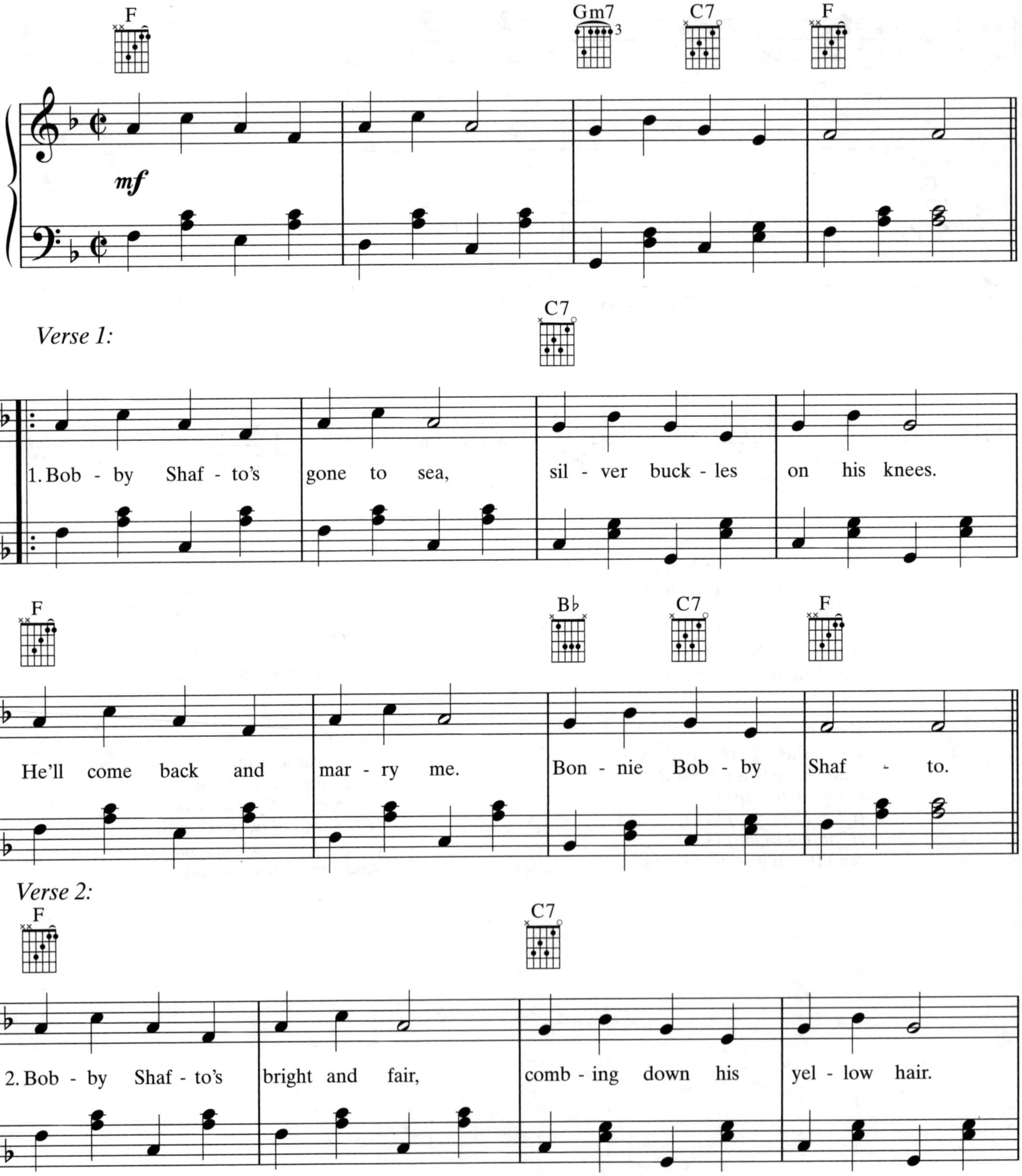
F
Gm7
C7
F
mf
Verse 1:
C7
1. Bob - by Shaf - to's gone to sea, sil - ver buck - les on his knees.
F
B♭
C7
F
He'll come back and mar - ry me. Bon - nie Bob - by Shaf - to.
Verse 2:
F
C7
2. Bob - by Shaf - to's bright and fair, comb - ing down his yel - low hair.

F
Gm7
C7
F
He's my own for - ev - er - more. Bon - nie Bob - by Shaf - to.
1.
Gm7
C7
F
2.
C7
F

Boys and Girls Come Out to Play

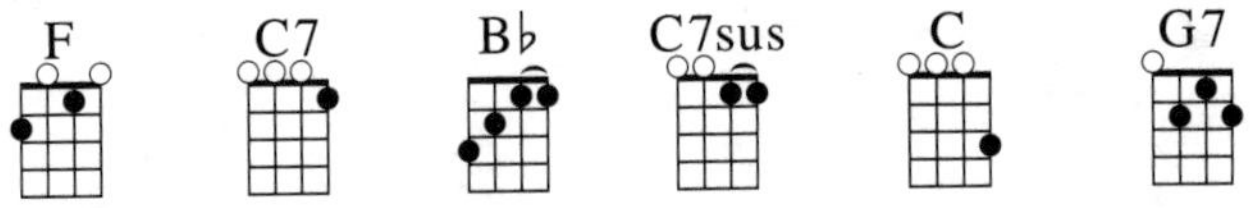
F
C7
B♭
C7sus
C
G7

Moderately (♩. = 84)

Traditional

F
C7
F
C7
B♭
F
C7sus
mf
F
C7
F
C7
F
Boys and girls come out to play. The moon doth shine_ as bright as day.
C7
F
C7
F
Leave your sup - per, and leave your sleep, and join your play - fel - lows in the street.

C G7 C G7 C
Come with a whoop and come with a call.
Come with a good will or not at all,
G7 C G7 C C7
Up the lad - der and down the wall, a pen - ny loaf will serve us all.
F C7 F C7 F
Boys and girls come out to play. The moon doth shine as bright as day.
1. D.C.
C7 F C7 F
Leave your sup - per, and leave your sleep, and join your play - fel - lows in the street
2.
F C7 F C7 B♭ C7 F
in the street.
8va
f

Brahms' Lullaby
(Lullaby and Goodnight)

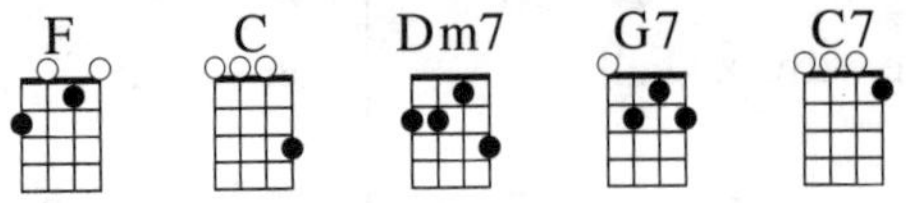
F
C
Dm7
G7
C7

Gentle lullaby (♩ = 82)

Traditional

F
C/E
Dm7
G7
mp
(with pedal)
C
*
Lul - la - by, and good - night, with
Gut - en a - bend, gut' nacht, mit
G7
ros - es be - dight, with lil - ies be - spread is
ro - sen be - dacht, mit näg - lein be - steckt, schlupf
C
F
C/E
ba - by's wee bed. Lay thee down now and rest, may that
un - ter die deck. Mor - gen früh, wenn Gott will, wirst du

*The original German lyric is provided in italic.

Dm7 G7 C/E C7 F C/E
16
slum - ber be blessed. Lay thee down now, and rest, may thou
wie - der ge - weckt. Mor - gen früh, wenn Gott will, wirst du
Dm7 G7 C F C/E
20
1.
slum - ber be blessed.
wie - der ge - weckt.
Dm7 G7 C C
24
2.
Lul - la - blessed.
Gu - ten weckt.
F C/E Dm7 G7 C
28
rit. e dim.
p

BRUSH YOUR TEETH

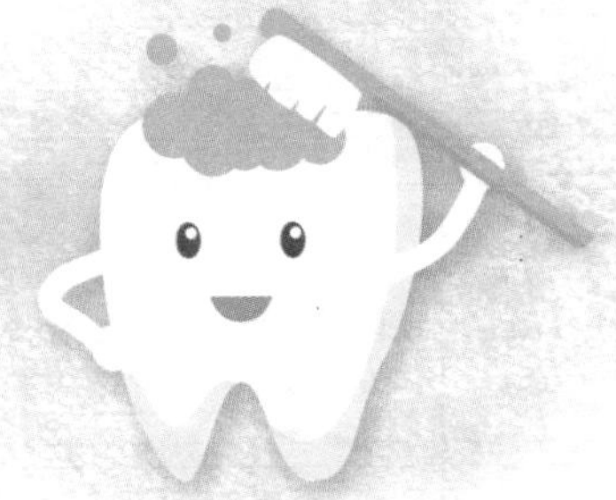

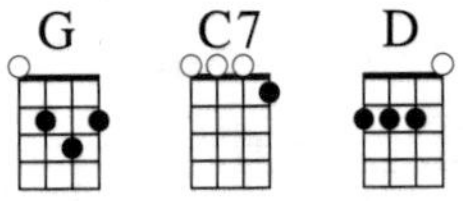
G
C7
D

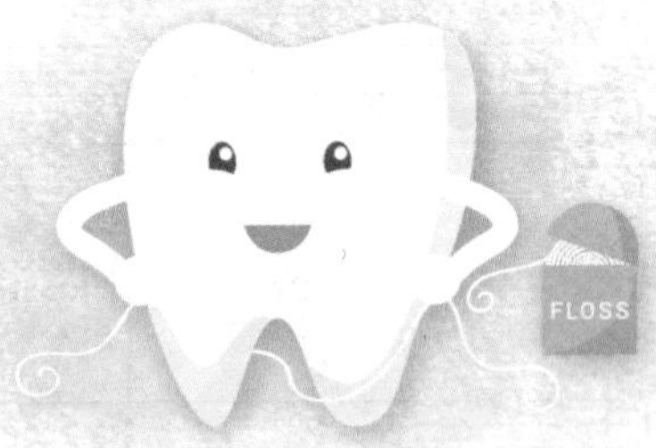

Moderately bright (♩ = 144) (♫ = ♩♪ triplet)

Traditional

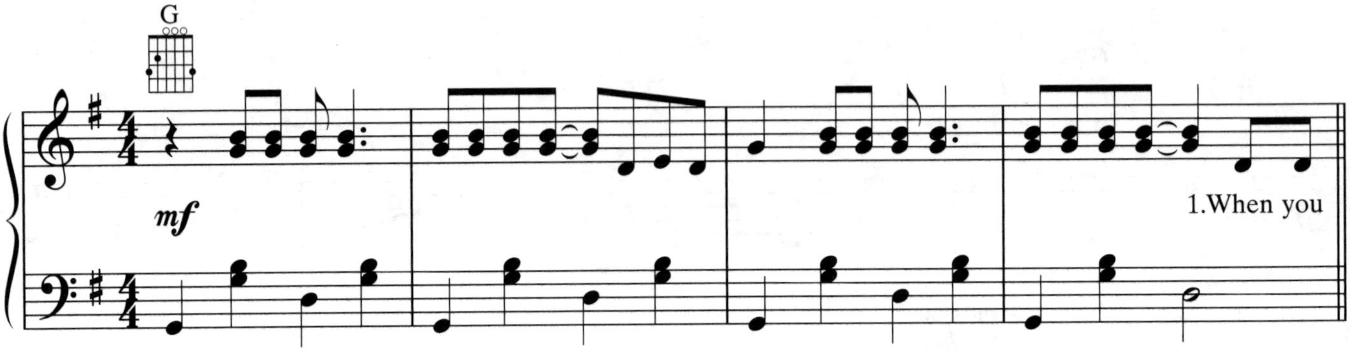
G
mf
1.When you

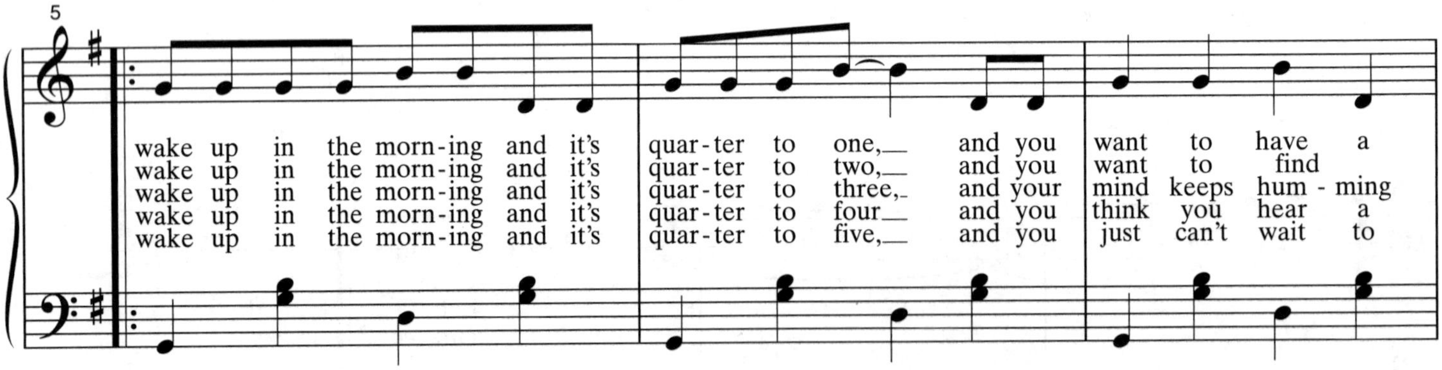
5
wake up in the morn-ing and it's quar-ter to one,__ and you want to have a
wake up in the morn-ing and it's quar-ter to two,__ and you want to find
wake up in the morn-ing and it's quar-ter to three,_ and your mind keeps hum - ming
wake up in the morn-ing and it's quar-ter to four__ and you think you hear a
wake up in the morn-ing and it's quar-ter to five,__ and you just can't wait to

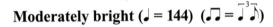

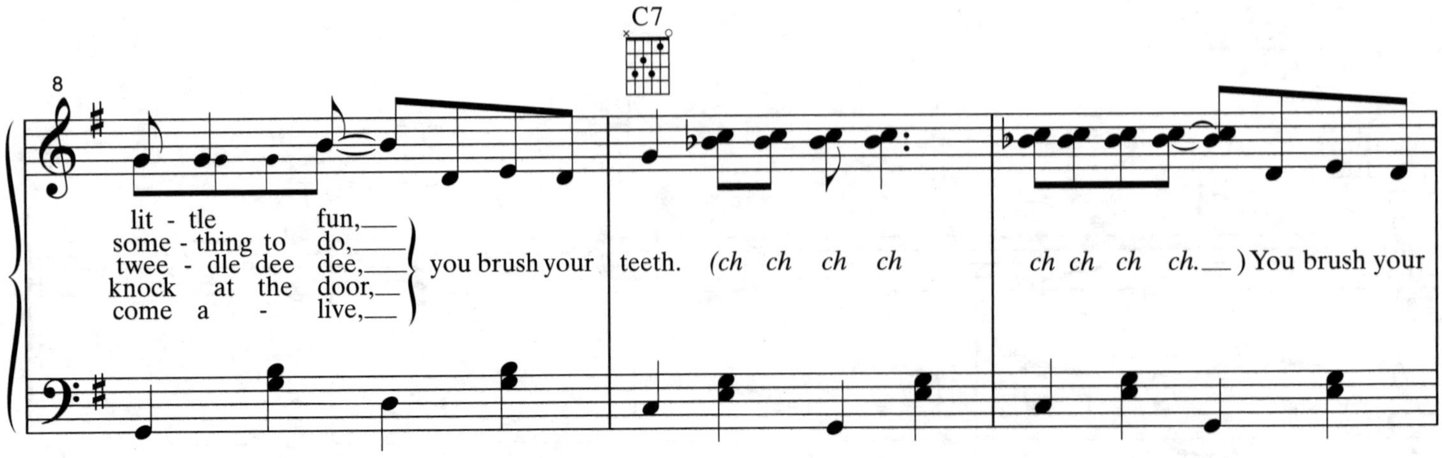
8
C7
lit - tle fun,__
some - thing to do,__
twee - dle dee dee,__
knock at the door,__
come a - live,__
you brush your teeth. (ch ch ch ch ch ch ch ch.__) You brush your

G
1.2.4.
3.
11
teeth. (ch ch ch ch
ch ch ch ch.___)
2. When you
3. When you
5. When you
ch ch ch ch___) You brush your
C7
G
14
teeth. (ch ch ch ch
ch ch ch ch.___) You brush your
teeth. (ch ch ch ch
5.
C7
17
ch ch ch ch.___) 4.When you
ch ch ch ch___) You brush your
teeth. (ch ch ch ch
G
D G
20
ch ch ch ch.___) You brush your
teeth. (ch ch ch ch
ch ch ch ch.___)

Cockles and Mussels
(Molly Malone)

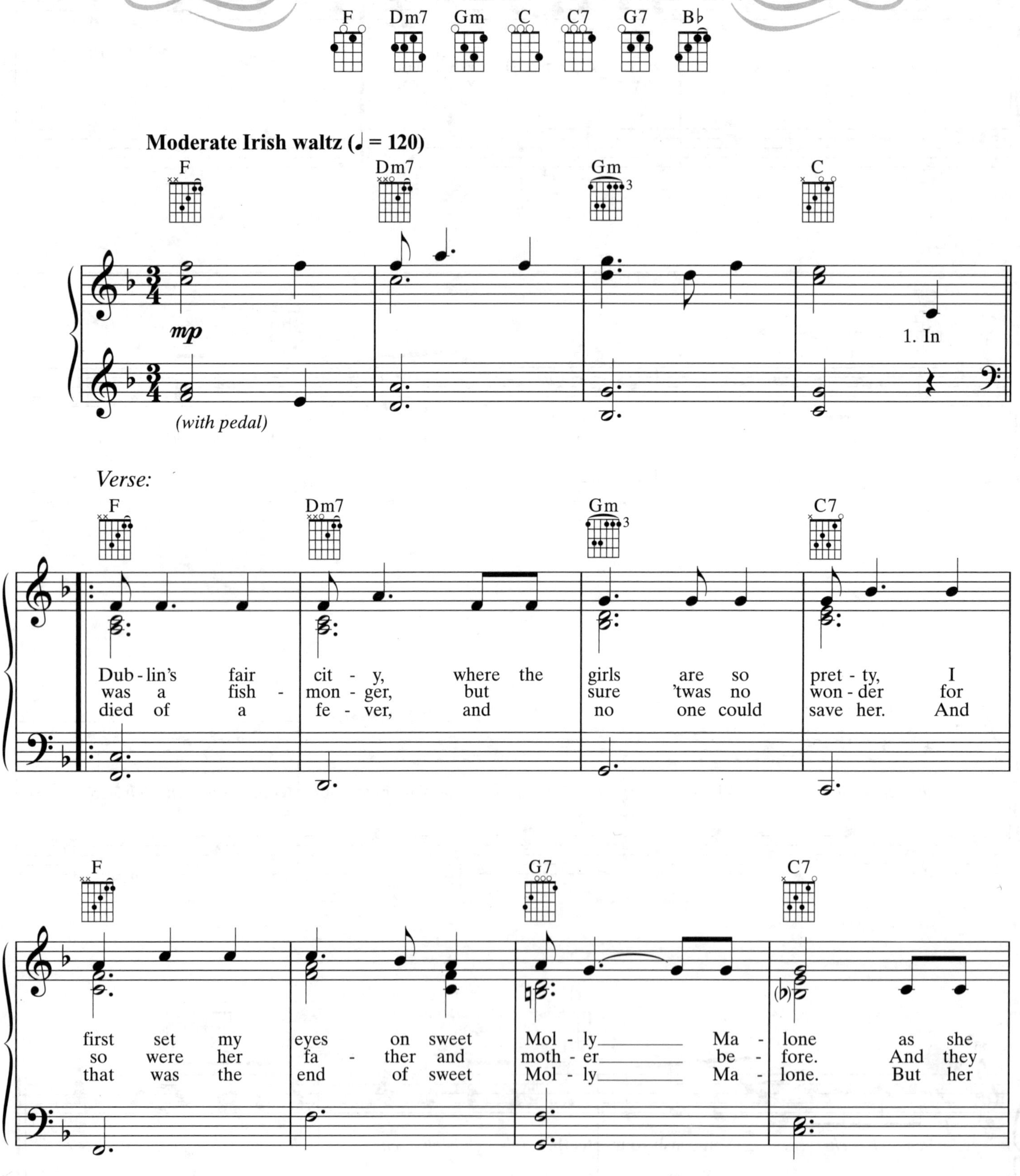
F Dm7 Gm C C7 G7 B♭
Moderate Irish waltz (♩ = 120)
F Dm7 Gm C
mp
(with pedal)
1. In
Verse:
F Dm7 Gm C7
Dub - lin's fair cit - y, where the girls are so pret - ty, I
was a fish - mon - ger, but sure 'twas no won - der for
died of a fe - ver, and no one could save her. And
F G7 C7
first set my eyes on sweet Mol - ly Ma - lone as she
so were her fa - ther and moth - er be - fore. And they
that was the end of sweet Mol - ly Ma - lone. But her

F Dm7 Gm C
wheeled her wheel - bar - row through streets broad and nar - row,
wheeled their bar - rows through the streets broad and nar - row,
ghost wheels her bar - row through streets broad and nar - row,
cry - ing,
F B♭ F/C C7 F
"Cock - les and mus - sels, a - live, a - live, oh." "A -
cresc.
Chorus:
Dm7 Gm C7
mf live, a - live, oh, a - live, a - live, oh. Cry - ing,
F B♭ 1.2. F/C C7 F
"Cock - les and mus - sels, a - live, a - live, oh." 2. She 3. She
dim.
3. F/C C7 F Dm7 Gm C F
live, a - live, oh."
mp
rit. e dim.
p

Come Little Leaves

Words by
George Cooper

Music by
Thomas J. Crawford

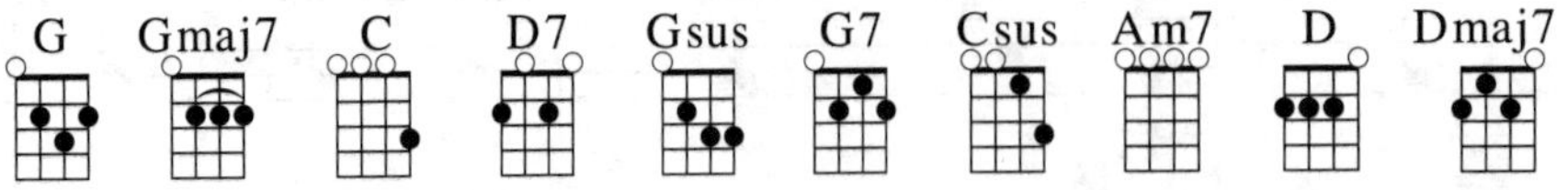
G
Gmaj7
C
D7
Gsus
G7
Csus
Am7
D
Dmaj7

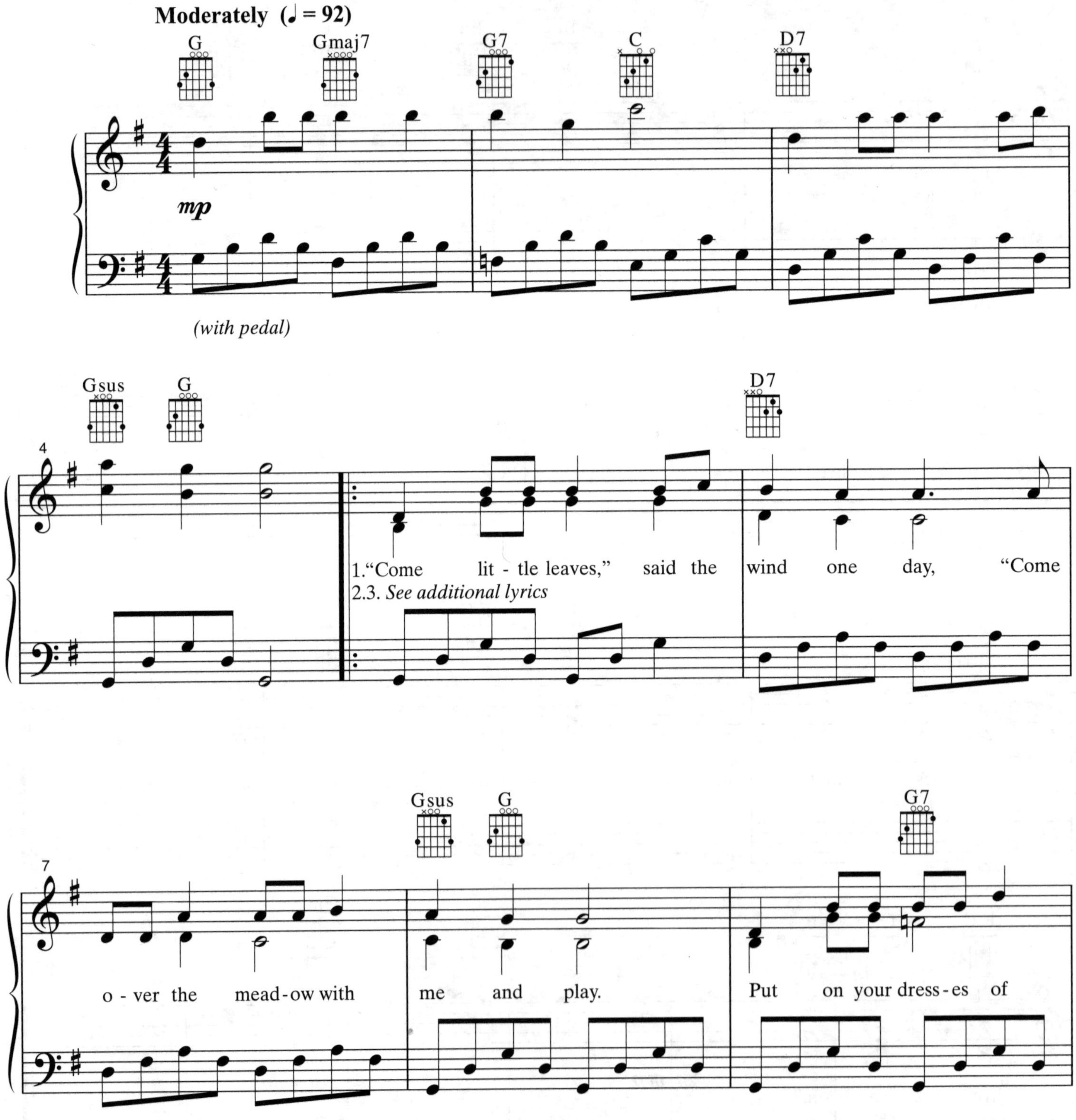
Moderately (♩ = 92)
G
Gmaj7
G7
C
D7
mp
(with pedal)
Gsus
G
D7
4
1."Come lit - tle leaves," said the wind one day, "Come
2.3. See additional lyrics
7
Gsus
G
G7
o - ver the mead - ow with me and play. Put on your dress - es of

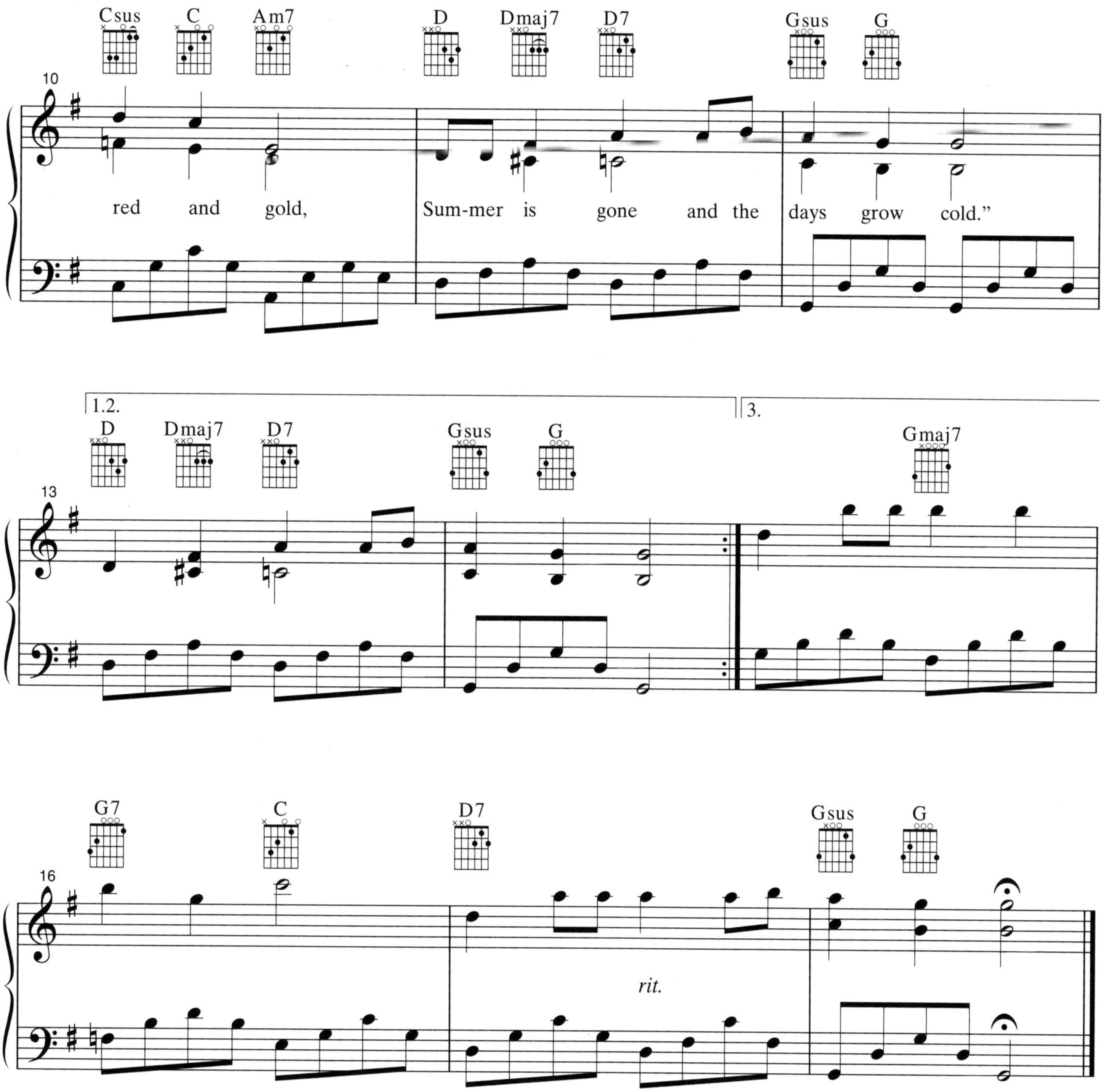
Csus C Am7 D Dmaj7 D7 Gsus G
10
red and gold, Sum-mer is gone and the days grow cold."
1.2.
D Dmaj7 D7 Gsus G
13
3.
Gmaj7
G7 C D7 Gsus G
16
rit.

Verse 2:
Soon as the leaves heard the wind's loud call,
Down they came fluttering, one and all;
Over the brown fields they danced and flew,
Singing the soft little songs they knew.

Verse 3:
Dancing and twirling the little leaves went,
Winter had called them and they were content;
Soon fast asleep in their earthly beds,
The snow laid a soft mantle over their heads.

Deck the Hall

English lyric by
Thomas Oliphant

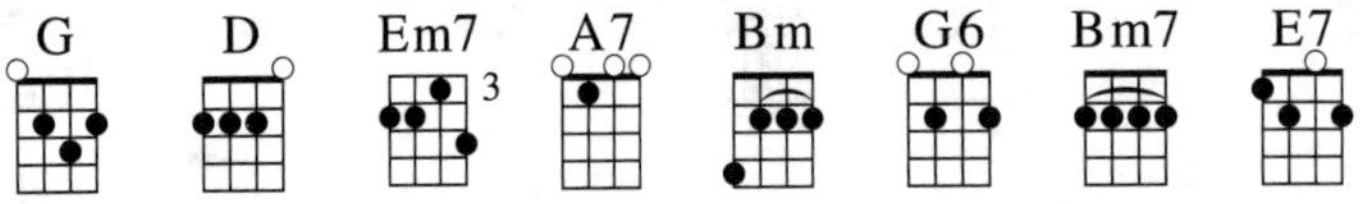
G
D
Em7
A7
Bm
G6
Bm7
E7
3

Original Welsh words by
John Jones
(a.k.a. Talhaiarn)

Brightly (𝅗𝅥 = 72) (♩ = 144)

Traditional

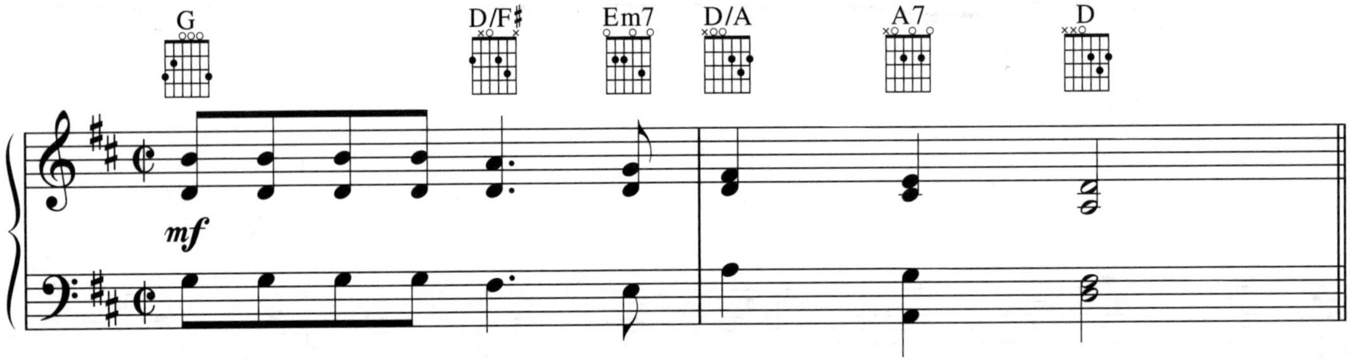
G
D/F♯
Em7
D/A
A7
D
mf

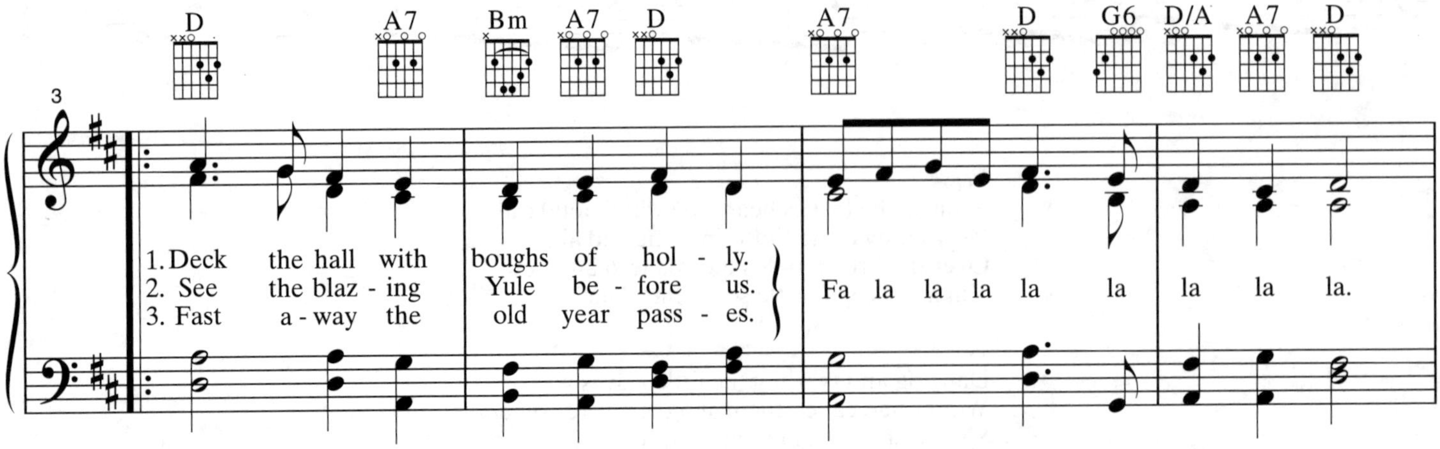
3
D
A7
Bm
A7
D
A7
D
G6
D/A
A7
D
1. Deck the hall with boughs of hol - ly.
2. See the blaz - ing Yule be - fore us.
3. Fast a - way the old year pass - es.
Fa la la la la la la la la.

D A7 Bm A7 D A7 D G6 D/A A7 D
7
'Tis the sea - son to be jol - ly.
Strike the harp and join the cho - rus.
Hail the new, ye lads and lass - es.
Fa la la la la la la la la.
A7 D A/C♯ Bm7 E7
11
Don we now our gay ap - par - el.
Fol - low me in mer - ry mea - sure,
Sing we joy - ous all to - geth - er,
Fa la la la la la
A E7 A7 D A7 Bm A7 D
14
la la la.
Troll the an - cient Yule - tide car - ol.
while I tell of Yule - tide trea - sure.
heed - less of the wind and weath - er.
G D/F♯ Em7 D/A A7 D D/A A7 D
1.2.
3.
17
Fa la la la la la la la la.
la la la.
rit.

Did You Ever See a Lassie?

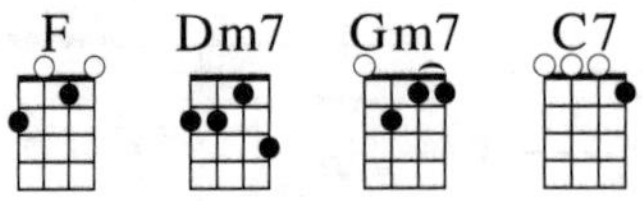
F
Dm7
Gm7
C7

Moderately (♩ = 144)

Traditional

F
Dm7
Gm7
C7
F
mf
1. Did you
(with pedal)
C7
F
ev - er see a las - sie, a las - sie, a las - sie? Did you
ev - er see a lad - die, a lad - die, a lad - die? Did you
Dm7
Gm7
C7
F
ev - er see a las - sie go this way or that? Go
ev - er see a lad - die go this way or that? Go

C7 F C7 F
this way and that way, go this way and that way. Did you
this way or that way, go this way or that way. Did you
Dm7 Gm7 C7 1. F
ev - er see a las - sie go this way or that?
ev - er see a lad - die go this way or
Dm7 Gm7 C7 F
2. Did you
2. F Dm7 Gm7 C7 F
that?

Do Your Ears Hang Low

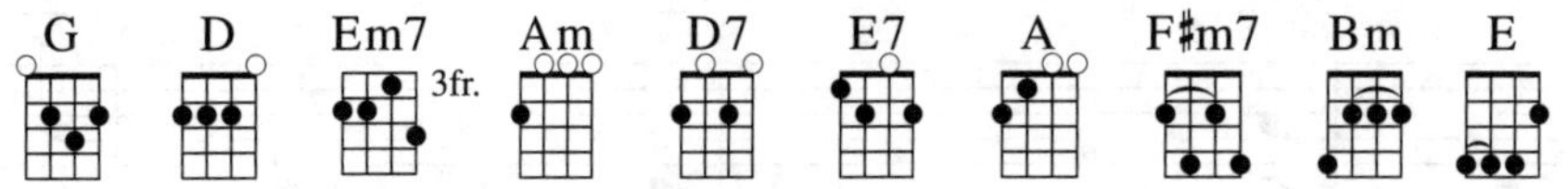
G D Em7 Am D7 E7 A F♯m7 Bm E
3fr.

Moderately (𝅗𝅥 = 74) (♪♪ = ♩♪ triplet)

Traditional

G
G/D
D
G
mf
1. Do your

Em7
ears hang low? Do they wob - ble to and fro? Can you tie 'em in a knot? Can you
ears stand high? Do they reach up to the sky? Do they droop when they are wet? Do they
ears flip - flop? Can you use them as a mop? Are they string - y at the bottom? Are they

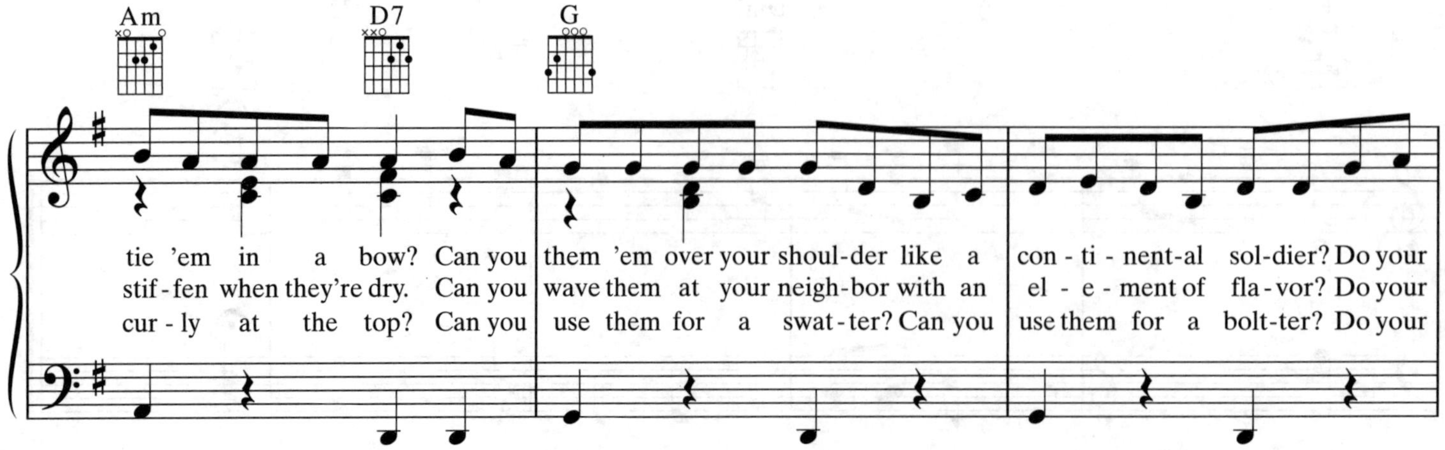
Am
D7
G
tie 'em in a bow? Can you them 'em over your shoul-der like a con - ti - nent-al sol-dier? Do your
stif - fen when they're dry. Can you wave them at your neigh-bor with an el - e - ment of fla - vor? Do your
cur - ly at the top? Can you use them for a swat - ter? Can you use them for a bolt-ter? Do your

1.2.
3.
G/D D G D7 G
ears hang low.
ears stand - high?
ears flip
2. Do your
3. Do your
G E7
flop?
Do your
A F♯m7
ears stick out? Can you wag - gle them a - bout? Can you flap them up and down as you
Bm E7 A
fly a - round the town? Can you shut them up for sure when you hear an aw - ful bore? Do your
A/E E A
ears stick out?
8va
f

Down by the Bay

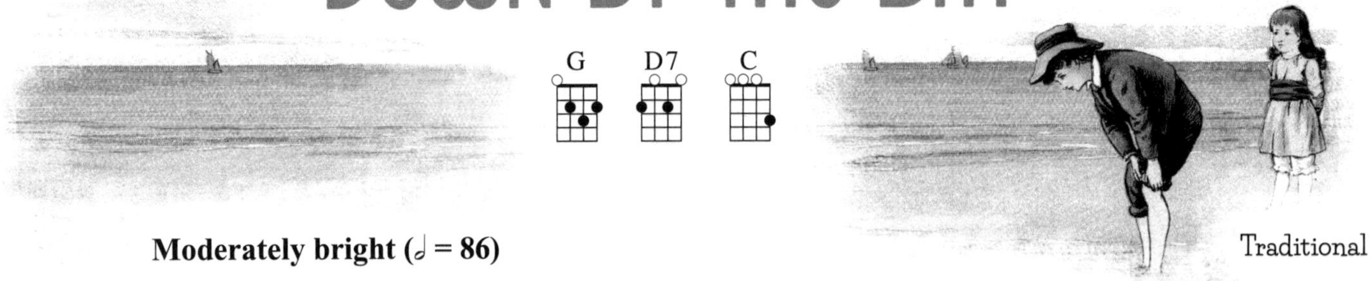
G
D7
C

Moderately bright (𝅗𝅥 = 86)

Traditional

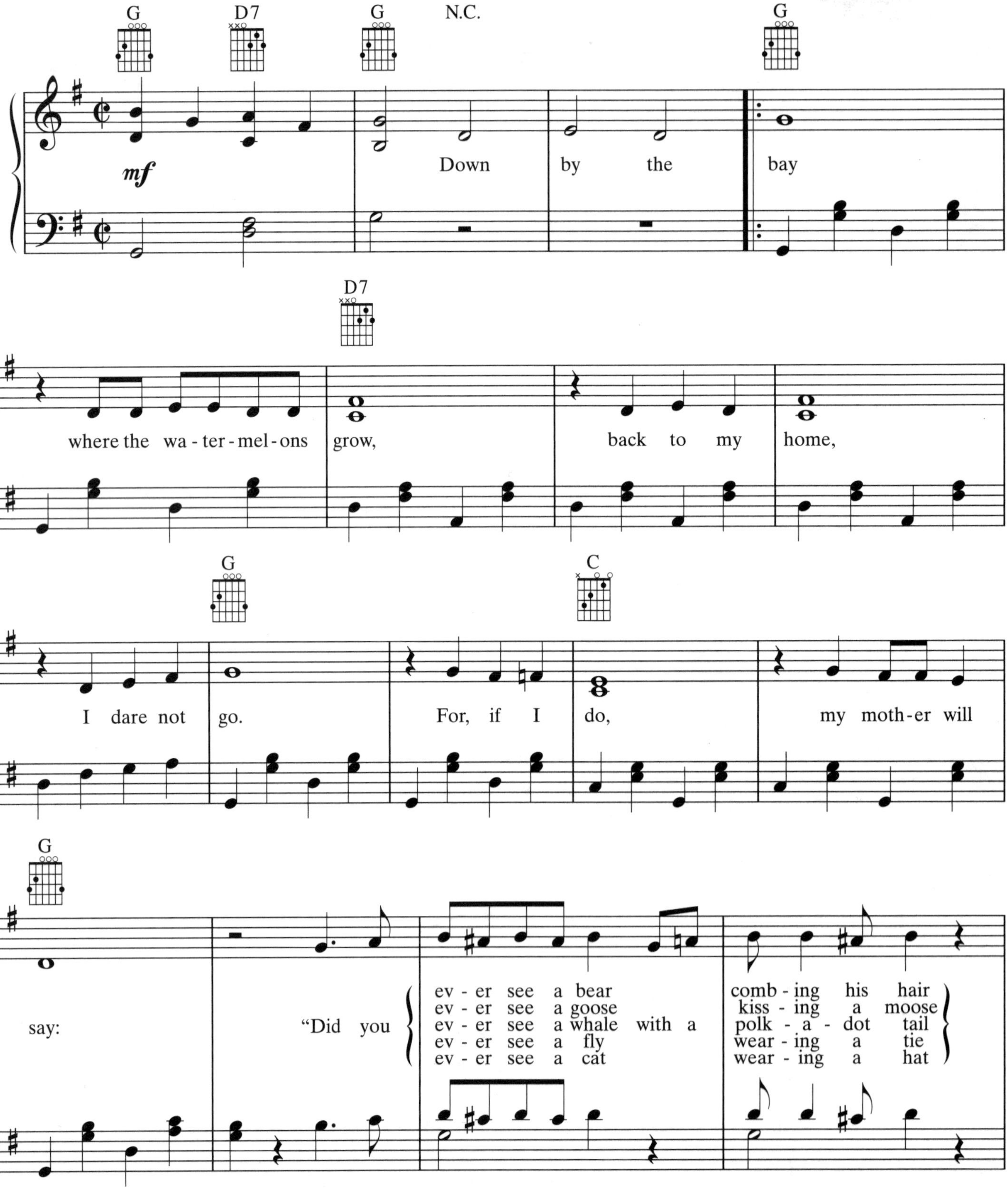
G
D7
G
N.C.
G
mf
Down by the bay
where the wa - ter - mel - ons grow,
back to my home,
D7
G
C
I dare not go.
For, if I do,
my moth - er will
say:
"Did you
ev - er see a bear
ev - er see a goose
ev - er see a whale with a
ev - er see a fly
ev - er see a cat
comb - ing his hair
kiss - ing a moose
polk - a - dot tail
wear - ing a tie
wear - ing a hat

1.–4.
5.
D7
G
G
down by the bay?" Down by the bay?" Down by the
D7
bay where the wa - ter - mel - ons grow, back to my
G
home, I dare not go. For if, I
C
G
do, my moth - er will say: "Did you
rit.
D7
G
ev - er have a time when you could - n't find a rhyme down by the bay."
a tempo
8vb

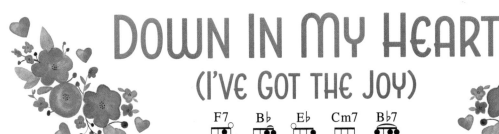

Down In My Heart
(I've Got the Joy)

F7 B♭ E♭ Cm7 B♭7
Moderately, with spirit (♩ = 112)
Verse:
Composed by
George W. Cooke
F7 B♭ E♭ B♭
mf
1. I've got the
joy, joy, joy, joy
2.–4. See additional lyrics
F7 B♭
4
down in my heart. (Where?)
Down in my heart. (Where?)
Down in my heart. I've got the
F7
7
joy, joy, joy, joy
down in my heart. (Where?)
Down in my heart to
Chorus:
B♭ E♭ B♭ E♭ B♭
10
stay. And I'm so
hap - py, so ver - y
hap - py. I

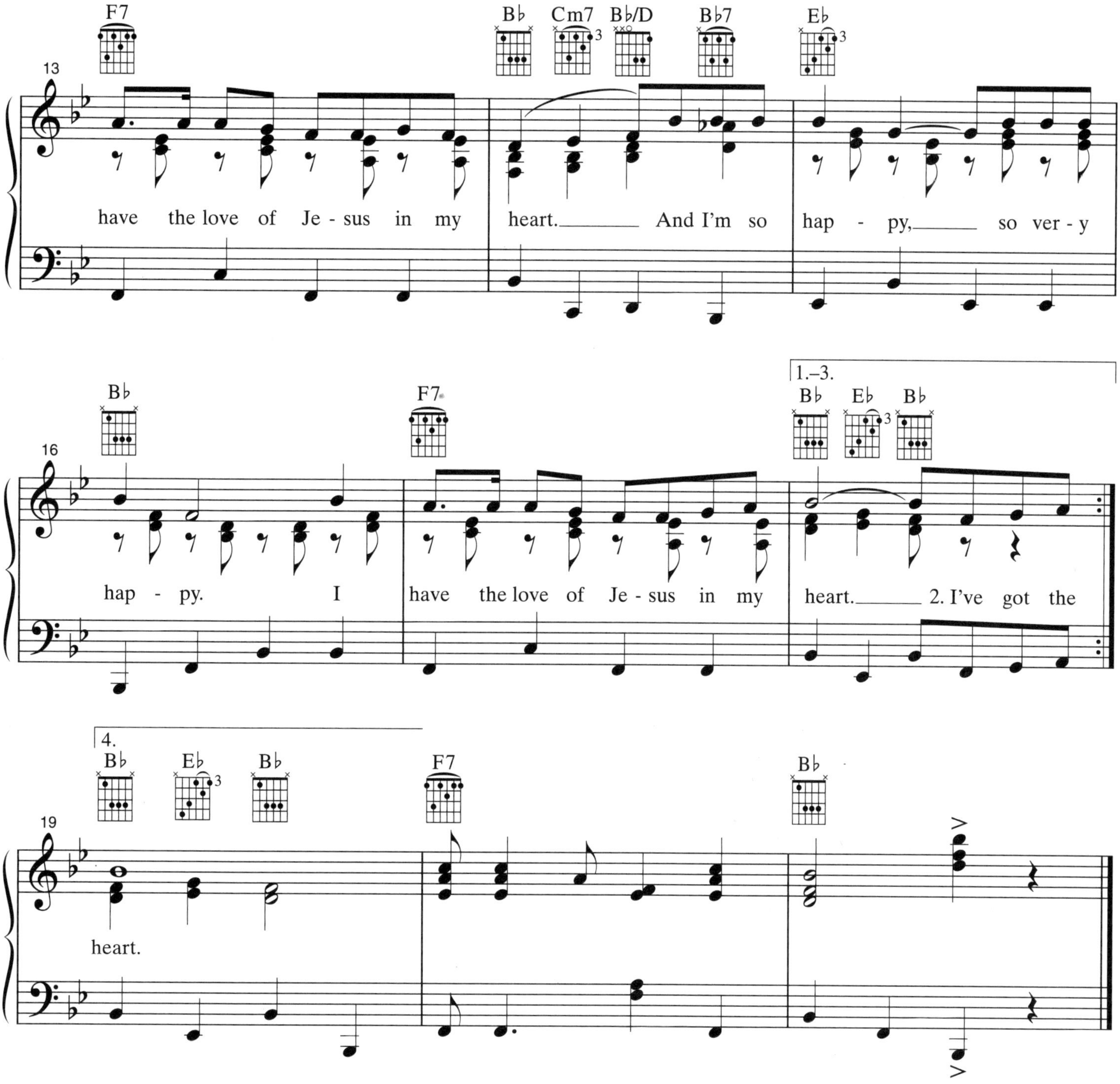
13
F7
B♭ Cm7 B♭/D B♭7
E♭
have the love of Je - sus in my heart. And I'm so hap - py, so ver - y
16
B♭
F7
1.–3.
B♭ E♭ B♭
hap - py. I have the love of Je - sus in my heart. 2. I've got the
4.
19
B♭ E♭ B♭
F7
B♭
heart.

Verse 2:
I've got the peace that passes understanding down in my heart,
Down in my heart, down in my heart.
I've got the peace that passes understanding down in my heart,
Down in my heart to stay.
(To Chorus:)

Verse 3:
I've got the love of Jesus, love of Jesus down in my heart,
Down in my heart, down in my heart.
I've got the love of Jesus, love of Jesus down in my heart,
Down in my heart to stay.
(To Chorus:)

Verse 4:
For there is therefore now no condemnation down in my heart,
Down in my heart, down in my heart.
For there is therefore now no condemnation down in my heart,
Down in my heart to stay.
(To Chorus:)

Eency Weency Spider

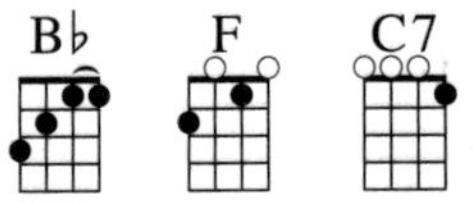
B♭
F
C7

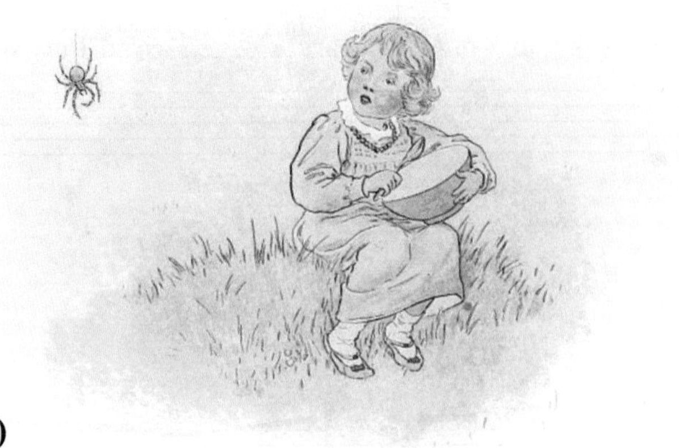

Moderately (♩. = 104)

Traditional

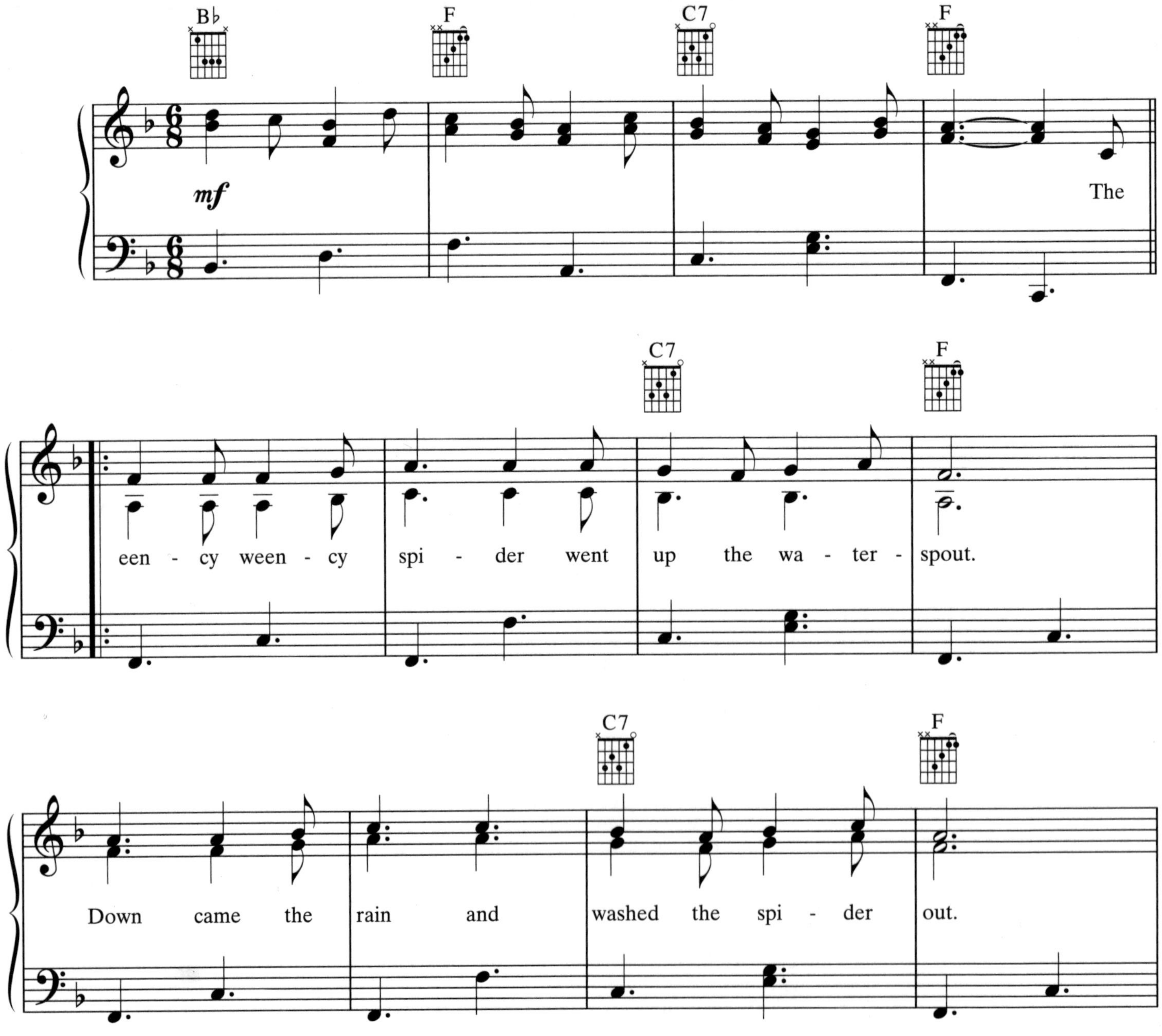
B♭
F
C7
F
mf
The
C7
F
een - cy ween - cy spi - der went up the wa - ter - spout.
C7
F
Down came the rain and washed the spi - der out.

C7
F
Out came the sun and dried up all the rain. And the
C7
F
B♭
een - cy ween - cy spi - der went up the spout a - gain.
F
1.
C7
F
The
2.
C7
F
8va

The Farmer in the Dell

Eb
Bb7
F
C7
Moderately (♩. = 108)
Traditional
Eb
mf
1. The
Verses 1–5:
farm - er in the dell, the farm - er in the dell,
farm - er takes a wife, the farm - er takes a wife,
3.4.5. See additional lyrics
Bb7
1.–4.
Eb
hi - ho, the der - ry - o, the farm - er in the dell. 2. The
hi - ho, the der - ry - o, the farm - er takes a wife. 3. The
5.
Eb
F
dog.
6. The

Verses 6–9:

dog takes the cat, the dog takes the cat, hi - ho, the
7.8.9. See additional lyrics

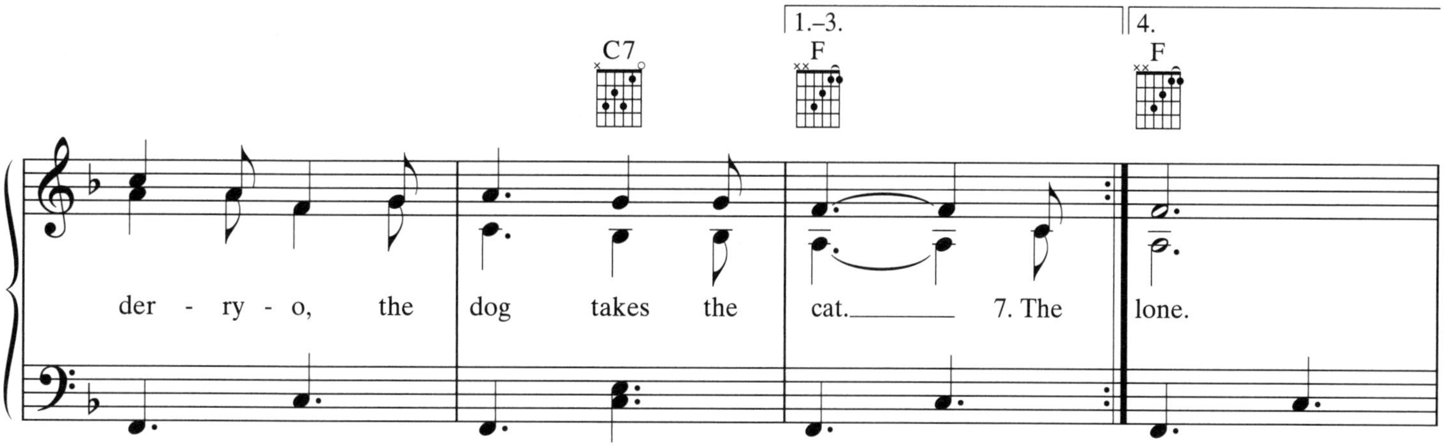
1.–3.
4.
C7
F
F
der - ry - o, the dog takes the cat. 7. The
lone.

C7
F

Verse 3:
The wife takes a child,
The wife takes a child,
Hi-ho, the derry-o,
The wife takes a child.

Verse 4:
The child takes a nurse,
The child takes a nurse,
Hi-ho, the derry-o,
The child takes a nurse.

Verse 5:
The nurse takes the dog,
The nurse takes the dog,
Hi-ho, the derry-o,
The nurse takes the dog.
(To Verse 6:)

Verse 7:
The cat takes the rat,
The cat takes the rat,
Hi-ho, the derry-o,
The cat takes the rat.

Verse 8:
The rat takes the cheese,
The rat takes the cheese,
Hi-ho, the derry-o,
The rat takes the cheese.

Verse 9:
The cheese stands alone,
The cheese stands alone,
Hi-ho, the derry-o,
The cheese stands alone.

Father's Whiskers

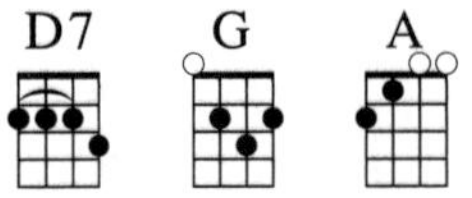
D7
G
A

Moderately bright (𝅗𝅥 = 120)

Traditional

D7
G
mf
1. I
Verse:
A
have a dear old fa - ther for whom I night - ly pray, he's
2.–4. See additional lyrics
D7
G
got a set of whisk - ers, they're al - ways in the way. They're
Chorus:
A
al - ways in the way, the cows eat them for hay, they

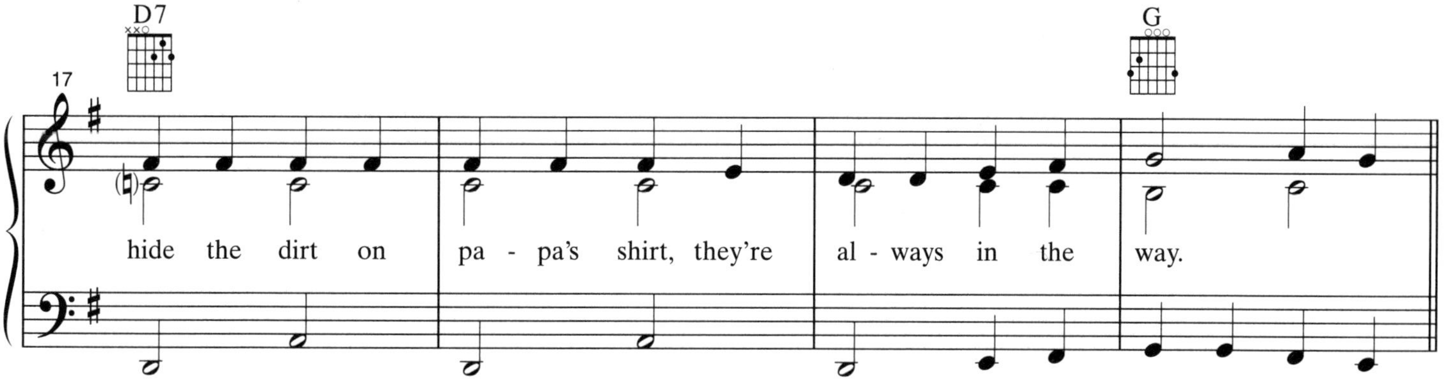
D7
17
G
hide the dirt on pa - pa's shirt, they're al - ways in the way.

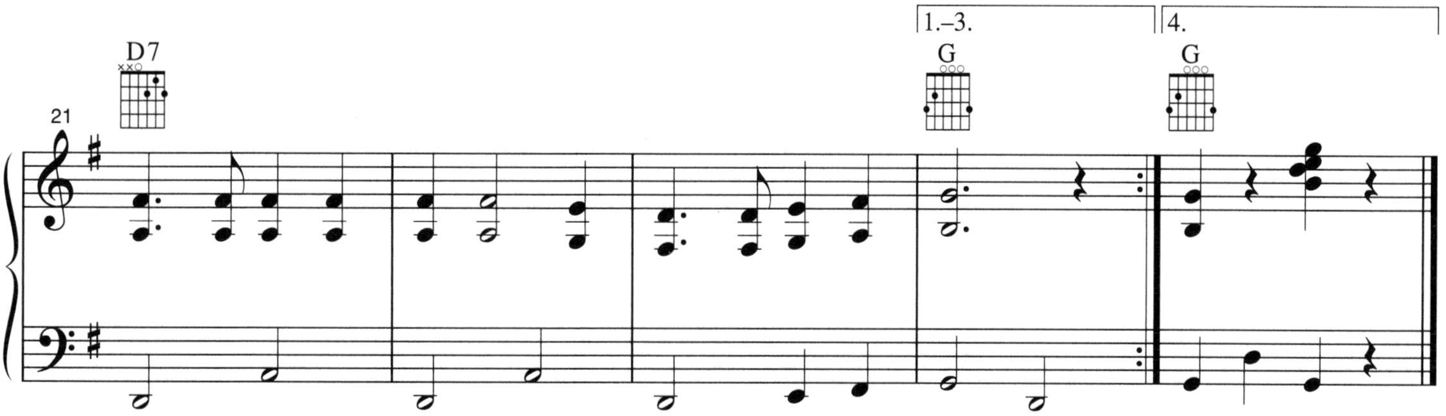
1.–3.
4.
D7
21
G
G

Verse 2:
Father had a strong back,
Now it's all caved in,
He stepped upon his whiskers
And walked up to his chin.
(To Chorus:)

Verse 3:
Father has a daughter,
Her name is Ella Mae,
She climbs up father's whiskers
And braids them all the way.
(To Chorus:)

Verse 4:
I have a dear old mother,
She likes the whiskers, too,
She uses them for dusting
And cleaning out the flue.
(To Chorus:)

Five Little Monkeys

F
C7
Gm7

Moderately bright (♩ = 144)

Traditional

F
mf
Verses 1–4:
C7
1. Five
2. Four
3. Three
4. Two
lit - tle mon - keys jump - ing on the bed, one fell off and
F
Gm7
bumped his head. Ma - ma called the doc - tor, and the doc - tor said,
C7
F
"No more mon - keys jump - ing on the bed!"

1.–3.
4.
14
Verse 5:
17
C7
5. One lit - tle mon - key jump - ing on the bed, he fell off and
F
20
Gm7
bumped his head. Ma - ma called the doc - tor, and the doc - tor said,
C7
23
F
C7
F
"Put those mon - keys right to bed!"

Frère Jacques/ Are You Sleeping

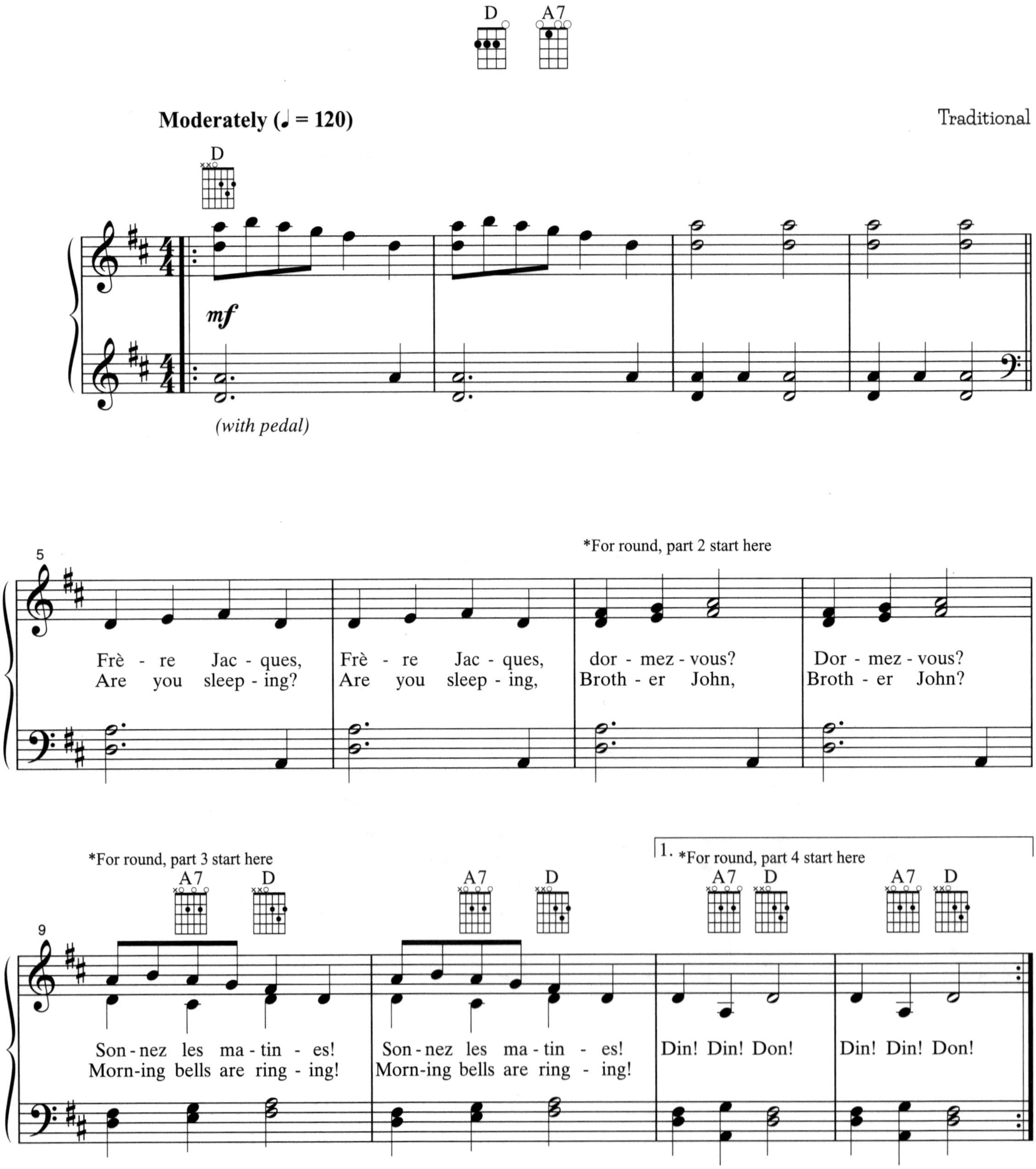
D
A7
Moderately (♩ = 120)
Traditional
D
mf
(with pedal)
5
*For round, part 2 start here
Frè - re Jac - ques, Frè - re Jac - ques, dor - mez - vous? Dor - mez - vous?
Are you sleep - ing? Are you sleep - ing, Broth - er John, Broth - er John?
*For round, part 3 start here
1. *For round, part 4 start here
A7 D A7 D A7 D A7 D
9
Son - nez les ma - tin - es! Son - nez les ma - tin - es! Din! Din! Don! Din! Din! Don!
Morn-ing bells are ring - ing! Morn-ing bells are ring - ing!

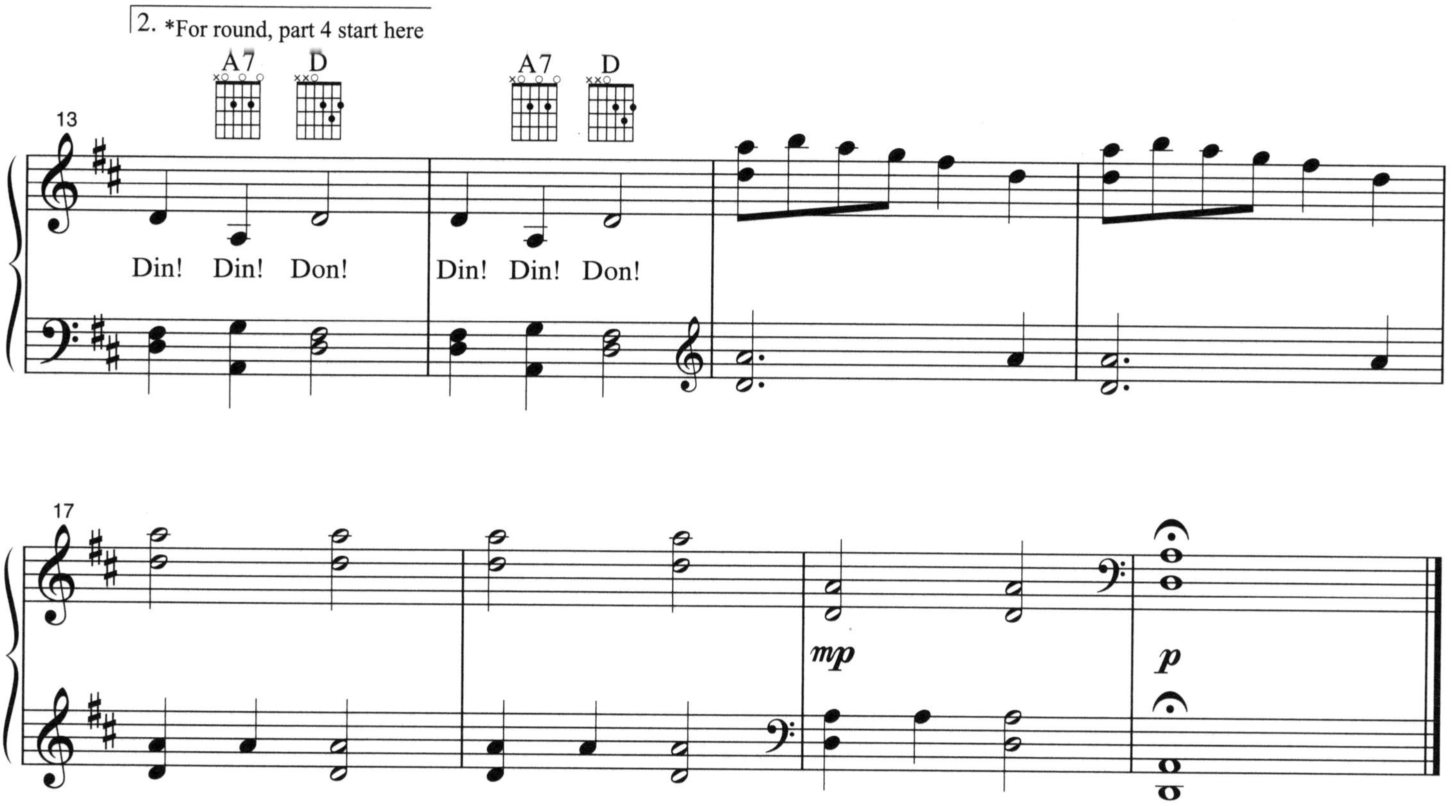
2. *For round, part 4 start here
A7
D
13
Din! Din! Don!
Din! Din! Don!
17
mp
p

Frog Went A-Courtin'

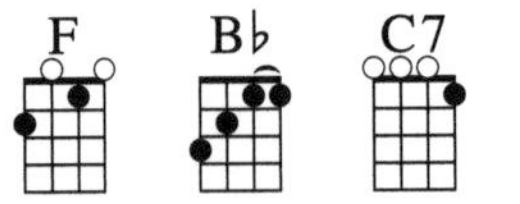
F
B♭
C7

Traditional

Moderately bright (𝅗𝅥 = 116)

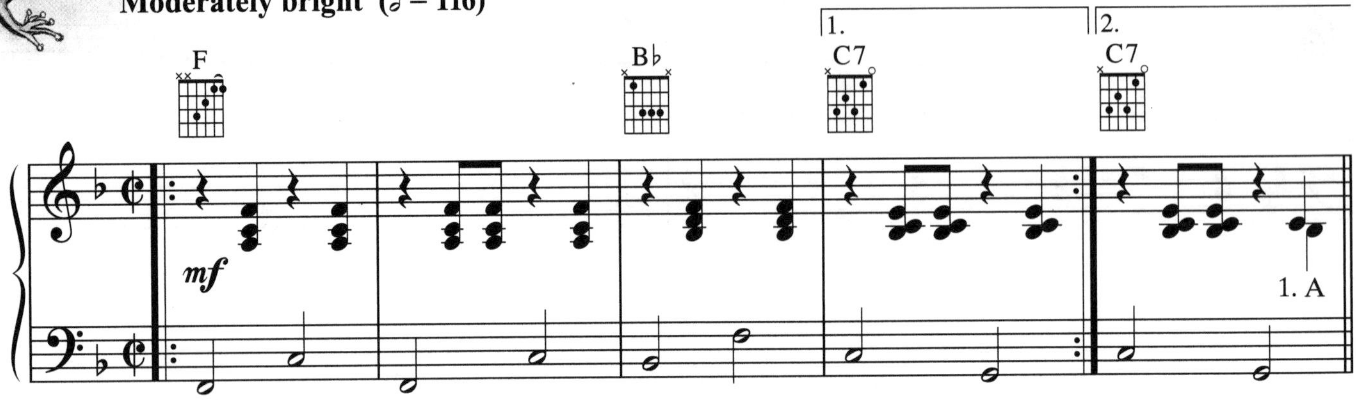
F
B♭
1.
C7
2.
C7
mf
1. A

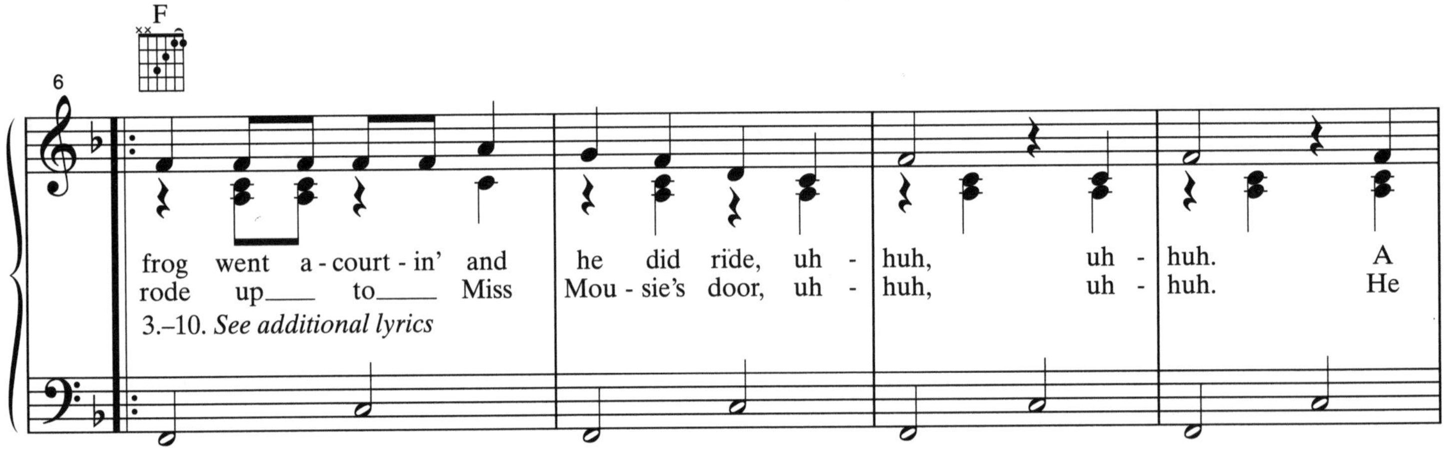
F
6
frog went a - court - in' and he did ride, uh - huh, uh - huh. A
rode up___ to___ Miss Mou - sie's door, uh - huh, uh - huh. He
3.–10. See additional lyrics

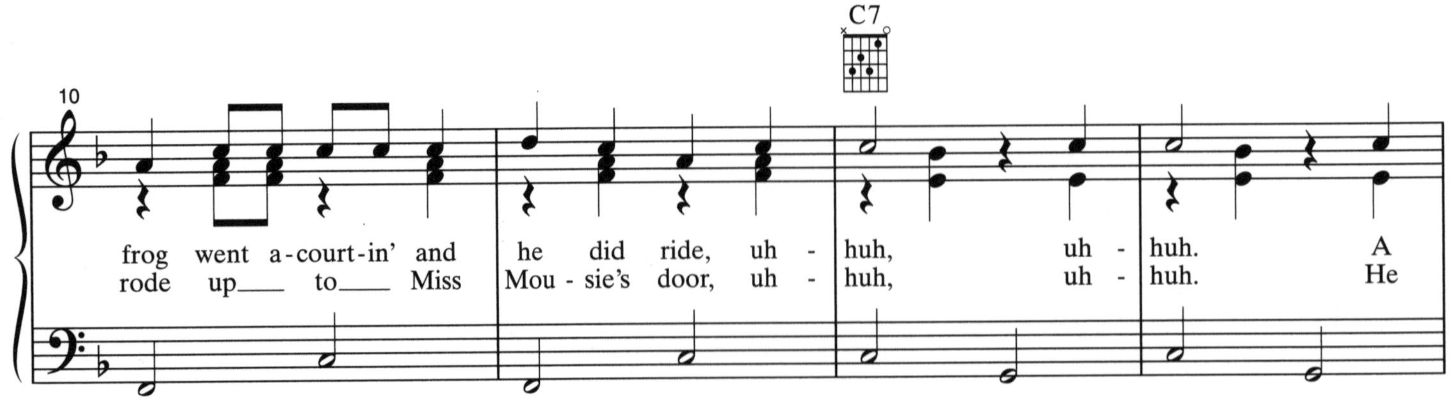
C7
10
frog went a - court - in' and he did ride, uh - huh, uh - huh. A
rode up___ to___ Miss Mou - sie's door, uh - huh, uh - huh. He

F
B♭
C7
14
frog went a-court-in' and he did ride, with sword and pis - tol by his side, uh -
rode up___ to___ Miss Mou - sie's door,___ where he'd of - ten been be - fore, uh -
F
1.–10.
C7
11.
C7
F
F7
18
huh, uh - huh. 2. He huh, uh - huh.
huh, uh - huh. 3. He
8vb

Verse 3:
He took Miss Mousie upon his knee, uh-huh, uh-huh.
He took Miss Mousie upon his knee, uh-huh, uh-huh.
He took Miss Mousie upon his knee,
Said "Miss Mousie, will you marry me?" Uh-huh, uh-huh.

Verse 4:
"I'll have to ask my Uncle Rat, uh-huh, uh-huh.
I'll have to ask my Uncle Rat, uh-huh, uh-huh.
I'll have to ask my Uncle Rat,
See what he has to say to that, uh-huh, uh-huh."

Verse 5:
Well, Uncle Rat laughed and shook his fat sides, uh-huh, uh-huh.
Well, Uncle Rat laughed and shook his fat sides, uh-huh, uh-huh.
Well, Uncle Rat laughed and shook his fat sides,
To think his niece would be a bride, uh-huh, uh-huh.

Verse 6:
Well, Uncle Rat rode off to town, uh-huh, uh-huh.
Well, Uncle Rat rode off to town, uh-huh, uh-huh.
Well, Uncle Rat rode off to town
To get his niece a wedding gown, uh-huh, uh-huh.

Verse 7:
"Where will the wedding supper be?" Uh-huh, uh-huh.
"Where will the wedding supper be?" Uh-huh, uh-huh.
"Where will the wedding supper be?"
"Way down yonder in the hollow tree." Uh-huh, uh-huh.

Verse 8:
The first to come was a little white moth, uh-huh, uh-huh.
The first to come was a little white moth, uh-huh, uh-huh.
The first to come was a little white moth,
She laid out the tablecloth, uh-huh, uh-huh.

Verse 9:
Next to come was a bumblebee, uh-huh, uh-huh.
Next to come was a bumblebee, uh-huh, uh-huh.
Next to come was a bumblebee,
Played the fiddle upon his knee, uh-huh, uh-huh.

Verse 10:
Next to come was Missus Cow, uh-huh, uh-huh.
Next to come was Missus Cow, uh-huh, uh-huh.
Next to come was Missus Cow,
Tried to dance but didn't know how, uh-huh, uh-huh.

Verse 11:
Next to come was the old gray cat, uh-huh, uh-huh.
Next to come was the old gray cat, uh-huh, uh-huh.
Next to come was the old gray cat,
He swallowed the frog, the mouse and the rat, uh-huh, uh-huh.

Go In and Out the Window

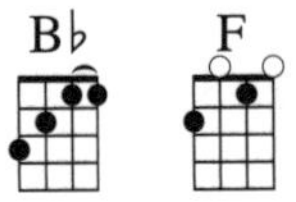
B♭
F
C7

Moderately, in two (𝅗𝅥 = 84)

Traditional

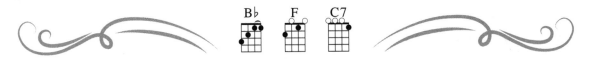

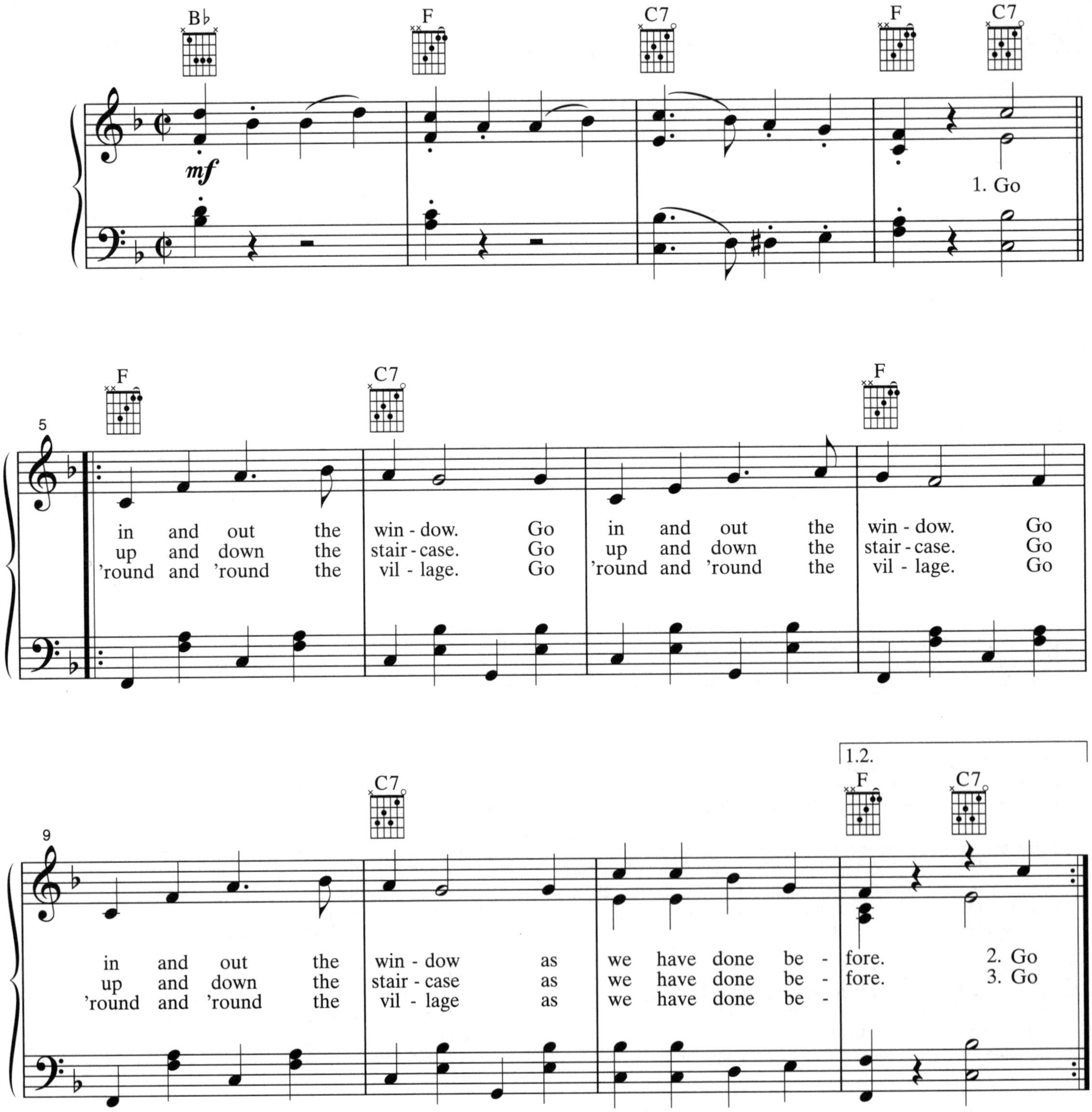
B♭ F C7 F C7
mf
1. Go
5
F C7 F
in and out the win - dow. Go in and out the win - dow. Go
up and down the stair - case. Go up and down the stair - case. Go
'round and 'round the vil - lage. Go 'round and 'round the vil - lage. Go
9
C7
1.2.
F C7
in and out the win - dow as we have done be - fore.
up and down the stair - case as we have done be - fore.
'round and 'round the vil - lage as we have done be -
2. Go
3. Go

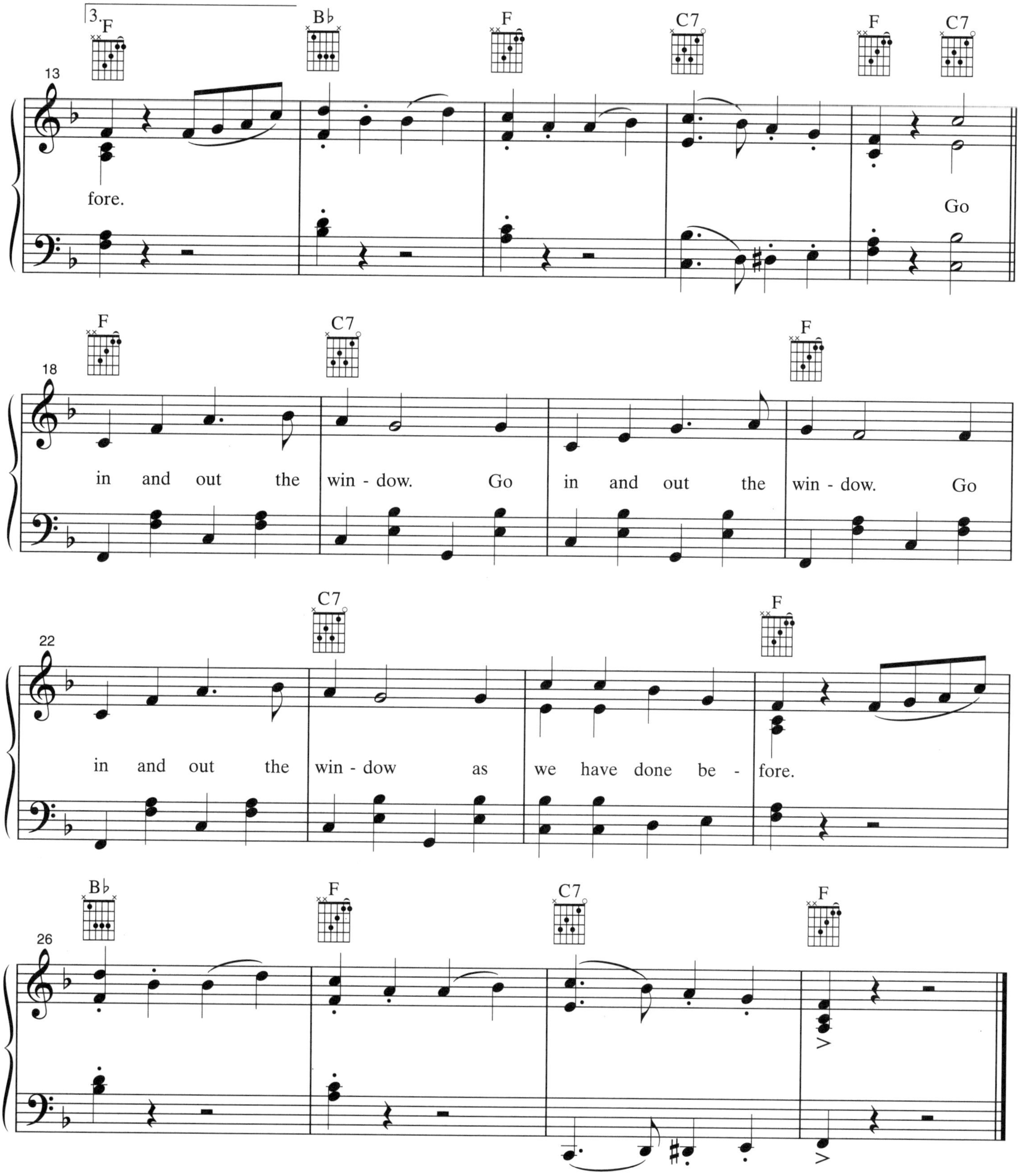
3.
F Bb F C7 F C7
13
fore. Go
F C7 F
18
in and out the win - dow. Go in and out the win - dow. Go
C7 F
22
in and out the win - dow as we have done be - fore.
Bb F C7 F
26

Goodnight, Ladies

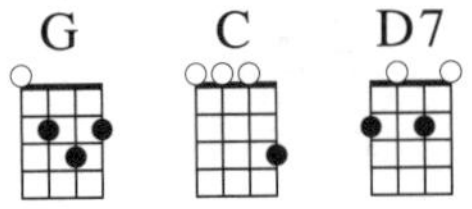
G
C
D7

Moderately bright (♩ = 160)

Traditional

G
C
G
D7
G
mf
Verse:
D7
1. Good - night, la - dies, good night, la - dies,
2. Fare - well, la - dies, fare - well, la - dies,
3. Sweet dreams, la - dies, sweet dreams, la - dies,
C
G
D7
G
good night, la - dies,
fare - well, la - dies,
sweet dreams, la - dies,
we're go - ing to leave you now.

D7
G
Mer - ri - ly we roll a - long, roll a - long, roll a - long.
D7
Mer - ri - ly we roll a - long, o'er the dark blue
1.2.
G
D7
G
sea.
3.
G
sea.
C
G
D7
G

The Grande Olde Duke of York

D7 G C
Moderate march (𝅗𝅥 = 92)
Traditional
N.C.
f
D7 G D7
Oh, the
mf
G D7
Grande Olde Duke of York, he had ten thou - sand men. He
G C G/D D7 G
marched them up to the top of the hill and he marched them down a - gain. And

D7
15
when they were up, they were up. And when they were down, they were down. And
G C G/D D7
1.
G
19
when they were on - ly half - way up, they were nei - ther up nor down.
C G/D D7 G D7
23
Oh, the
2.
G
N.C.
D7 G
27
down.
f

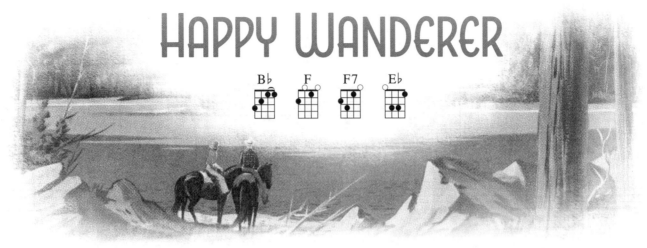

Happy Wanderer

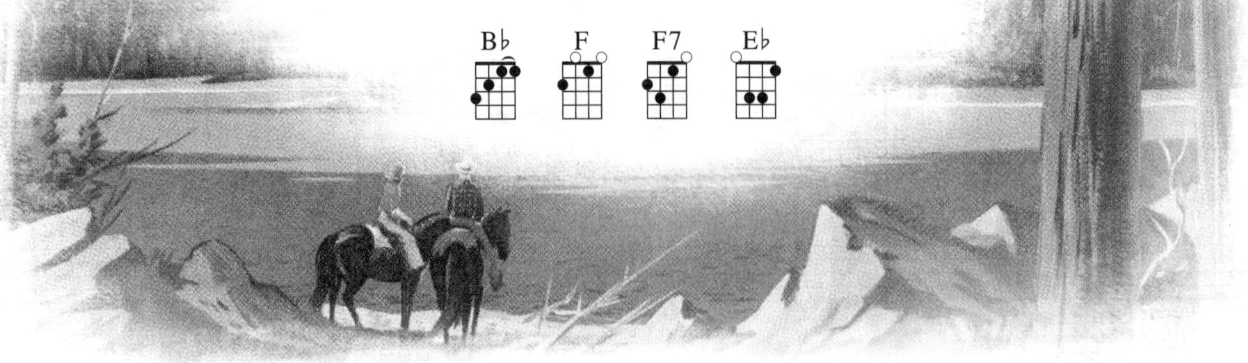
B♭
F
F7
E♭

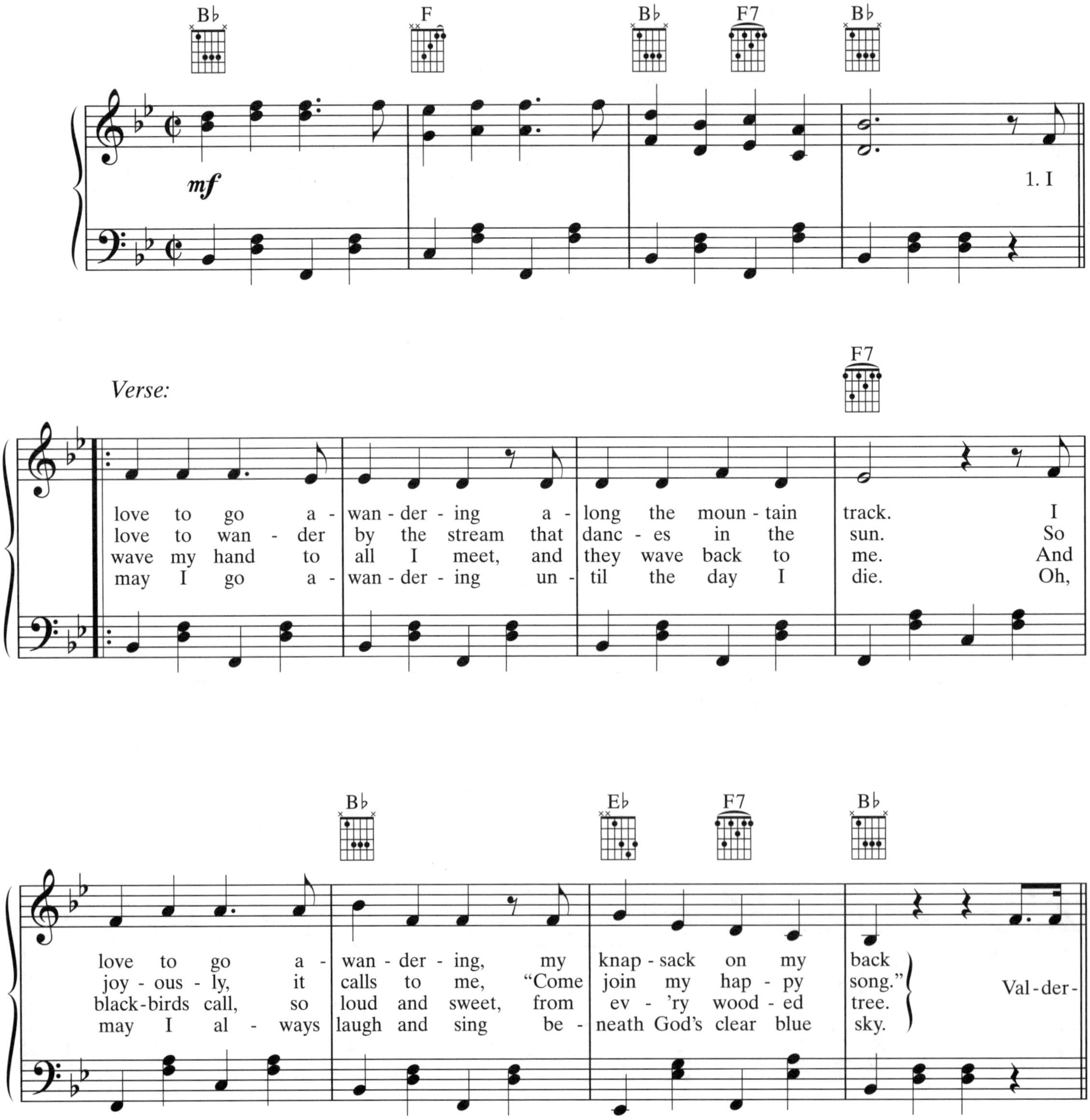
B♭
F
B♭
F7
B♭
mf
1. I
Verse:
F7
love to go a - wan - der - ing a - long the moun - tain track. I
love to wan - der by the stream that danc - es in the sun. So
wave my hand to all I meet, and they wave back to me. And
may I go a - wan - der - ing un - til the day I die. Oh,
B♭
E♭
F7
B♭
love to go a - wan - der - ing, my knap - sack on my back
joy - ous - ly, it calls to me, "Come join my hap - py song."
black-birds call, so loud and sweet, from ev - 'ry wood - ed tree.
may I al - ways laugh and sing be - neath God's clear blue sky.
Val - der -

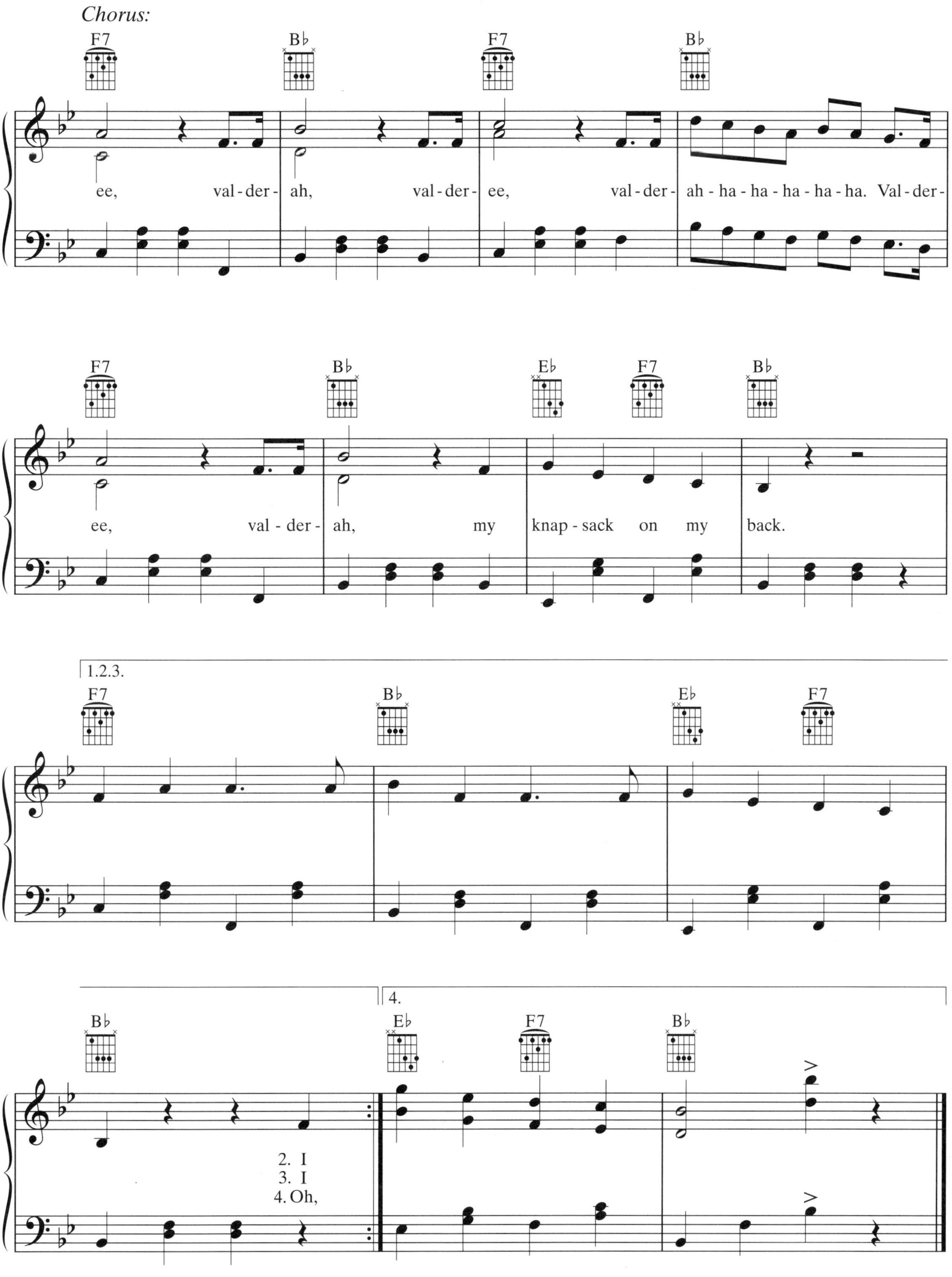
Chorus:
F7 B♭ F7 B♭
ee, val - der - ah, val - der - ee, val - der - ah - ha - ha - ha - ha - ha. Val - der -
F7 B♭ E♭ F7 B♭
ee, val - der - ah, my knap - sack on my back.
1.2.3.
F7 B♭ E♭ F7
B♭
2. I
3. I
4. Oh,
4.
E♭ F7 B♭

Billy Boy

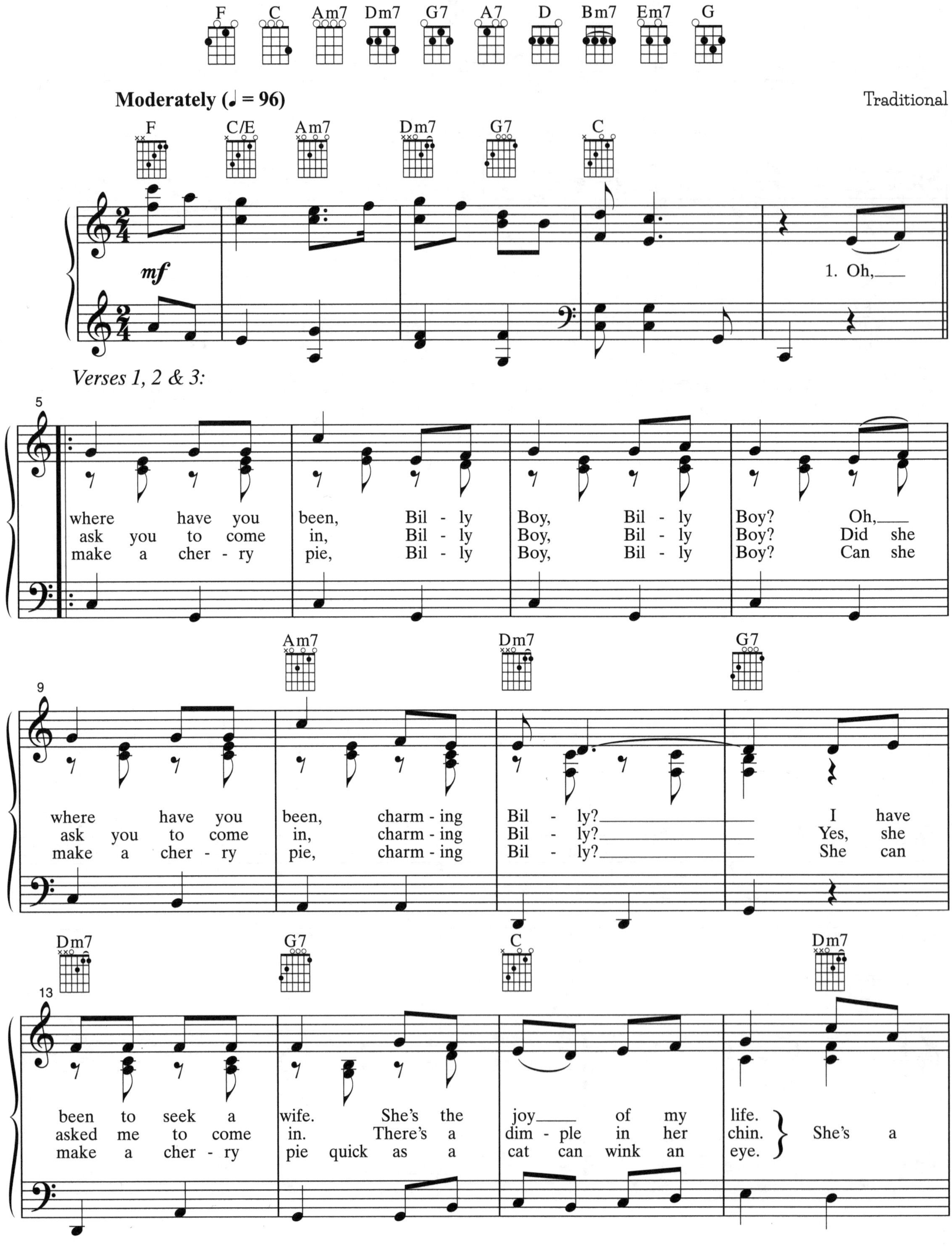
F C Am7 Dm7 G7 A7 D Bm7 Em7 G
Moderately (♩ = 96)
Traditional
F C/E Am7 Dm7 G7 C
mf
1. Oh,
Verses 1, 2 & 3:
where have you been, Bil - ly Boy, Bil - ly Boy? Oh,
ask you to come in, Bil - ly Boy, Bil - ly Boy? Did she
make a cher - ry pie, Bil - ly Boy, Bil - ly Boy? Can she
Am7 Dm7 G7
where have you been, charm - ing Bil - ly? I have
ask you to come in, charm - ing Bil - ly? Yes, she
make a cher - ry pie, charm - ing Bil - ly? She can
Dm7 G7 C Dm7
been to seek a wife. She's the joy of my life.
asked me to come in. There's a dim - ple in her chin.
make a cher - ry pie quick as a cat can wink an eye.
She's a

1.2.
C/E Am7 Dm7 G7 C F C/E Am7
17
young thing and can - not leave her moth - er.
Dm7 G7 C
3.
C F
22
2. Did she
3. Can she
moth - er.
C/E Am7 Dm7 G7 Em7 A7
27
f
4. How
Verse 4:
D
31
old is she now, Bil - ly Boy, Bil - ly Boy? How

Bm7
Em7
A7
35
old is she now, charm - ing Bil - ly? Three times
Em7
A7
D
Em7
39
six and four times seven, twen - ty - eight and e - leven. She's a
D/F#
Bm7
Em7
A7
D
G
43
young thing and can - not leave her moth - er.
D/F#
Bm7
Em7
A7
D
47

He's Got the Whole World
(In His Hands)

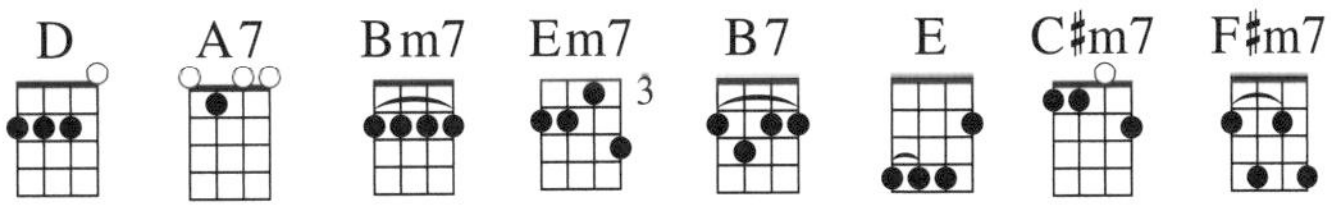
D
A7
Bm7
Em7
B7
E
C♯m7
F♯m7

Moderately (♩ = 120)
Traditional
D
A7
D
mf
He's got the
Chorus:
Bm7
Em7
A7
whole world_ in His hands.__ He's got the whole world_
Em7
A7
D
Bm7
in His hands._ He's got the whole world_ in His hands._ He's got the

Verse:
Em7
A7
D
whole world in His hands.
He's got the
He's got the
He's got
wind and the rain
ti - ny lit - tle ba - by
you and me, broth - er,
in His hands. He's got the
in His hands. He's got the
in His hands. He's got
1, 2.
He's got the
whole world in His hands.
3.
B7
cresc.

Chorus:
E
C♯m7
F♯m7
B7
whole world_ in His hands._ He's got the whole world_
f
F♯m7
B7
E
C♯m7
in His hands._ He's got the whole world_ in His hands._ He's got the
F♯m7
B7
E
C♯m7
F♯m7
B7
E
whole world in His hands.___ He's got the whole world in His hands.___

Head, Shoulders, Knees and Toes

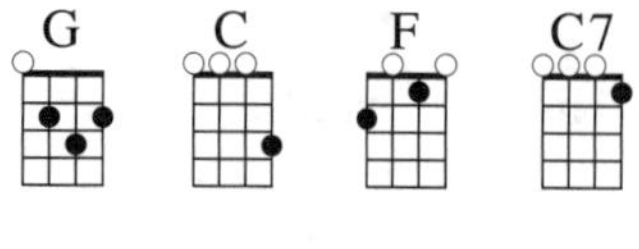
G
C
F
C7

*Moderately (♩ = 100)

Traditional

G
C
F
C
mf
Head, shoul-ders, knees and
4
toes, knees and toes.
Head, shoul-ders, knees and
G
toes, knees and toes.
C
C7
F
G
7
Eyes and ears and
mouth and nose.
Head and shoul-ders, knees and

*Sing and play faster 2nd and 3rd times.

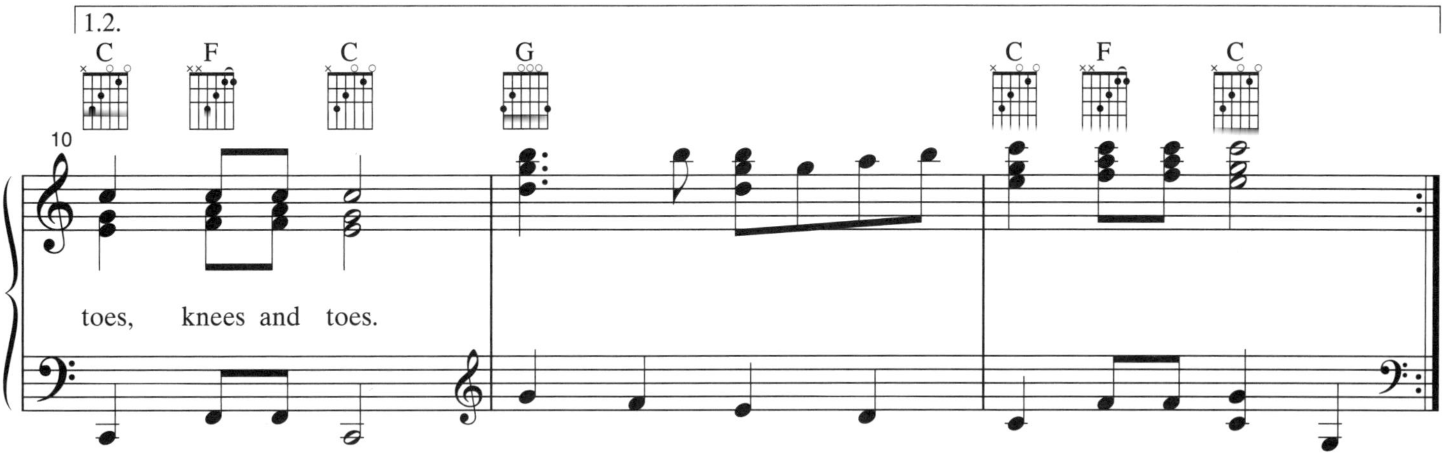
1.2.
C F C G C F C
10
toes, knees and toes.

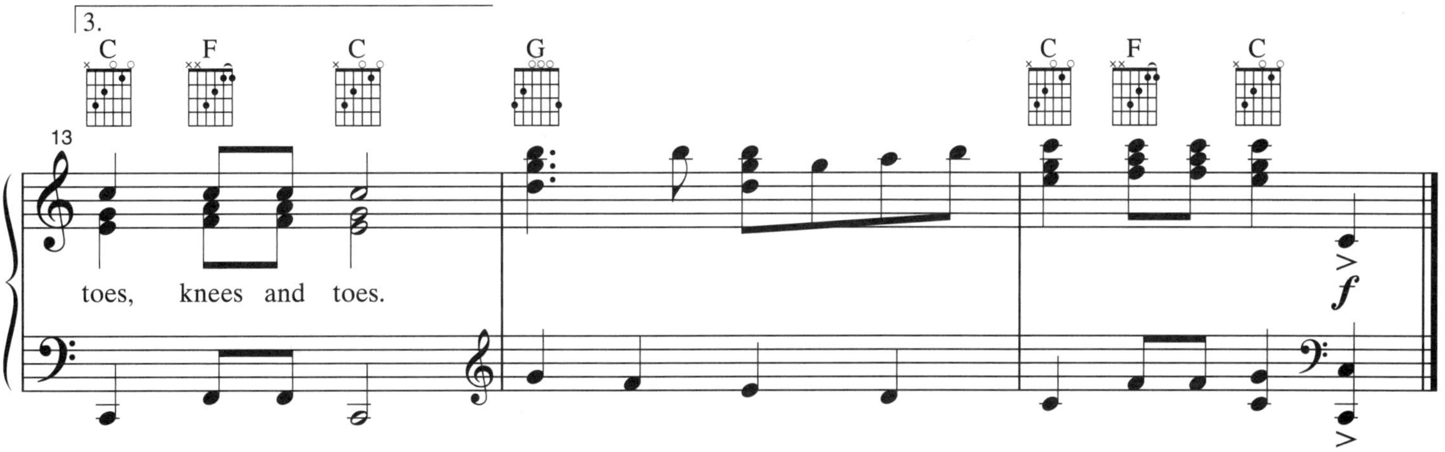
3.
C F C G C F C
13
toes, knees and toes.
f

Here We Go 'Round the Mulberry Bush

Moderately (♩. = 80)

Traditional

Gm
C7
F
mf
1. Here we go 'round the mul - berry bush,
2. This is the way we wash our clothes,
3.–8. See additional lyrics
5
mul - berry bush, mul - berry bush.
wash our clothes wash our clothes.
Here we go 'round the mul - berry bush so
This is the way we wash our clothes so
1.–7.
8.
9
ear - ly in the morn - ing.
ear - ly Mon - day morn - ing.
ear - ly Sun - day morn - ing.

Verse 3:
This is the way we iron our clothes,
Iron our clothes, iron our clothes.
This is the way we iron our clothes
So early Tuesday morning.

Verse 4:
This is the way we mend our clothes,
Mend our clothes, mend our clothes.
This is the way we mend our clothes
So early Wednesday morning.

Verse 5:
This is the way we scrub the floor,
Scrub the floor, scrub the floor.
This is the way we scrub the floor
So early Thursday morning.

Verse 6:
This is the way we sweep the house,
Sweep the house, sweep the house.
This is the way we sweep the house
So early Friday morning.

Verse 7:
This is the way we bake our bread,
Bake our bread, bake our bread.
This is the way we bake our bread
So early Saturday morning.

Verse 8:
This is the way we go to church,
Go to church, go to church.
This is the way we go to church
So early Sunday morning.

Here We Go Looby-Loo

D
Bm7
Em7
A7
G
3

Traditional

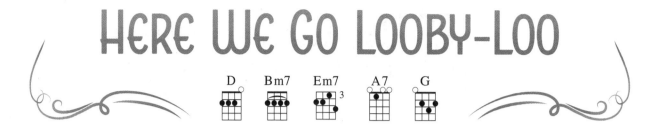

Moderately (♩. = 100)
D
mf
Chorus:
Bm7
Em7
A7
Here we go loo - by - loo
Here we go loo - by - light.
D
Em7
A7
D
Here we go loo - by - loo
all on a Sat - ur - day night.
1. You
Verse:
G
D
put your right hand / left hand / right foot / left foot / whole self in.
You take your right hand / left hand / right foot / left foot / whole self out.
You

Em7 D G D/A A7 D A7
give your hand your hand your foot your foot your-self a shake, shake shake, and turn your-self a-bout. Oh,
Chorus:
Bm7 Em7 A7
here we go loo-by-loo. Here we go loo-by-light.
1.–4.
D Em7 A7 D
Here we go loo-by-loo all on a Sat-ur-day night. 2.3.4.5. You
5.
Em7 A7 Em7 A7 Em7 A7 D
all on a Sat-ur-day, all on a Sat-ur-day night.
f

Hey Diddle Diddle

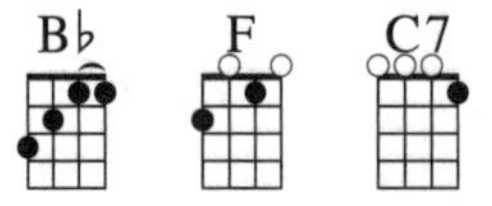
B♭
F
C7

Moderately slow (♩. = 60)

Traditional

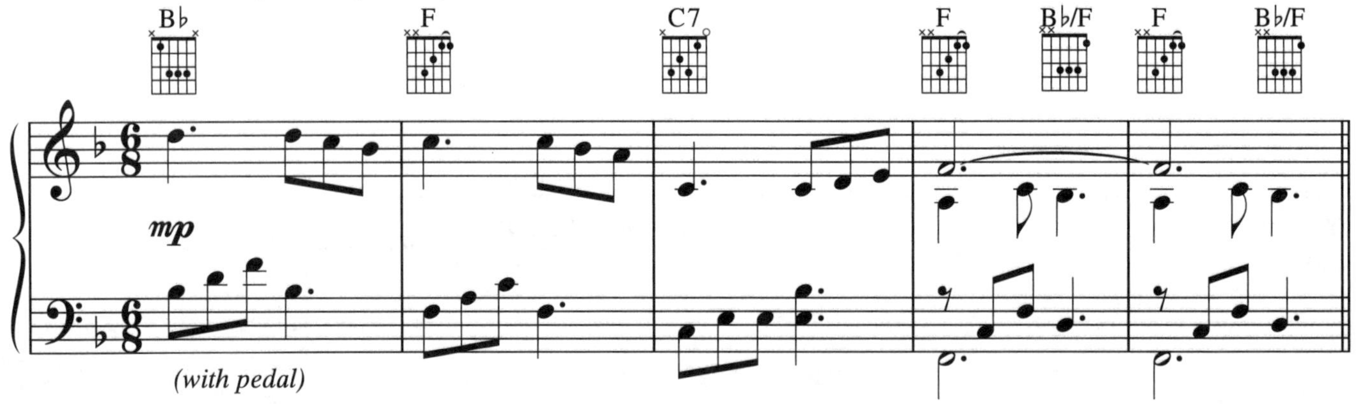
B♭
F
C7
F
B♭/F
F
B♭/F
mp
(with pedal)

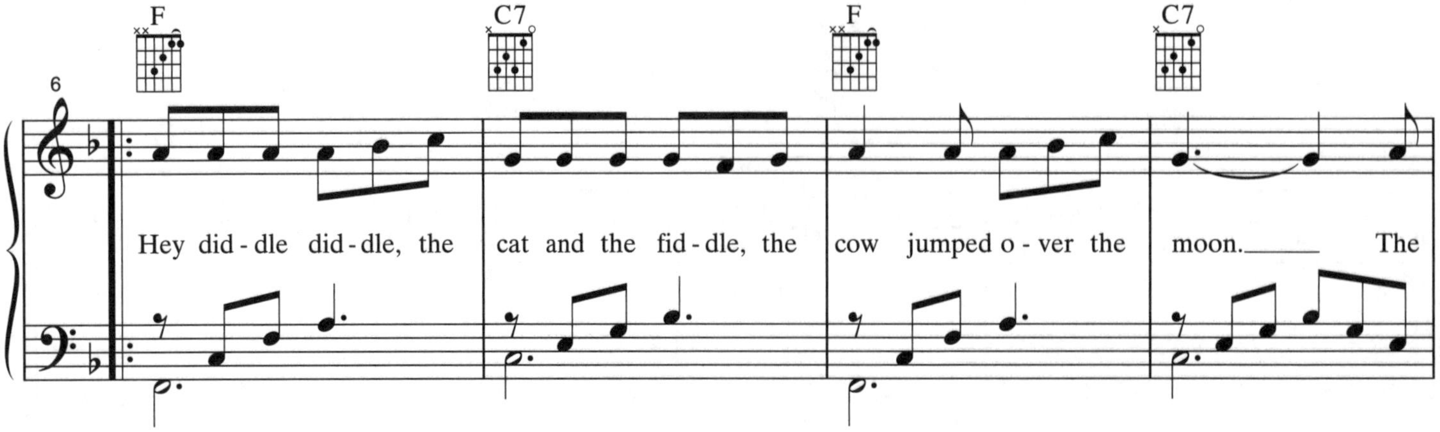
F
C7
F
C7
6
Hey did - dle did - dle, the cat and the fid - dle, the cow jumped o - ver the moon.___ The

B♭
F
C7
10
lit - tle dog laughed_ to see such sport, and the dish ran a - way with the
F
B♭/F
F
B♭/F
B♭
F
13
spoon.
1.
C7
F
B♭/F
F
B♭/F
17
2.
C7
F
20
8va
rit. e dim.
p
pp

Hickory Dickory Dock

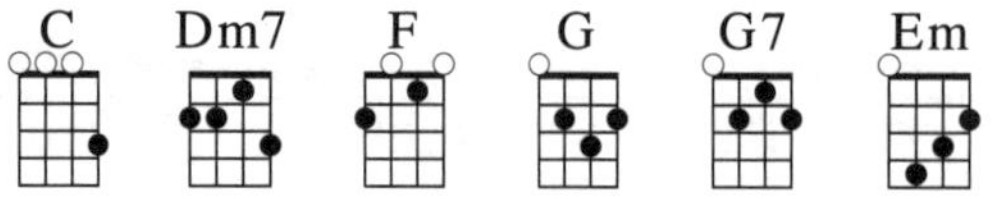
C
Dm7
F
G
G7
Em

Moderately (♩. = 84)

Traditional

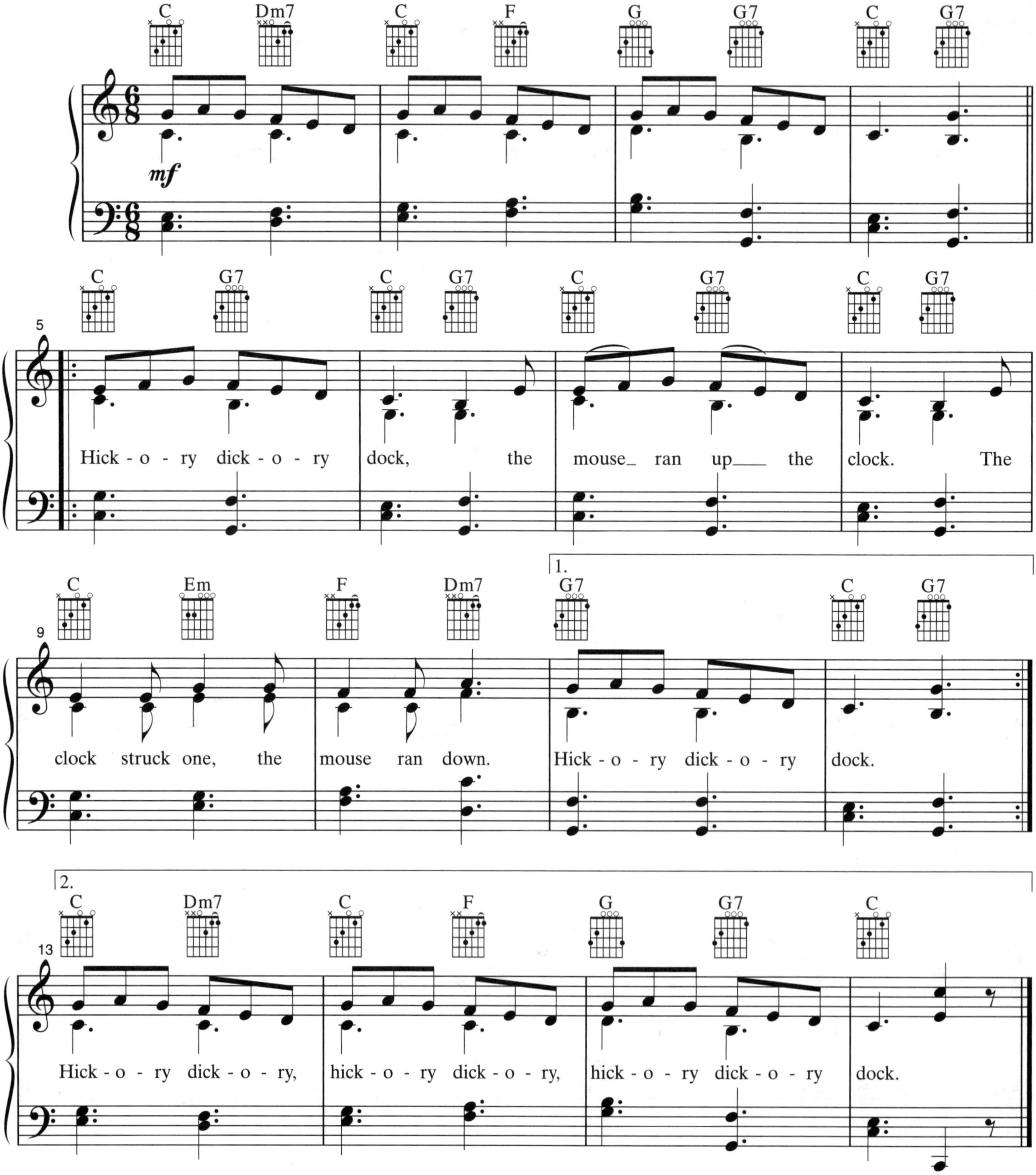
C Dm7 C F G G7 C G7
mf
C G7 C G7 C G7 C G7
Hick - o - ry dick - o - ry dock, the mouse ran up the clock. The
C Em F Dm7
clock struck one, the mouse ran down.
1.
G7 C G7
Hick - o - ry dick - o - ry dock.
2.
C Dm7 C F G G7 C
Hick - o - ry dick - o - ry, hick - o - ry dick - o - ry, hick - o - ry dick - o - ry dock.

Home on the Range

B♭
F
C7
B♭m
Dm7
G7
Gm7

Moderately (♩ = 108)

Traditional

B♭
F/C
C7
B♭
F
mp
Oh,
(with pedal)
Verse:
6
B♭
B♭m
give me a home where the buf - fa - lo roam, where the
10
F
Dm7
G7
C7
deer and the an - te - lope play.
Where

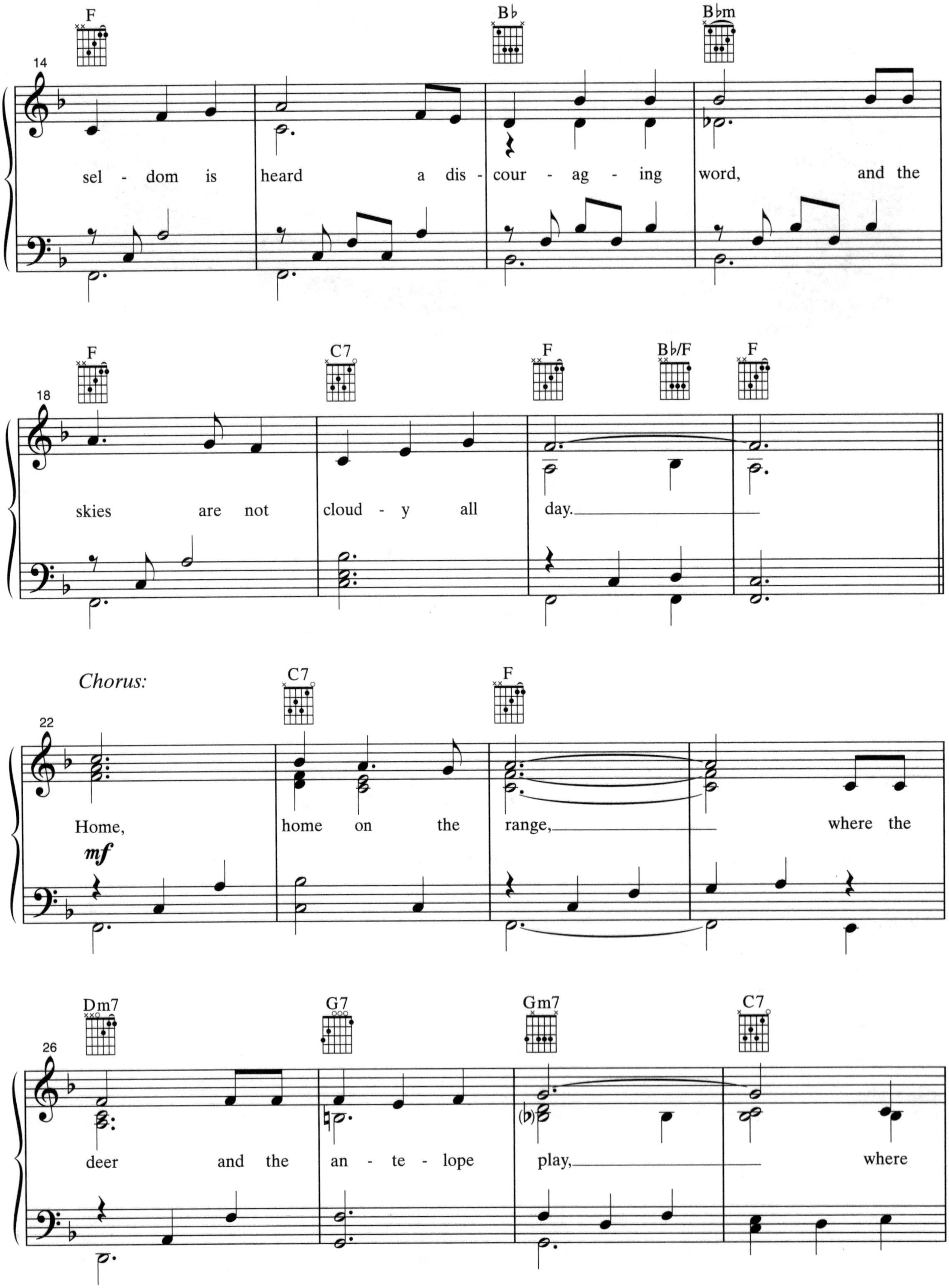
F
B♭
B♭m
14
sel - dom is heard a dis - cour - ag - ing word, and the
F
C7
F
B♭/F
F
18
skies are not cloud - y all day.
Chorus:
C7
F
22
Home, home on the range, where the
mf
Dm7
G7
Gm7
C7
26
deer and the an - te - lope play, where

F
B♭
B♭m
30
sel - dom is heard a dis - cour - ag - ing word, and the
F/C
1.
C7
B♭
F
34
skies are not cloud - y all day. Oh,
2.
C7
Dm
B♭m
F/C
38
cloud - y all day, and the skies are not
C7
B♭
F
42
cloud - y all day.

Hot Cross Buns

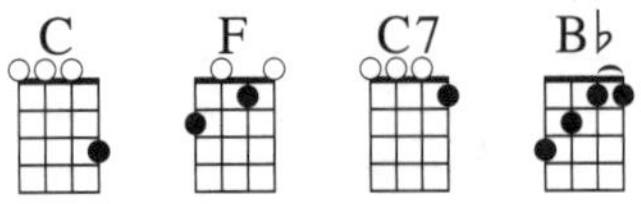
C
F
C7
B♭

Moderately (♩ = 116)

Traditional

C
F
C7
F
F
C7
F
mf
Hot cross buns!
4
C7
F
C
F
C7
F
Hot cross buns!
One a pen-ny, two a pen-ny.
Hot cross buns!
7
C
F
C
F
C
Give them to your daugh-ters,
give them to your sons.
One a pen-ny, two a pen-ny.
1.
2.
F
C7
F
B♭
F
C7
F
C7
F
10
Hot cross buns!
rit.

HUMPTY DUMPTY

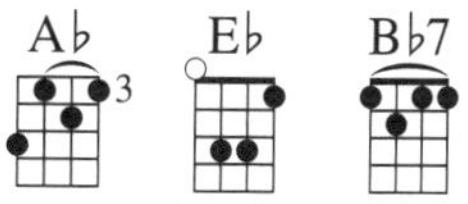
A♭
E♭
B♭7

Moderately (♩. = 84)

Traditional

A♭ E♭ B♭7 E♭ B♭7 E♭ B♭7 E♭
mf
B♭7 E♭ B♭7 E♭
Hump - ty Dump - ty sat on the wall,
Hump - ty Dump - ty had a great fall.
A♭ E♭ B♭7 E♭ B♭7 E♭ B♭7 E♭
All the king's hors - es and all the king's men
could - n't put Hump - ty to - geth - er a - gain.
1.
A♭ E♭ B♭7 E♭ B♭7 E♭ B♭7 E♭
2.
B♭7 E♭ B♭7 E♭
rit.

Hush, Little Baby

G
Am
D7
F
C

Traditional

Moderately (♩ = 92)

G
Am
D7
(with pedal)
G
Am
1. Hush, lit - tle ba - by! Don't say a word.
2. If that__ dia - mond ring turns__ brass,
3. If that__ bil - ly goat won't__ pull,
4. If that__ dog named Rov - er won't bark,
D7
G
Ma - ma's gon - na buy you a mock - ing - bird. If that mock - ing
ma - ma's gon - na buy you a look - ing glass. If that look - ing
ma - ma's gon - na buy you a cart and bull. If that cart and
ma - ma's gon - na buy you a horse and cart. If that horse and

Am
D7
1.3.
G
bird won't sing, ma - ma's gon - na buy you a dia - mond ring.
glass gets broke, ma - ma's gon - na buy you a dog named Rover.
bull turns over, ma - ma's gon - na buy you a
cart fall down, you'll still be the sweet - est
D7
G
2.
G
F
bil - ly goat.
C
G
D7
4.
G
D7
G
ba - by in town.
rit.

I Have a Little Dreidel

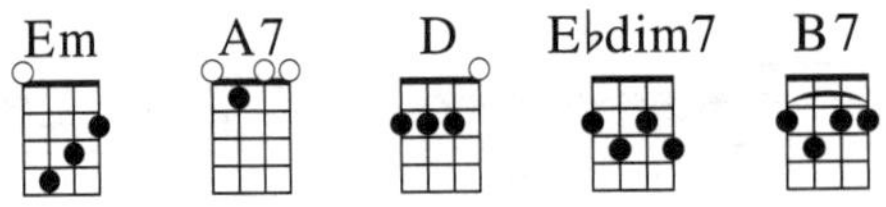
Em
A7
D
E♭dim7
B7

Traditional

Moderately (𝅗𝅥 = 86)
Em
A7
mf
D
A7
Verse:
D
A7
D
1. I
have a lit - tle drei - del, I
has a love - ly bod - y, with
drei - del's al - ways play - ful, it
E♭dim7
Em
B7
made it out of clay; and when it's dry and
legs so short and thin; and when it gets all
loves to dance and spin. A hap - py game of
Em
A7
D
A7
read - y, then drei - del I shall play. My
ti - red, it drops and then I win! My
drei - del, come play now let's be - gin. My

Chorus:
D
E♭dim7
13
drei - del, drei - del, drei - del, I made it out of
drei - del, drei - del. drei - del, with legs so short and
drei - del, drei - del, drei - del, it loves to dance and
Em
16
clay; and when it's dry and read - y, then
thin. Oh, drei - del, drei - del, drei - del, it
spin. Oh, drei - del, drei - del, drei - del, come
1.2.
3.
A7
D
A7
D
19
drei - del I shall play! 2. It gin.
drops and then I win! 3. My
play now let's be -

I'm a Little Teapot

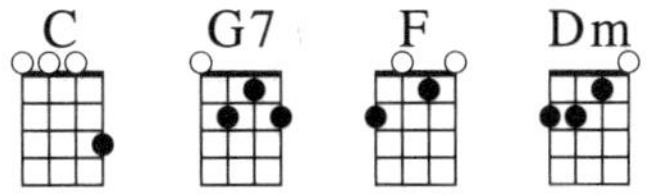
C
G7
F
Dm

Moderately (♩ = 120)

Traditional

C G7 C F C
mf
1. I'm a lit-tle tea-pot, short and stout.
2. I'm a spe-cial tea-pot, it is true.
G7 C G7 C
Here is my han-dle, here is my spout. When I get all steamed up,
Here, let me show you what I can do. I can change my han-dle
F C Dm G7 C
hear me shout, "Just tip me o-ver and pour me out!"
and my spout, "Just tip me o-ver and pour me out!"
1. Dm G7 C
2. G7 C
rit.

I'm a Nut

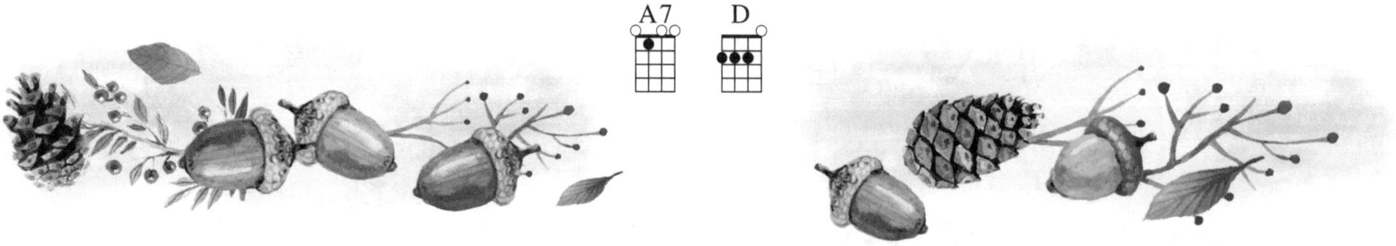
A7
D

Very bright (♩ = 200)

Traditional

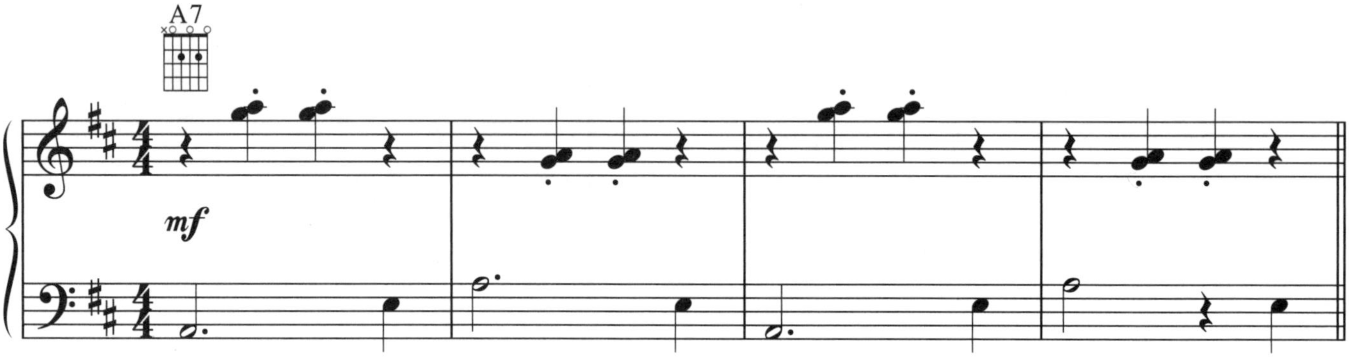
A7
mf

Verse:

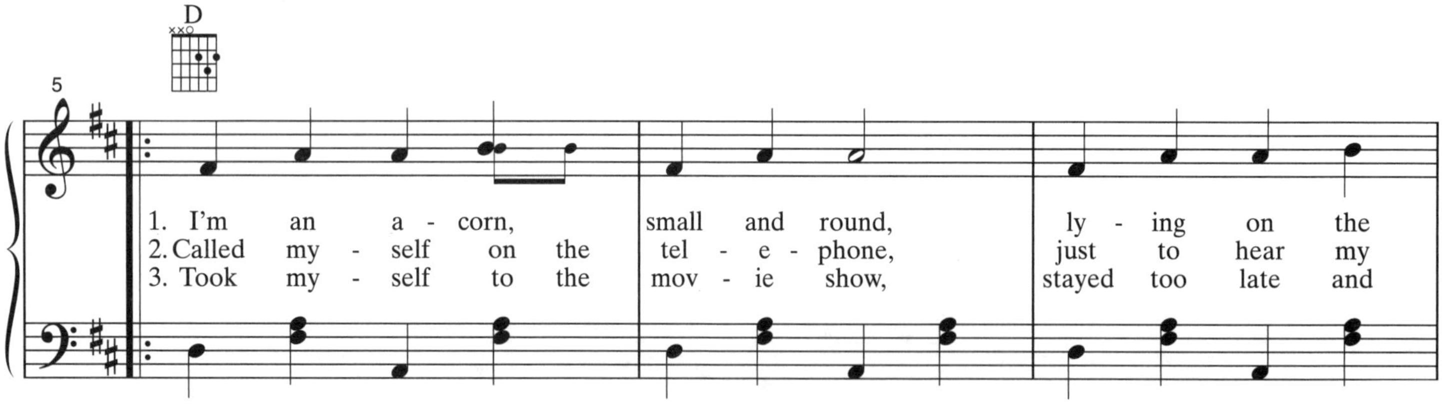
D
5
1. I'm an a - corn, small and round, ly - ing on the
2. Called my - self on the tel - e - phone, just to hear my
3. Took my - self to the mov - ie show, stayed too late and

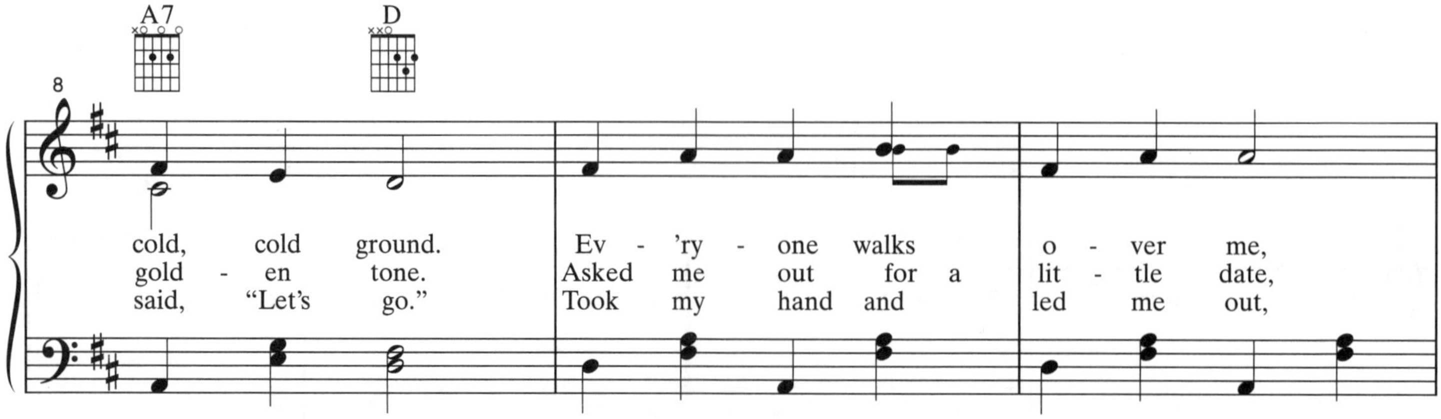
A7
D
8
cold, cold ground. Ev - 'ry - one walks o - ver me,
gold - en tone. Asked me out for a lit - tle date,
said, "Let's go." Took my hand and led me out,

A7
D
11
that is why I'm cracked, you see.
picked me up 'bout half past eight. I'm a
drove me home and gave a shout!
Chorus:
A7
D
A7
13
nut! (Click, click) I'm a nut! (Click, click) I'm a nut! (Click, click) I'm a
D
A7
16
nut!
1.2.
3.
D
19
8va

I'm H-A-P-P-Y!

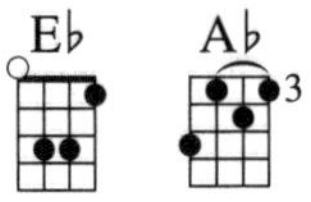
E♭
A♭
B♭7

Moderately (𝅗𝅥 = 84)

Traditional

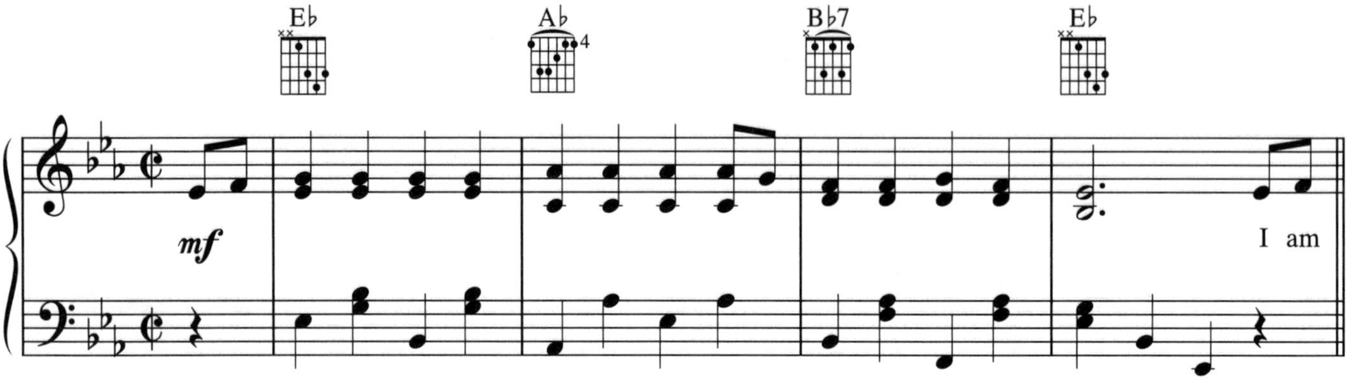
E♭
A♭
B♭7
E♭
mf
I am

Chorus:

A♭
B♭7
E♭
5
H - A - P - P - Y! I am H - A - P - P - Y! I

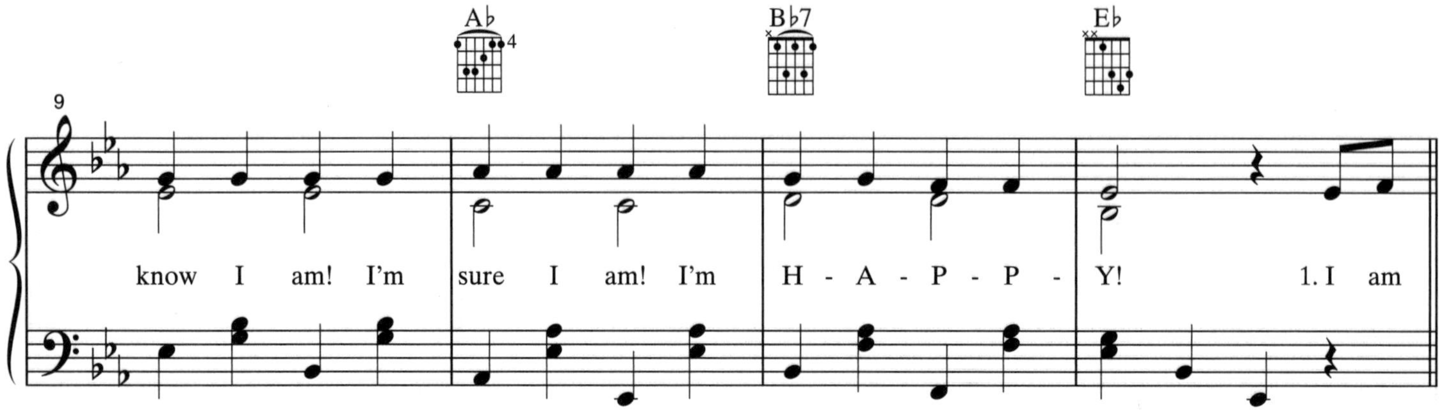
A♭
B♭7
E♭
9
know I am! I'm sure I am! I'm H - A - P - P - Y! 1. I am

Verse:
A♭
B♭7
(clap) - A - P - P - Y! I am (clap) - A - P - P -
2.–5. See additional lyrics
E♭
A♭
Y! I know I am! I'm sure I am! I'm
1.–4.
5.
B♭7
E♭
B♭7
E♭
(clap) - A - P - P - Y! I am (clap) - (clap) - (clap) - (clap) - (clap)!
rit.

Verse 2:
I am *(clap)*-*(clap)*-P-P-Y!
I am *(clap)*-*(clap)*-P-P-Y!
I know I am!
I'm sure I am!
I'm *(clap)*-*(clap)*-P-P-Y!

Verse 3:
I am *(clap)*-*(clap)*-*(clap)*-P-Y!
I am *(clap)*-*(clap)*-*(clap)*-P-Y!
I know I am!
I'm sure I am!
I'm *(clap)*-*(clap)*-*(clap)*-P-Y!

Verse 4:
I am *(clap)*-*(clap)*-*(clap)*-*(clap)*-Y!
I am *(clap)*-*(clap)*-*(clap)*-*(clap)*-Y!
I know I am!
I'm sure I am!
I'm *(clap)*-*(clap)*-*(clap)*-*(clap)*-Y!

Verse 5:
I am *(clap)*-*(clap)*-*(clap)*-*(clap)*-*(clap)*!
I am *(clap)*-*(clap)*-*(clap)*-*(clap)*-*(clap)*!
I know I am!
I'm sure I am!
I'm *(clap)*-*(clap)*-*(clap)*-*(clap)*-*(clap)*!

I've Been Working on the Railroad

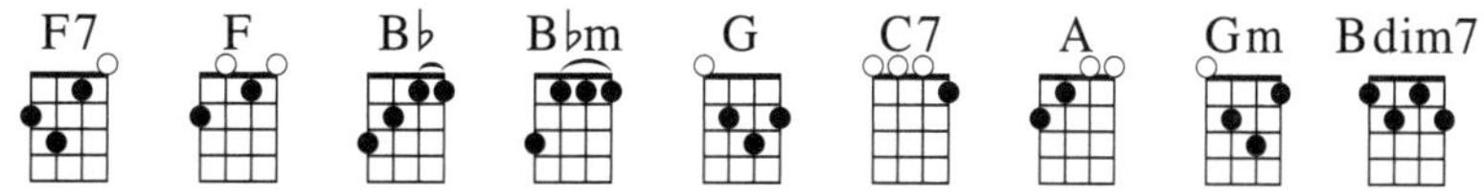
F7
F
B♭
B♭m
G
C7
A
Gm
Bdim7

Modertely (♩ = 120)

Traditional

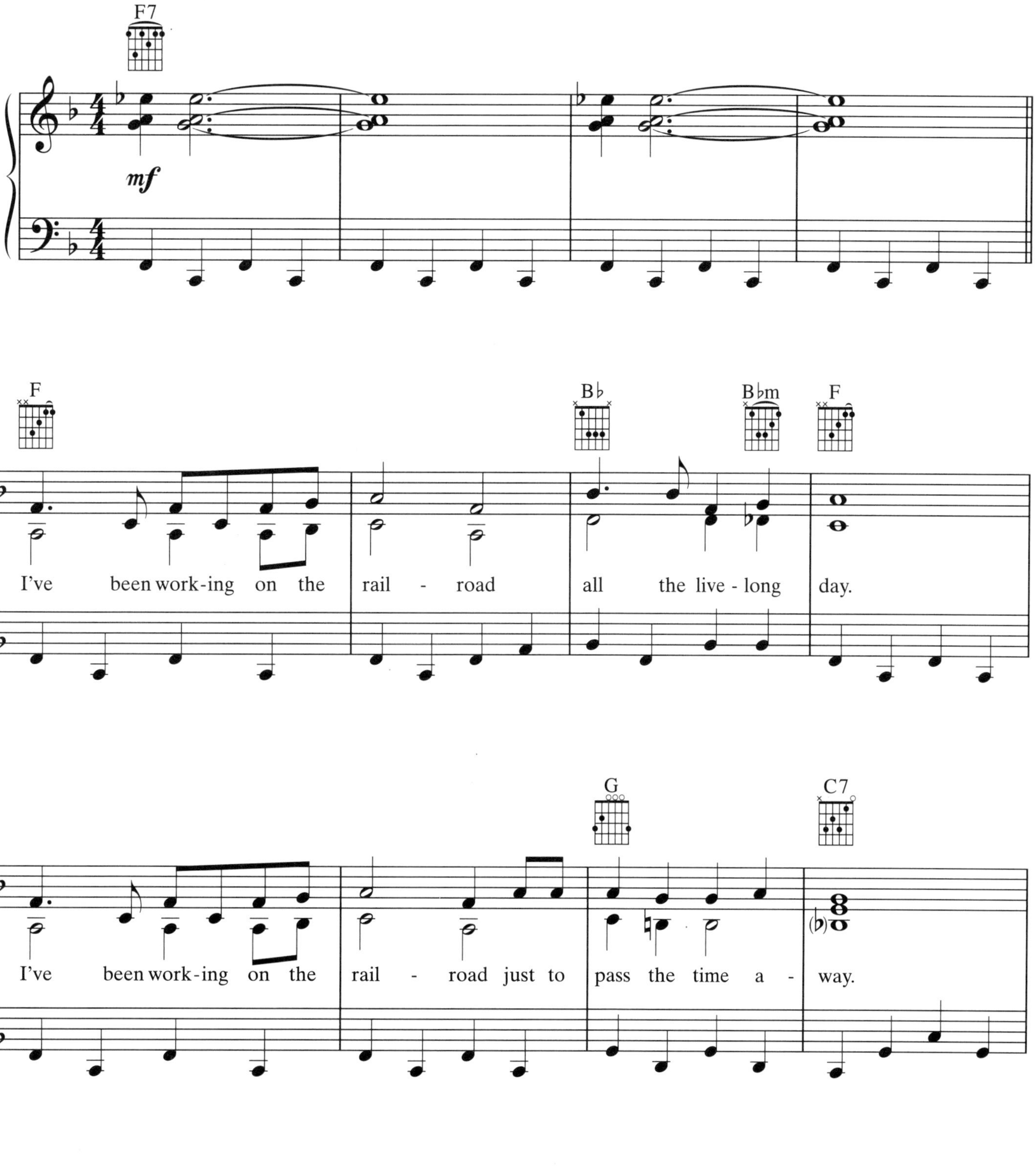
F7
mf
F
B♭
B♭m
F
I've been work-ing on the rail - road all the live - long day.
G
C7
I've been work-ing on the rail - road just to pass the time a - way.

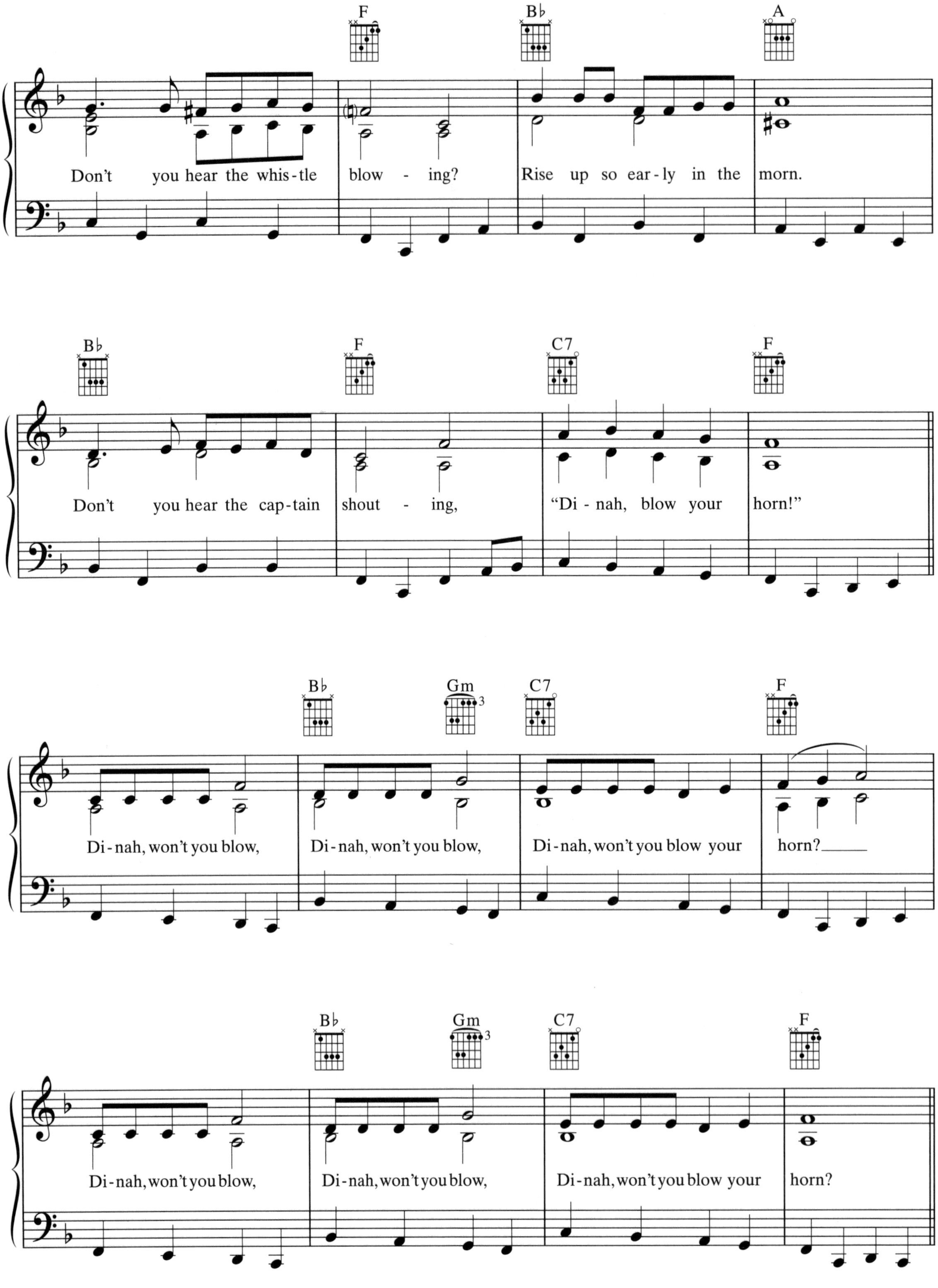
F Bb A
Don't you hear the whis-tle blow - ing? Rise up so ear-ly in the morn.
Bb F C7 F
Don't you hear the cap-tain shout - ing, "Di - nah, blow your horn!"
Bb Gm C7 F
Di-nah, won't you blow, Di-nah, won't you blow, Di-nah, won't you blow your horn?
Bb Gm C7 F
Di-nah, won't you blow, Di-nah, won't you blow, Di-nah, won't you blow your horn?

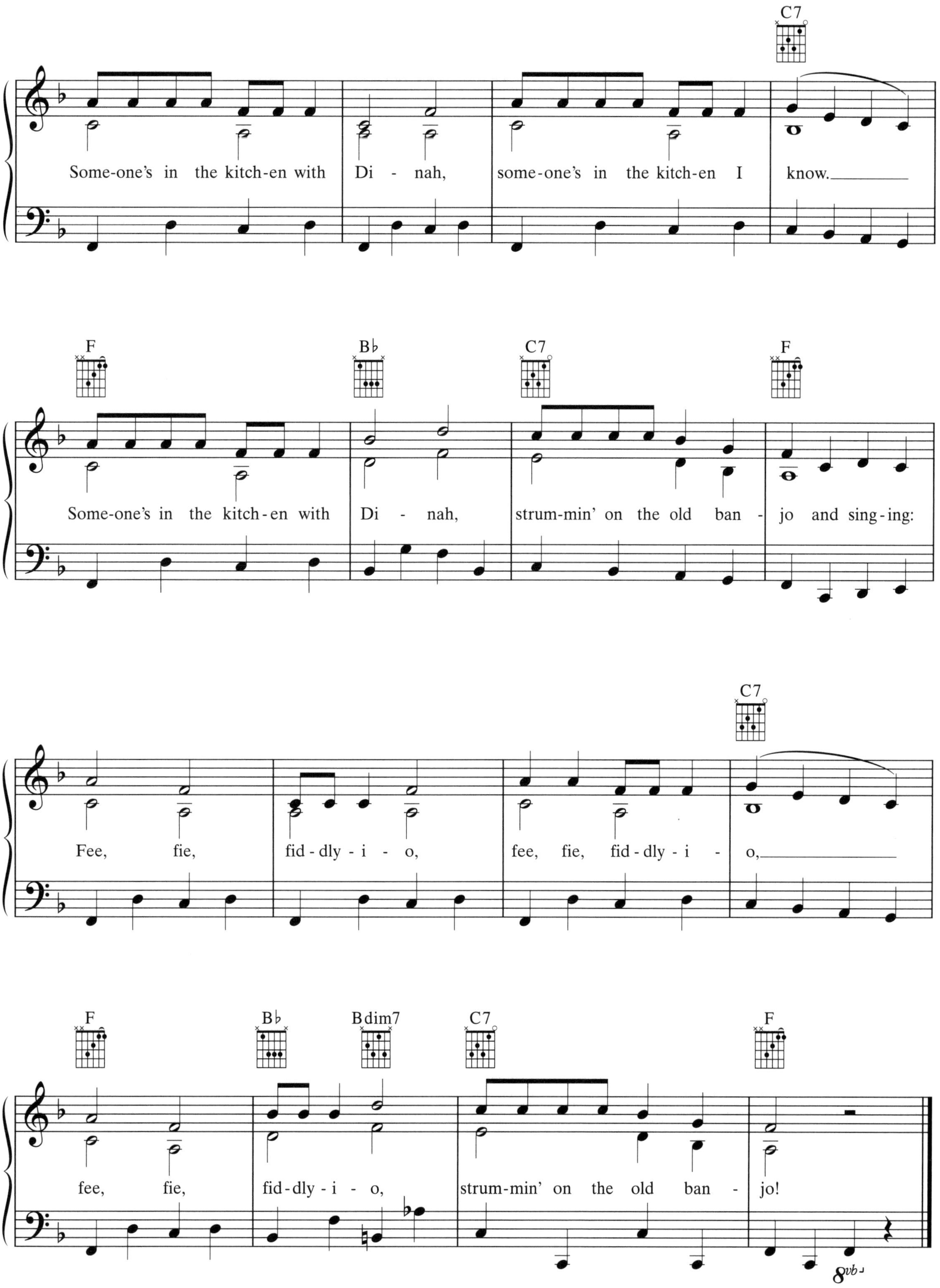
C7
Some-one's in the kitch-en with Di - nah, some-one's in the kitch-en I know.
F
B♭
C7
F
Some-one's in the kitch-en with Di - nah, strum-min' on the old ban - jo and sing-ing:
C7
Fee, fie, fid-dly-i - o, fee, fie, fid-dly-i - o,
F
B♭
Bdim7
C7
F
fee, fie, fid-dly-i - o, strum-min' on the old ban - jo!
8vb

If You're Happy
(And You Know It)

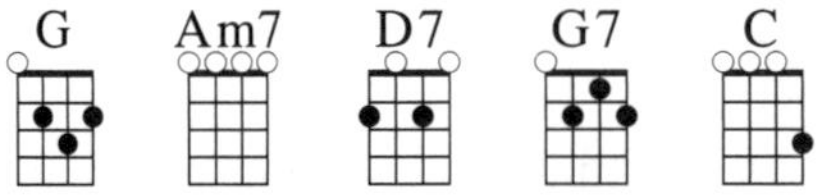
G
Am7
D7
G7
C

Traditional

Moderately (♩ = 110) (♫ = ♩³♪)

G
Am7
G
Am7
G
Am7
mf
4
G
Am7
G
*D7
1. If you're
hap - py and you know it, clap your
2.3.4. *See additional lyrics*
hands! (*Clap, clap.*) If you're
7
G
G7
C
hap - py and you know it, clap your
hands! (*Clap, clap.*) If you're
hap - py and you know it, then you

* For the last verse, do all three. (Clap, stomp, "hooray")

1.–3.
G
Am7
D7
G
Am7
G
10
real - ly ought to show it, if you're hap - py and you know it, clap your hands! (Clap, clap.)
C
G
Am7
D7
G
4.
G
Am7
G
13
2. If you're
three!
Am7
G
Am7
G
Am7
G
Am7
G
16

Verse 2:
If you're happy and you know it, stomp your feet! (*Stomp, stomp.)*
If you're happy and you know it, stomp your feet! (*Stomp, stomp.)*
If you're happy and you know it, then you really ought to show it,
If you're happy and you know it, stomp your feet! (*Stomp, stomp.)*

Verse 3:
If you're happy and you know it, say "hooray!" (*Shout, "hooray!"*)
If you're happy and you know it, say "hooray!" (*Shout, "hooray!"*)
If you're happy and you know it, then you really ought to show it,
If you're happy and you know it, say "hooray!" (*Shout, "hooray!"*)

Verse 4:
If you're happy and you know it, do all three!
If you're happy and you know it, do all three!
If you're happy and you know it, then you really ought to show it,
If you're happy and you know it, do all three!

It's Raining, It's Pouring

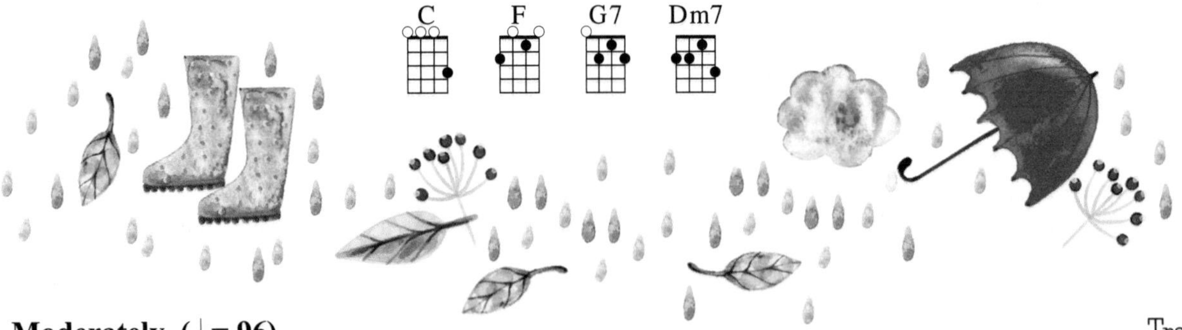
C
F
G7
Dm7

Moderately (♩ = 96)

Traditional

C F C F C F
mp
It's
(with pedal)
5
C F C G7 C F
rain - ing, it's pour - ing, the old man is
8
C Dm7 G7 Dm7 G7
snor - ing, he bumped his head and went to bed and

1.
Dm7
G7
C
F
G
11
could-n't get up in the morn - ing.
F
G
F
G
C
F
C
14
It's
2.
C
F
G
C
F
C
17
morn - ing.
rit.

JACK AND JILL

Cm7 F7 B♭ Gm7 Cm E♭
Moderately bright (♩. = 84)
Traditional
Cm7 F7 B♭ Gm7 Cm F7 B♭
mf
E♭ B♭
Jack and Jill went up the hill to fetch a pail of wa - ter.
Cm F7 B♭ Gm7 Cm7 F7
1. B♭
Jack fell down and broke his crown, and Jill came tum - bling af - ter.
2. B♭ Cm7 F7 B♭ Gm7 Cm F7 B♭
af - ter.
f

Jingle Bells

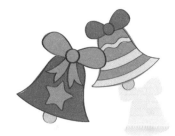

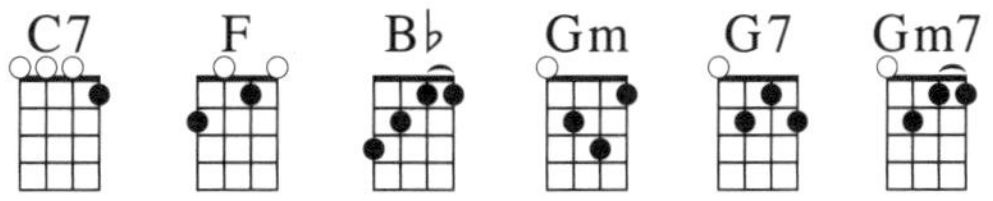
C7
F
B♭
Gm
G7
Gm7

Lively (𝅗𝅥 = 92)

Words and Music by
James Pierpont

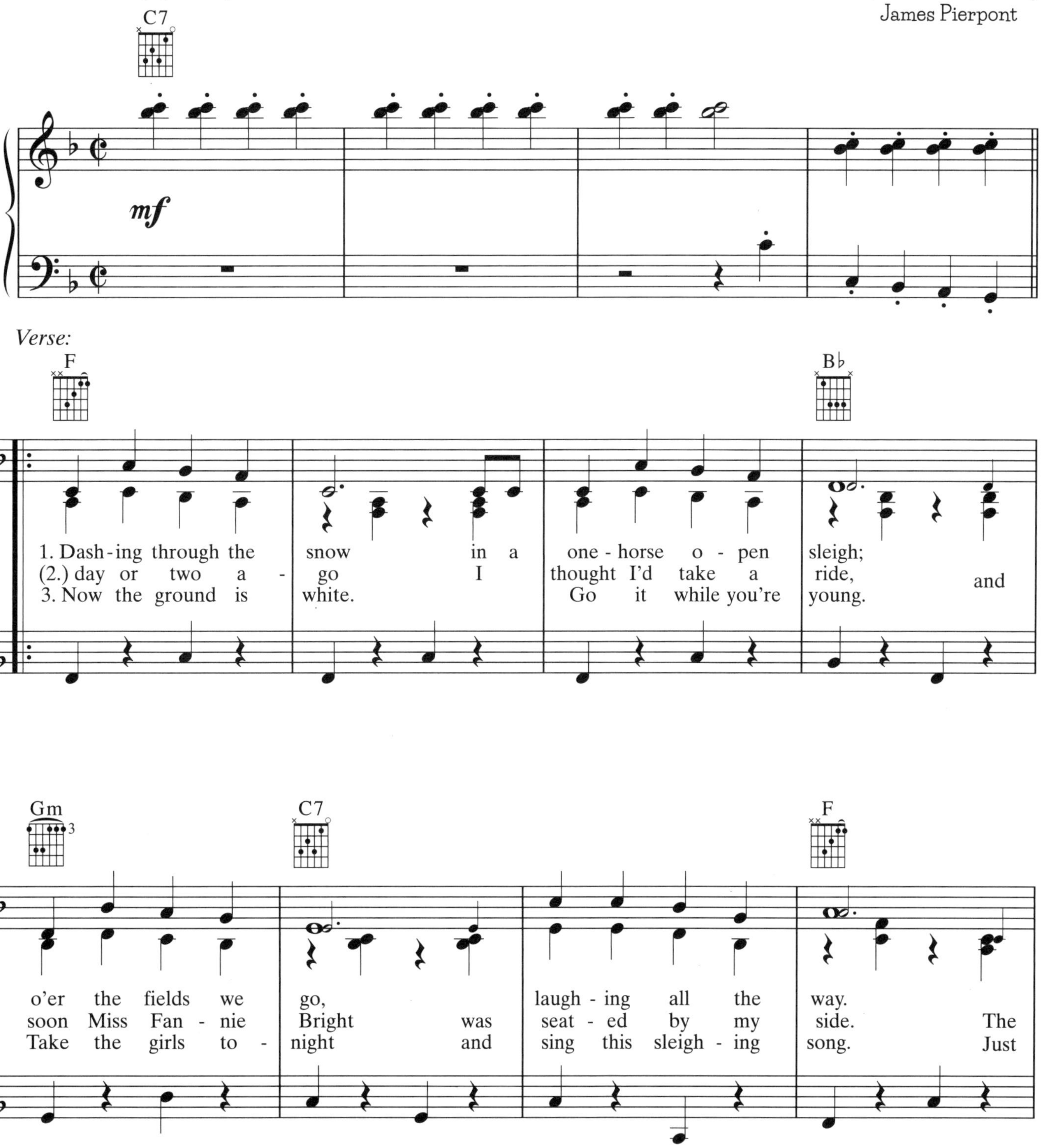
C7
mf
Verse:
F
B♭
1. Dash-ing through the snow in a one-horse o-pen sleigh;
(2.) day or two a-go I thought I'd take a ride, and
3. Now the ground is white. Go it while you're young.
Gm
C7
F
o'er the fields we go, laugh-ing all the way.
soon Miss Fan-nie Bright was seat-ed by my side. The
Take the girls to-night and sing this sleigh-ing song. Just

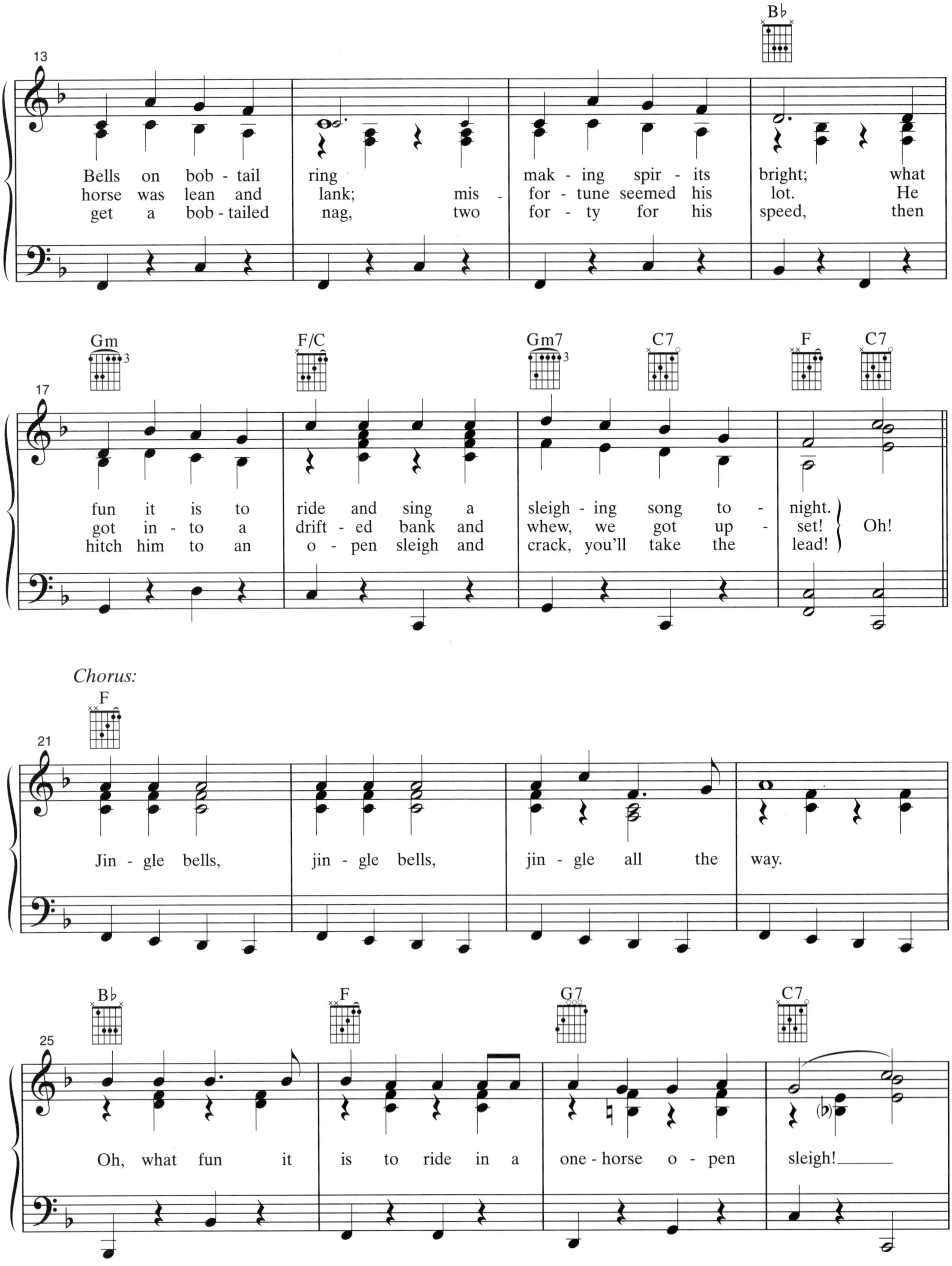
13
B♭
Bells on bob - tail ring mak - ing spir - its bright; what
horse was lean and lank; mis - for - tune seemed his lot. He
get a bob - tailed nag, two for - ty for his speed, then
Gm
F/C
Gm7
C7
F
C7
17
fun it is to ride and sing a sleigh - ing song to - night.
got in - to a drift - ed bank and whew, we got up - set! Oh!
hitch him to an o - pen sleigh and crack, you'll take the lead!
Chorus:
F
21
Jin - gle bells, jin - gle bells, jin - gle all the way.
B♭
F
G7
C7
25
Oh, what fun it is to ride in a one - horse o - pen sleigh!

F
29
Jin - gle bells,
jin - gle bells,
jin - gle all the way.
B♭
F
C7
1.2.
F
33
Oh, what fun it is to ride in a one - horse o - pen sleigh!
C7
3.
F
37
2. A
sleigh!

John Jacob Jingleheimer Schmidt

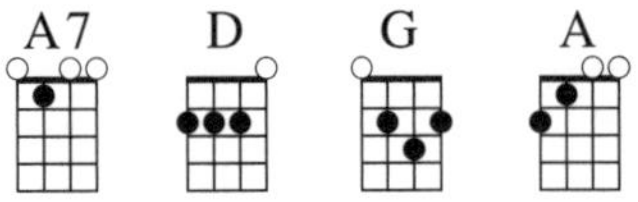
A7
D
G
A

Moderately bright (♩ = 112)

Traditional

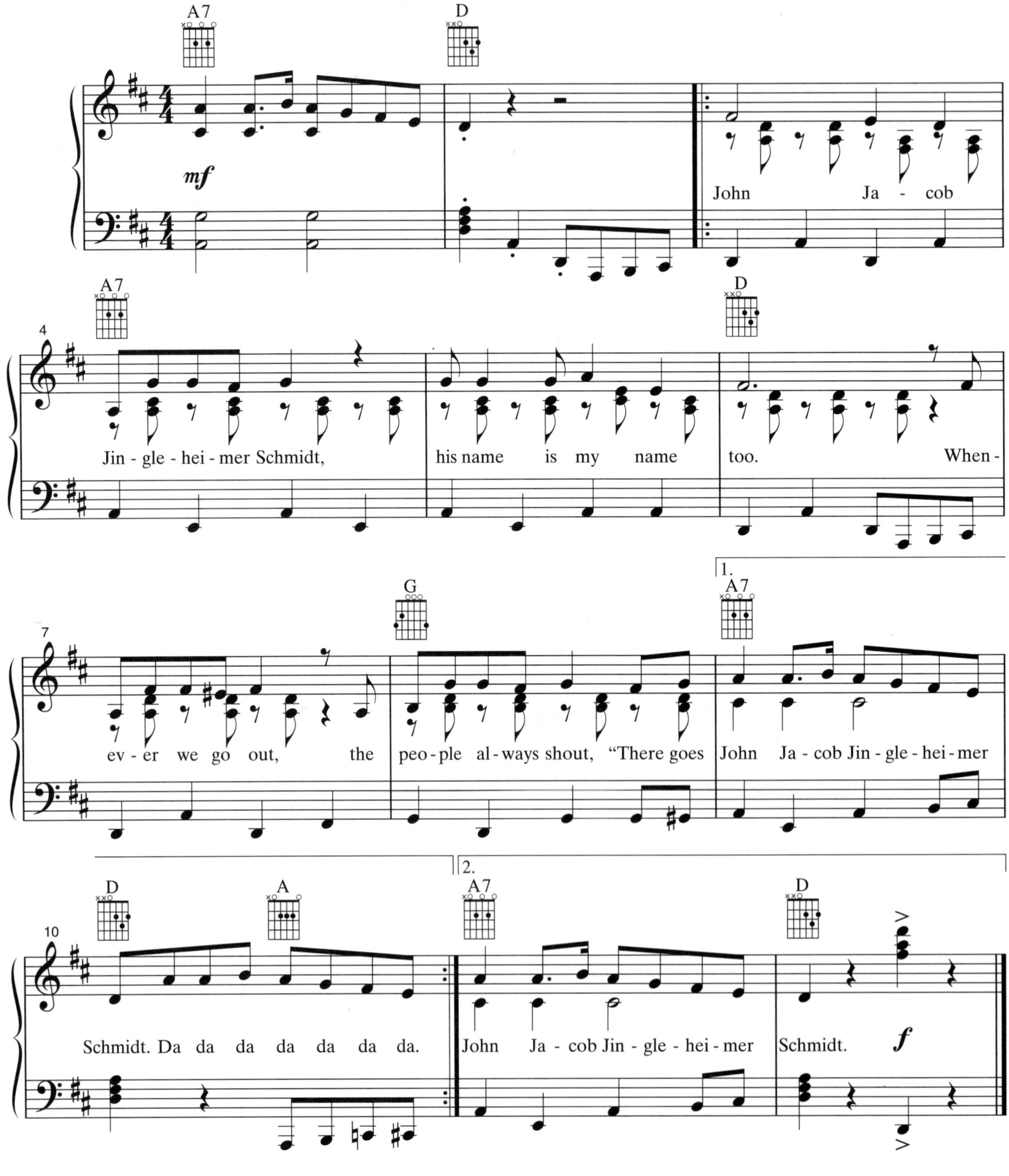
A7
D
mf
John Ja - cob
4
Jin - gle - hei - mer Schmidt,
his name is my name
too. When -
7
G
1.
ev - er we go out, the
peo - ple al - ways shout, "There goes
John Ja - cob Jin - gle - hei - mer
10
A
2.
Schmidt. Da da da da da da da.
John Ja - cob Jin - gle - hei - mer
Schmidt.
f

KUMBAYA

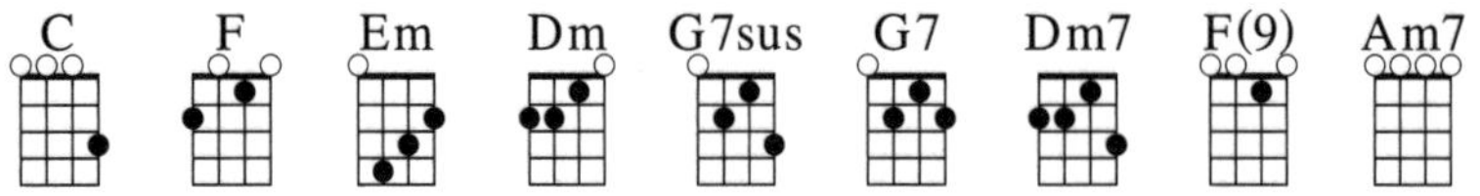
C
F
Em
Dm
G7sus
G7
Dm7
F(9)
Am7

Traditional

Moderately (♩ = 120)
1.
2.
C
F
C
mp
1. Kum-ba -
(with pedal)
6
F
C
ya, my Lord, kum - ba - ya. Kum - ba -
2.–4. See additional lyrics
10
Em
Dm
G7sus
G7
ya, my Lord, kum - ba - ya. Kum-ba -

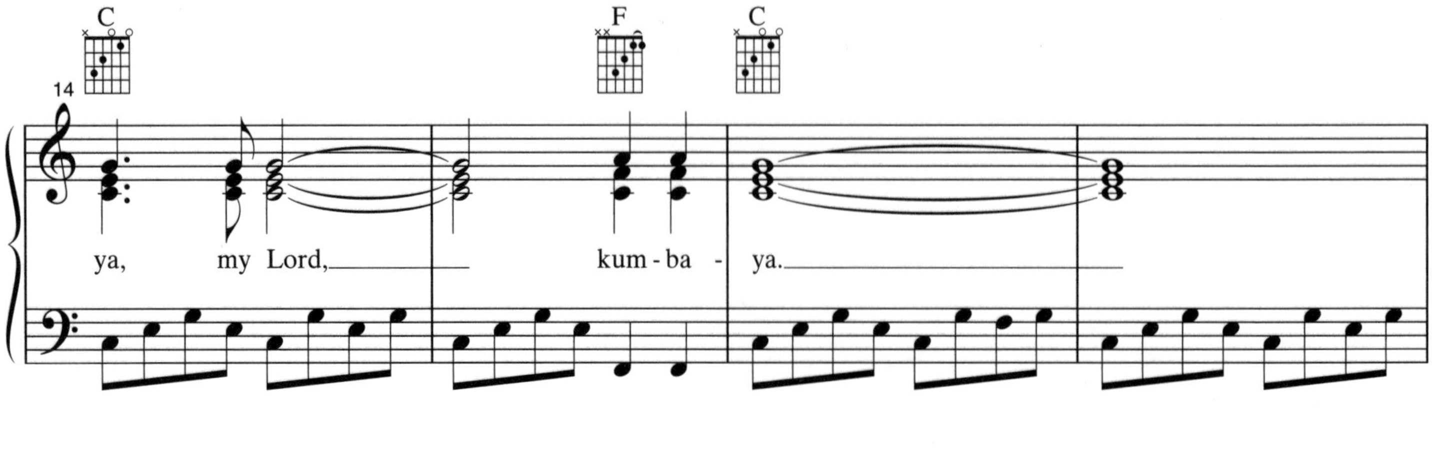
14
C
F
C
ya, my Lord, kum-ba - ya.

1.–3.
F C G7 C Dm7 C F(9)
18
Oh, Lord,__ kum - ba - ya.
4.
C Dm7 C Am7 F C
22
2. Some-one's ya. Oh, Lord,__
G7 C Dm7 C F(9) C
27
kum - ba - ya.
rit.

Verse 2:
Someone's singing, Lord, kumbaya.
Someone's singing, Lord, kumbaya.
Someone's singing, Lord, kumbaya.
Oh Lord, kumbayah.

Verse 3:
Someone's crying, Lord, kumbaya.
Someone's crying, Lord, kumbaya.
Someone's crying, Lord, kumbaya.
Oh Lord, kumbaya.

Verse 4:
Someone's praying, Lord, kumbaya.
Someone's praying, Lord, kumbaya.
Someone's praying, Lord, kumbaya.
Oh Lord, kumbaya.

Lavender's Blue

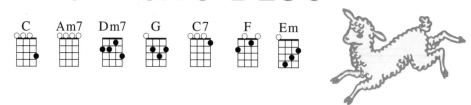

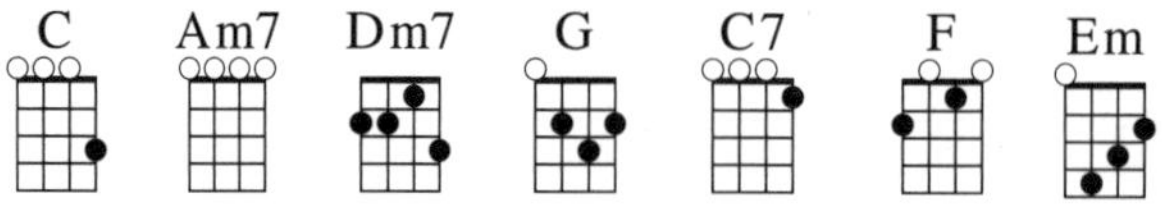
C
Am7
Dm7
G
C7
F
Em

Moderately (♩ = 108)

Traditional

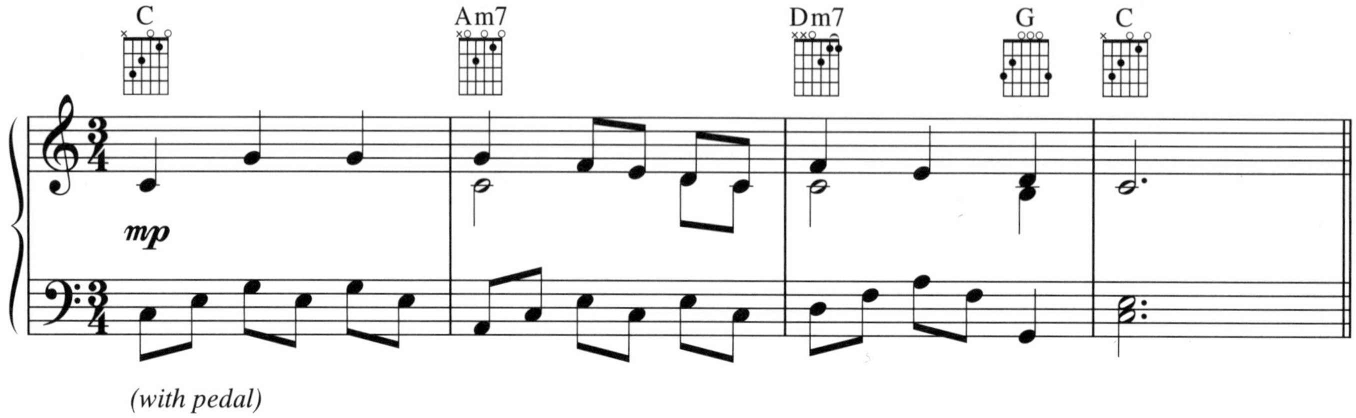
C
Am7
Dm7
G
C
mp
(with pedal)

Verses 1 & 3:

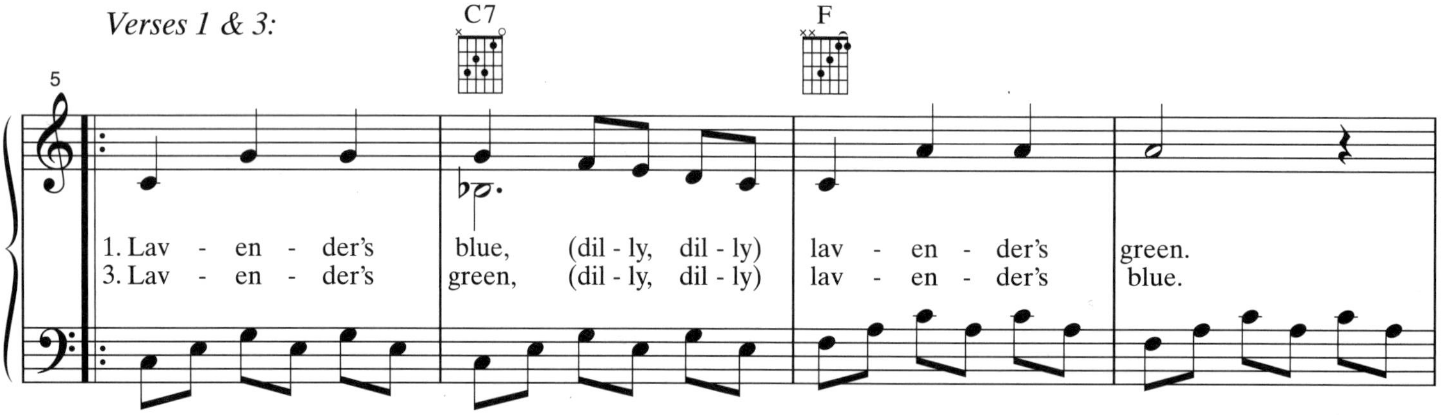
C7
F
5
1. Lav - en - der's blue, (dil - ly, dil - ly) lav - en - der's green.
3. Lav - en - der's green, (dil - ly, dil - ly) lav - en - der's blue.

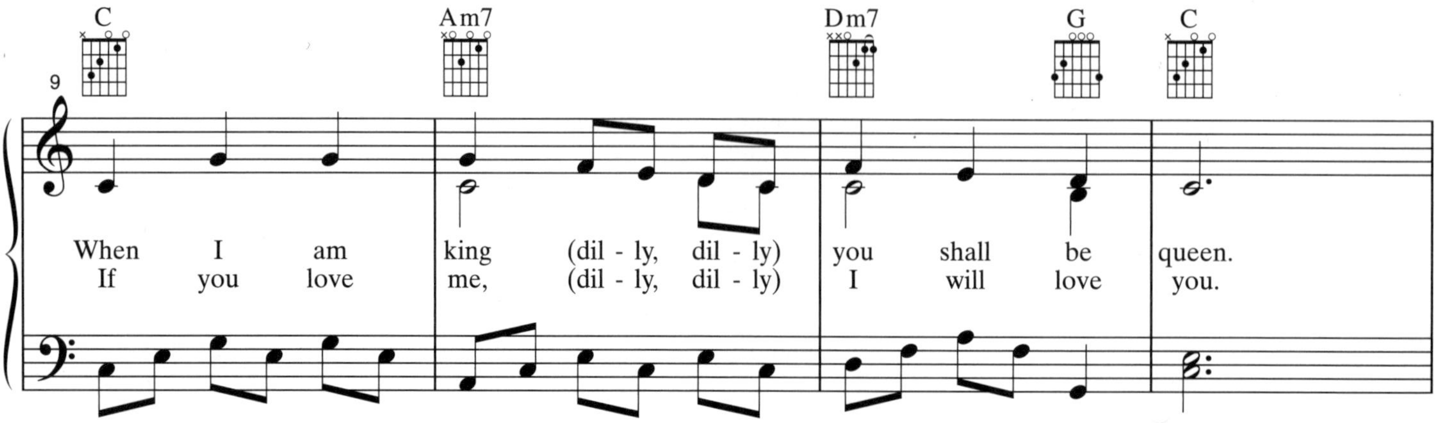
C
Am7
Dm7
G
C
9
When I am king (dil - ly, dil - ly) you shall be queen.
If you love me, (dil - ly, dil - ly) I will love you.

C7 F
13
Who told you so, (dil - ly, dil - ly) who told you so?
Let the birds sing, (dil - ly, dil - ly) and the lambs play.
C Am7 Dm7 G C
17
'Twas my own heart, (dil - ly, dil - ly) that told me so.
We shall be safe, (dil - ly, dil - ly) out of harm's way.
F C Dm7 G C
21
Verses 2 & 4:
C7 F
25
2. Call up your men, (dil - ly, dil - ly) set them to work.
4. I love to dance, (dil - ly, dil - ly) I love to sing.

C Am7 Dm7 G C
29
Some to the plow, (dil - ly, dil - ly) some to the cart.
When I am queen, (dil - ly, dil - ly) you'll be my king.
Em/B Am7 F
33
Some to make hay, (dil - ly, dil - ly) some to cut corn.
Who told me so, (dil - ly, dil - ly) who told me so?
C Am7 Dm7 G C F
37
Whilst you and I (dil - ly, dil - ly) keep our - selves warm.
I told my - self, (dil - ly, dil - ly) I told me so.
1. 2.
C Dm7 G C Dm7 G C
42
rit.

Limericks

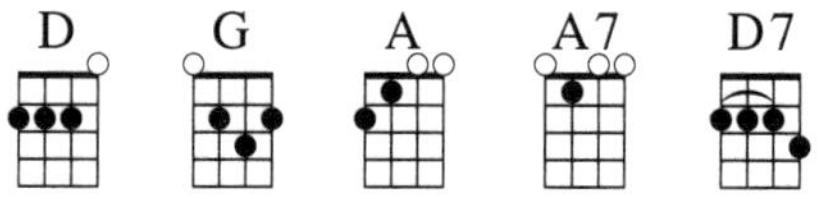
D G A A7 D7

Moderate waltz tempo (in one) (𝅗𝅥. = 53)

Traditional

D D/F♯ G
mf
(with pedal)
A A7 D
1. There
Verse:
A7
once was a la - dy from Ni - ger, who
once was two cats from Kil - ken - ny. Each
once was a man from Pe - ru, who
4.–7. See additional lyrics
D A7
rode on the back of a ti - ger. They re -
thought that one cat was too man - y. So they
dreamed he was eat - ing his shoe. He a -

D
D7
G
17
turned from a ride, with the la - dy in - side, and a
start - ed to fight, and to scratch and to bite. Now in -
woke in the night with a ter - ri - ble fright, and
A7
D
1.–5.
21
smile on the face of the ti - ger.
stead of two cats there aren't an - y.
found it was ac - tual - ly true.
2. There
3. There
4. A
6.
D
D/F♯
G
25
A
A7
D
29
7. There

7.
34
D/F♯
G
38
A
A7
D
f

Verse 4:
A mouse in her room woke Miss Dowd,
She was frightened it must be allowed,
But a happy thought hit her
To scare off the critter,
She sat up in the bed and meowed.

Verse 5:
There once was a girl who said, "Why
Can't I look in my ear with my eye?
If I put my mind to it,
I surely can do it,
You never can tell till you try."

Verse 6:
There once was a girl in the choir,
Whose voice rang higher and higher,
It reached such a height
It went clear out of sight,
And they found it next day in the spire.

Verse 7:
There was a young lady from Lynn,
Who was so excessively thin,
That when she essayed
To drink lemonade,
She looked down the straw and fell in.

Little Bo Peep

F
C7
Dm7
Gm7

Moderately (♩. = 72)

Traditional

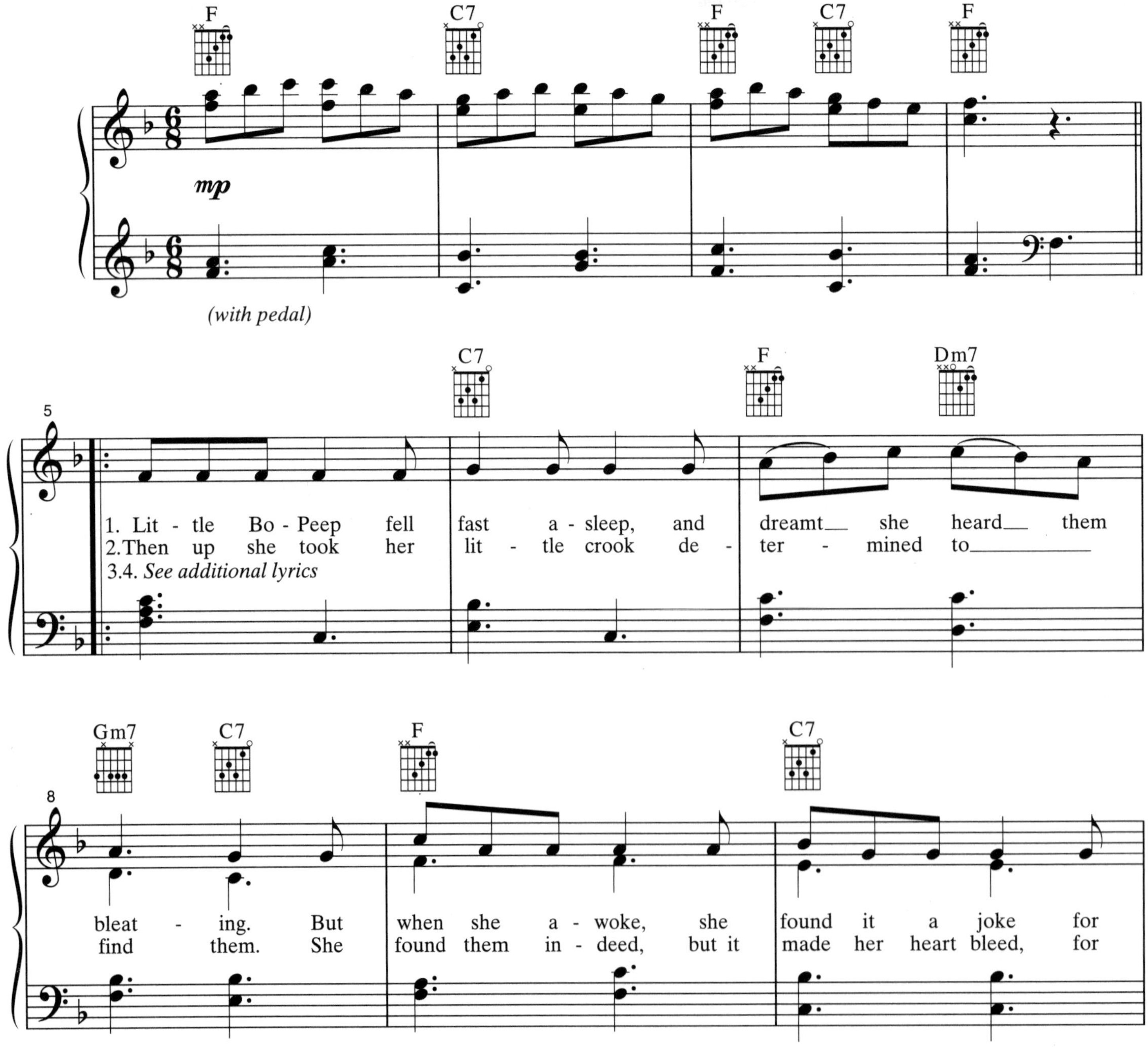
F
C7
F
C7
F
mp
(with pedal)
C7
F
Dm7
1. Lit - tle Bo - Peep fell fast a - sleep, and dreamt she heard them
2.Then up she took her lit - tle crook de - ter - mined to
3.4. See additional lyrics
Gm7
C7
F
C7
bleat - ing. But when she a - woke, she found it a joke for
find them. She found them in - deed, but it made her heart bleed, for

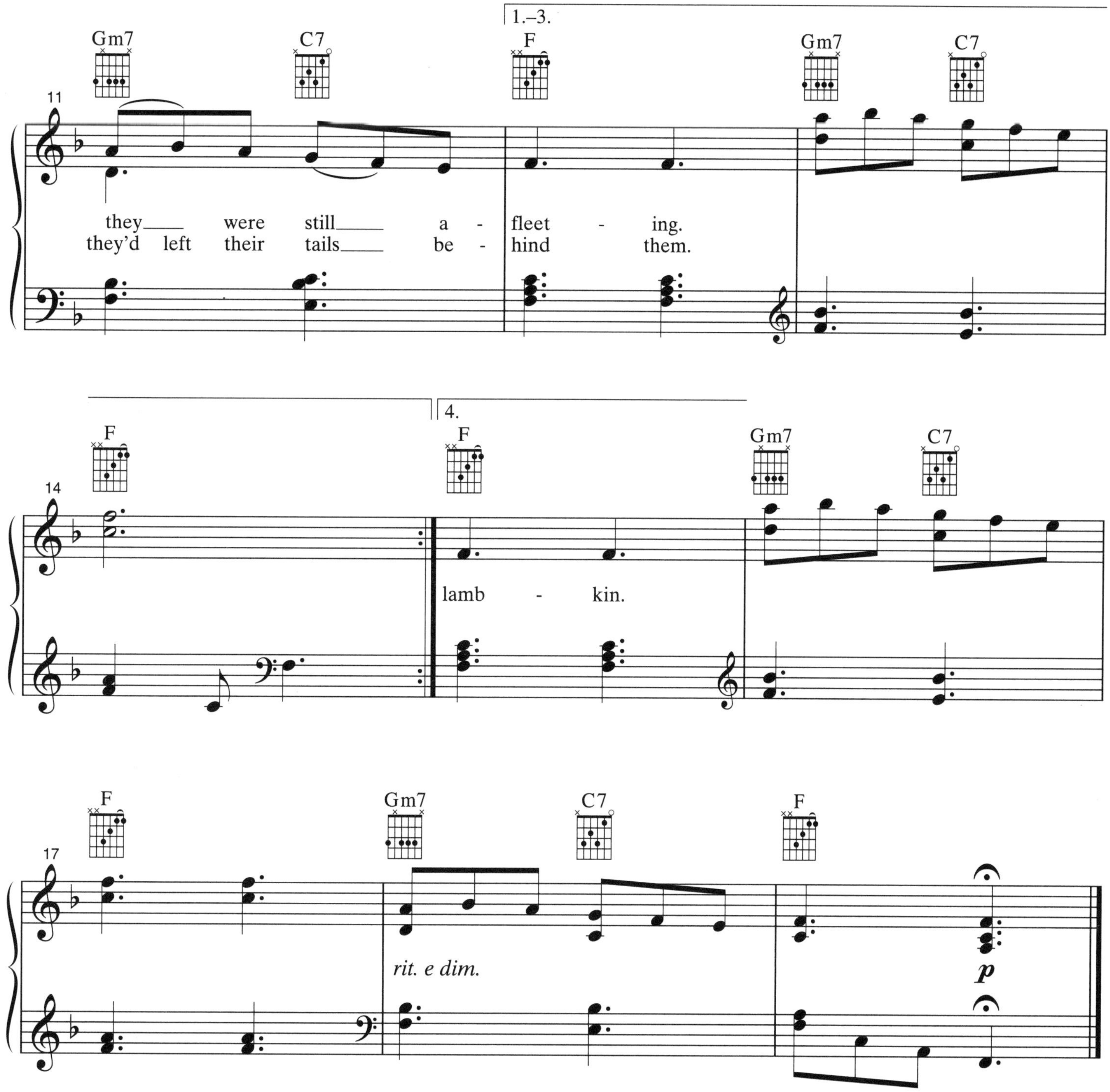
1.–3.
Gm7
C7
F
Gm7
C7
11
they___ were still___ a - fleet - ing.
they'd left their tails___ be - hind them.
4.
F
F
Gm7
C7
14
lamb - kin.
F
Gm7
C7
F
17
rit. e dim.
p

Verse 3:
It happened one day, as Bo-Peep did stray
Into a meadow hard by,
There she espied their tails side by side
All hung on a tree to dry.

Verse 4:
She heaved a sigh and wiped her eye,
And over the hillocks went rambling.
And tried what she could, as a shepherdess should
To tack each again to its lambkin.

Little Boy Blue

Traditional

F Bb C7 Dm7 G7 C Gm7
Moderately and flowing (♩. = 60)
F Bb F/C C7 F C7 F C7
mp
(with pedal)
Lit - tle boy blue, come blow_ your horn. There's
mf
F Dm7 G7 C F Bb C F
sheep in the mea-dow and cows in the corn. Where is the boy that looks af - ter the sheep? He's
Bb Gm7 F/C C7 F Bb F/C C7 F
1.
un - der the hay - stack fast a - sleep.
mp
2.
F/C C7 F F Bb F/C C7 F
fast a - sleep.
mp
rit. e dim.
p

Little Jack Horner

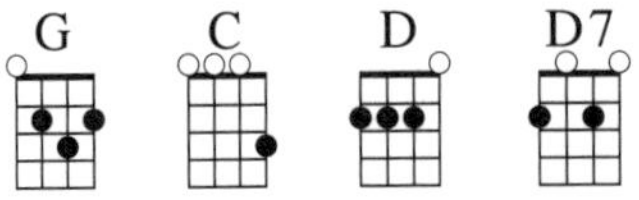
G
C
D
D7

Traditional

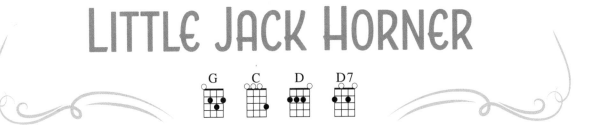

Allegretto (♩. = 60)
G G/B C D D7 G
mf
(with pedal)
G G/B C D D7 G
Lit - tle Jack Hor - ner sat in a cor - ner eat - ing a Christ - mas pie. He
G/B C D D7 1. G
put in his thumb, and pulled out a plum, and said, "What a good boy am I."

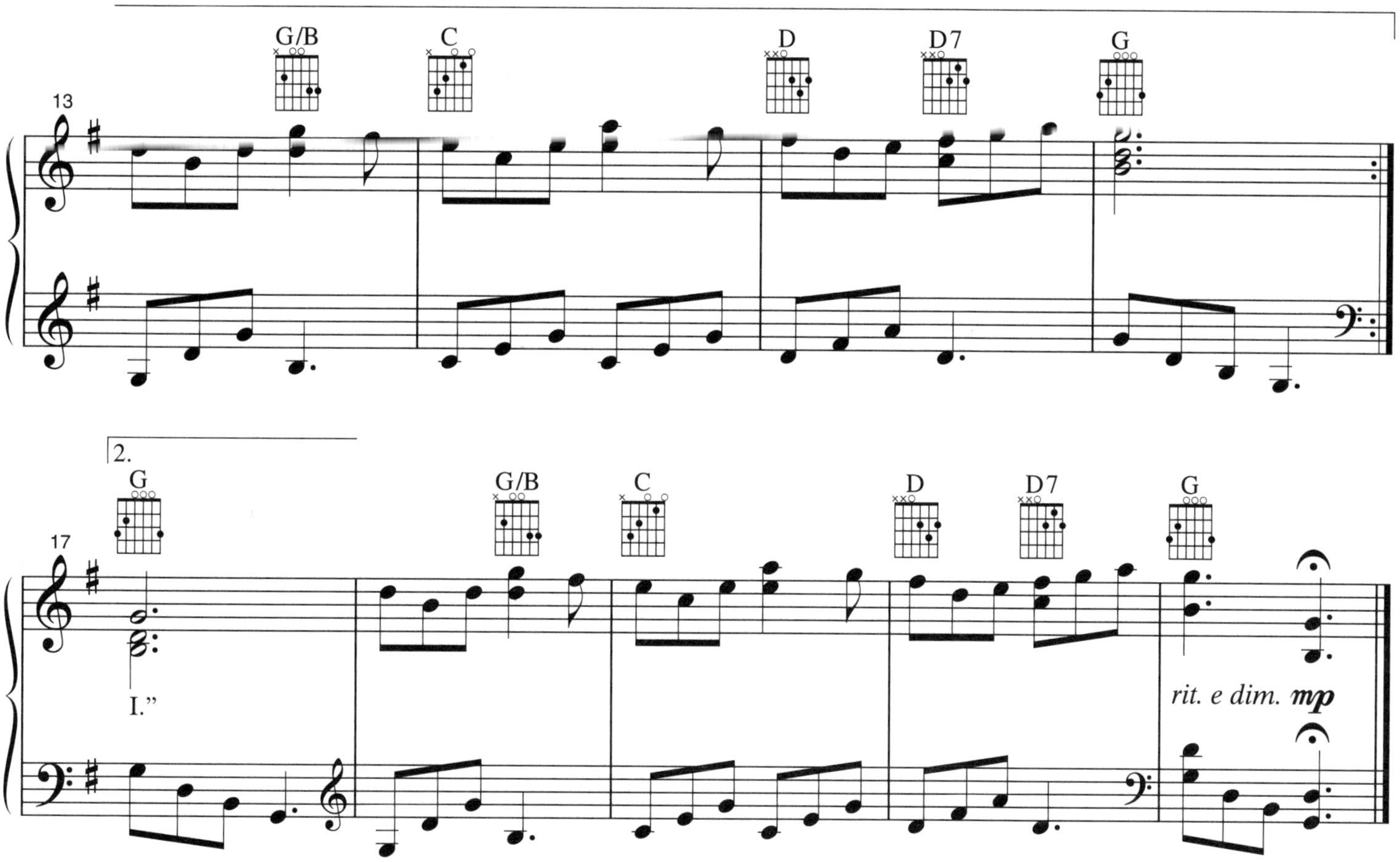
13
G/B
C
D
D7
G
2.
17
G
G/B
C
D
D7
G
I.”
rit. e dim. mp

London Bridge Is Falling Down

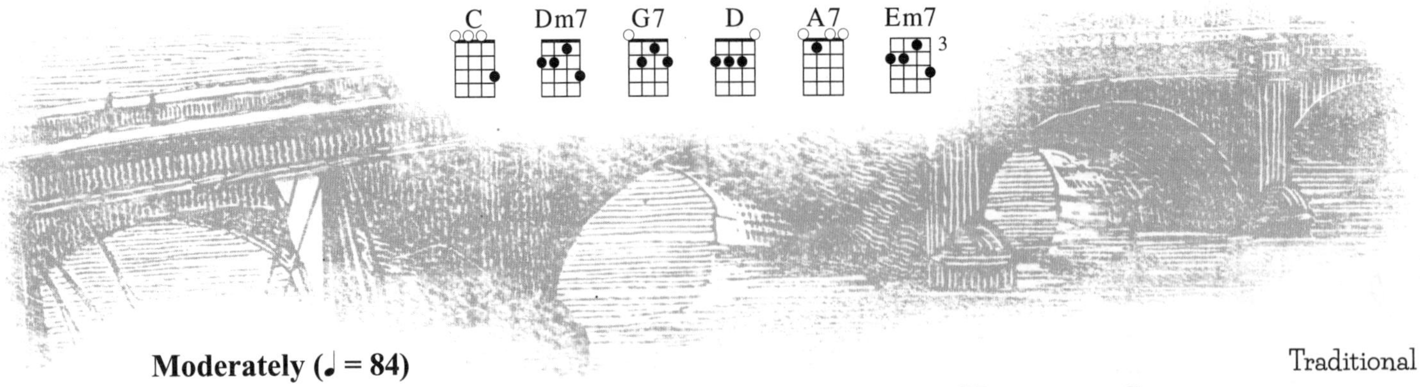
C
Dm7
G7
D
A7
Em7

Moderately (♩ = 84)

Traditional

C
Dm7
G7
C
mf
Verses 1–8:
G7
C
1. London Bridge is falling down, falling down, falling down.
2. Build it up with wood and clay, wood and clay, wood and clay.
3. Wood and clay will wash away, wash away, wash away.
4. Build it up with bricks and mortar, bricks and mortar, bricks and mortar.
5.–8. See additional lyrics
Dm7
G7
1.–7.
C
London Bridge is falling down, my fair lady.
Build it up with wood and clay, my fair lady.
Wood and clay will wash away, my fair lady.
Build it up with bricks and mortar, my fair lady.

Dm7 G7 C
8
C Dm7 G7 Em7 A7
13
la - dy.
cresc.
Verse 9:
D A7 D
18
9. London Bridge is falling down, falling down, falling down. London Bridge is
f
Em7 A7 D Em7 A7 D
23
falling down, my fair lady.

Verse 5:
Bricks and mortar will not stay,
Will not stay, will not stay.
Bricks and mortar will not stay,
My fair lady.

Verse 6:
Build it up with iron and steel,
Iron and steel, iron and steel.
Build it up with iron and steel,
My fair lady.

Verse 7:
Iron and steel will bend and bow,
Bend and bow, bend and bow.
Iron and steel will bend and bow,
My fair lady.

Verse 8:
Build it up with silver and gold,
Silver and gold, silver and gold.
Build it up with silver and gold,
My fair lady.
(To Verse 9:)

Mary Had a Little Lamb

Words by
Sarah Josepha Hale

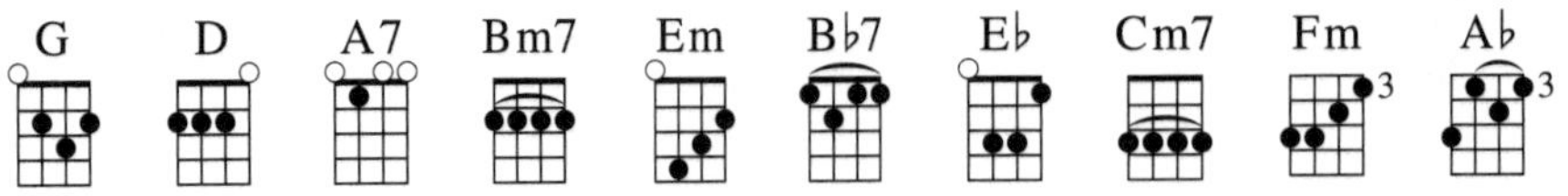
G
D
A7
Bm7
Em
B♭7
E♭
Cm7
Fm
A♭

Music by Lowell
Mason

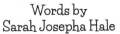

Moderately (𝅗𝅥 = 92)
G
D
A7
D
A7
mf
5
D
A7
D
1. Mar - y had a lit - tle lamb, lit - tle lamb, lit - tle lamb.
fol - lowed her to school one day, school one day, school one day. He
9
Bm7
Em
A7
D
Mar - y had a lit - tle lamb whose fleece was white as snow. And
fol - lowed her to school one day which was a - gainst the rules. It

A7
D
13
ev - 'ry-where that Mar - y went, Mar - y went, Mar - y went,
made the chil - dren laugh and play, laugh and play, laugh and play, it
Bm7
1.2.
Em
A7
17
ev - 'ry - where that Mar - y went the lamb was sure to
made the chil - dren laugh and play to
D
3.
Em
A7
D
B♭7
20
go. 2. He see a lamb at school.
E♭
B♭7
E♭
23
Mar - y had a lit - tle lamb, lit - tle lamb, lit - tle lamb.

Cm7 Fm B♭7 E♭
27
Mar - y had a lit - tle lamb whose fleece was white as snow. And
B♭7 E♭
31
ev - 'ry-where that Mar - y went, Mar - y went, Mar - y went,
Cm7 Fm B♭7 E♭
35
ev - 'ry-where that Mar - y went, the lamb was sure to go.
A♭ E♭ B♭7 E♭
39
f

MICHAEL FINNEGAN

F Gm7 Dm7 C7
Moderately, in two (𝅗𝅥 = 84)
Traditional
mf
1. There
was an old man named Mi - chael Fin - ne - gan. He had whis - kers on his chin - ne - gan.
was an old man named Mi - chael Fin - ne - gan. He went fish - ing with a pin - ne - gan.
was an old man named Mi - chael Fin - ne - gan. He grew fat and then grew thin a - gain.
They fell out and then grew in a - gain. Poor old Mi - chael Fin - ne - gan. be - gin a - gain.
Caught a fish and threw it in a - gain. Poor old Mi - chael Fin - ne - gan. Be - gin a - gain.
Then he died and had to be - gin a - gain. Poor old Mi - chael
1.2.
2. There
3. There
3.
Fin - ne - gan.
mp

Michael, Row the Boat Ashore

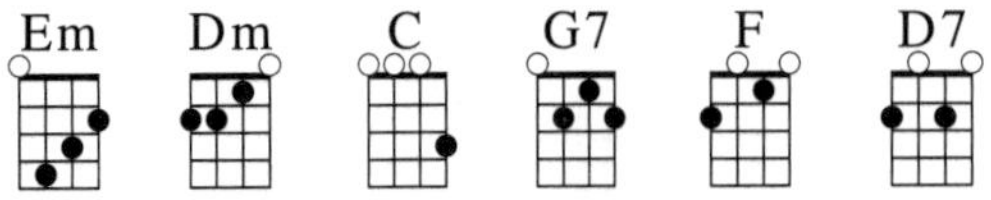
Em
Dm
C
G7
F
D7

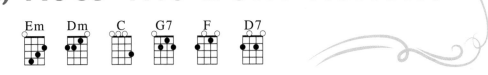

Moderately (♩ = 104)
Traditional
Em
Dm/F *
C/G
G7
C
Chorus:
mp
(with pedal)
Mi - chael, row the boat a - shore, hal - le - lu - jah. Mi - chael, row the boat a - shore, hal - le - lu - jah.
F
C
Em
Dm/F
C/G
G7
C
F
Sis - ter, help to trim the sail, hal - le - lu - jah. Sis - ter, help to trim the sail, hal - le - lu - jah. 1. The riv - er is
C
Em
Dm/F
C/G
G7
C

* "Slash" bass notes reflect pianinst's left hand.

Verse:
F C Em
deep and the riv - er is wide, hal - le - lu - jah. Green pas - tures on the oth - er
riv - er is chil - ly and cold, hal - le - lu - jah. Chills the bod - y but not the
deep and the riv - er is wide, hal - le - lu - jah. Milk and hon - ey on the oth - er
Dm/F C/G G7 C
Chorus:
side, hal - le - lu - jah.
soul, hal - le - lu - jah.
side, hal - le - lu - jah.
Mi - chael, row the boat a - shore, hal - le -
F C Em Dm/F C/G G7
lu - jah. Mi - chael, row the boat a - shore, hal - le - lu -
1. 2. 3.
C C C D7/F# C/G G7 C
jah. 2. Jor - dan's
jah. 3. The riv - er is
jah, hal - le - lu - jah.
rit.

The More We Get Together

F
C7

Moderately bright (♩ = 154)

Traditional

F
C7
F
mf
Oh, the
5
C7
F
more we get to - geth - er, to - geth - er, to - geth - er, oh, the
9
C7
F
more we get to - geth - er, the hap - pi - er we'll be. For

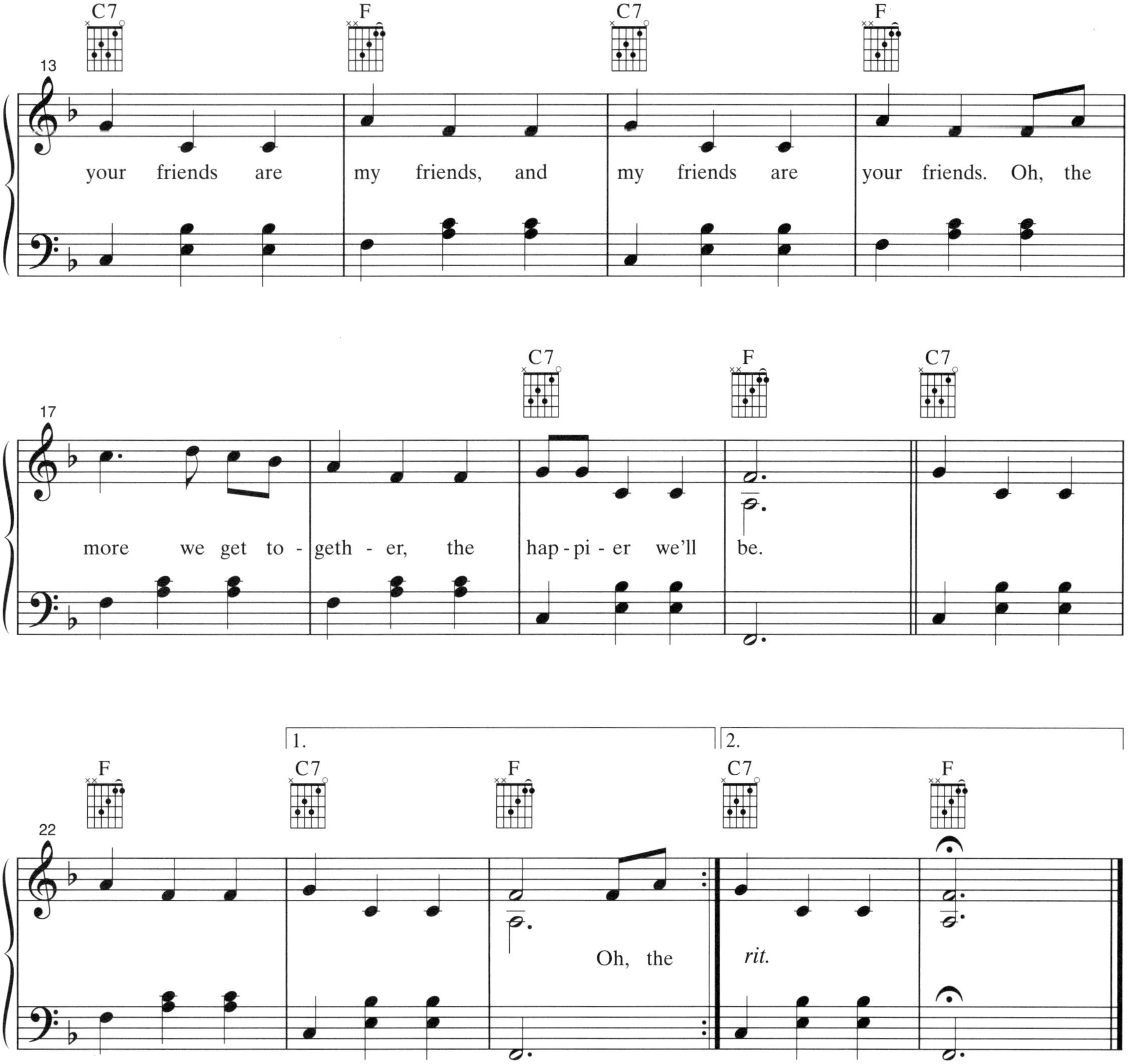
C7 F C7 F
13
your friends are my friends, and my friends are your friends. Oh, the
C7 F C7
17
more we get to - geth - er, the hap - pi - er we'll be.
1. 2.
F C7 F C7 F
22
Oh, the
rit.

The Muffin Man

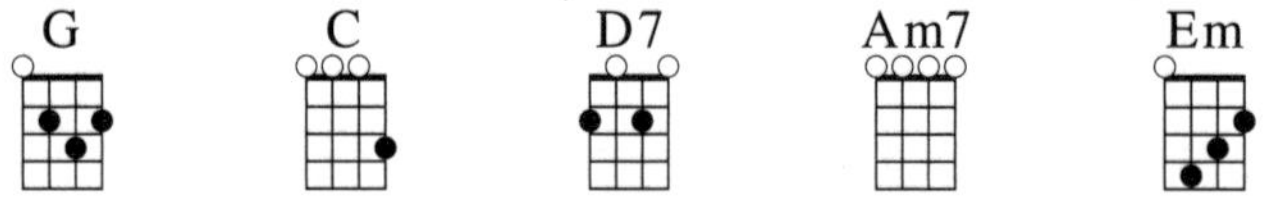
G
C
D7
Am7
Em

Moderately bright (♩ = 154)

Traditional

G
C
D7
G
D7
mf
1. Oh,
G
C
Am7
D7
5
do you know the muf - fin man, the muf - fin man, the muf - fin man? Oh,
G
C
D7
G
D7
9
do you know the muf - fin man that lives on Dru - ry Lane?
2. Oh,
3. Now
4. A
5. Now
G
C
Am7
D7
13
yes, I
two of us
few of us
we all
know the muf - fin man, the muf - fin man, the muf - fin man.
Oh,
Now
A
Now

1.–3.
G C D7 G D7
17
yes, I
two of us
few of us
we all
know the muf - fin man that lives on Dru - ry Lane.
G Em C D7 G D7
21
Oh,
4.
G D7 Am7 D7 G D7 G
25
lane. That lives on Dru - ry Lane.

My Bonnie Lies Over the Ocean

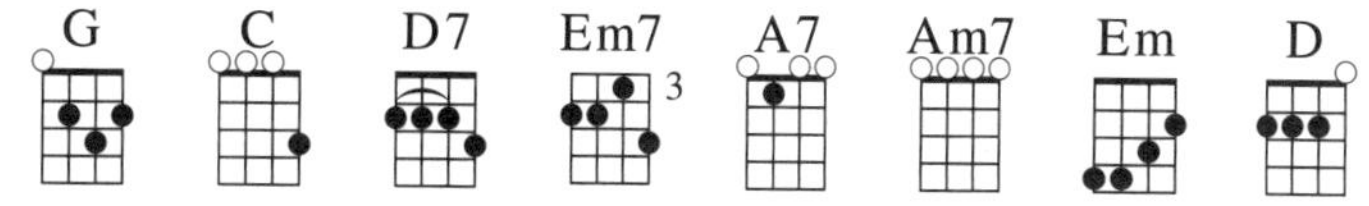
G
C
D7
Em7
A7
Am7
Em
D

Gently and flowing (♩ = 116)

Traditional

G C G D7
mp
1. My
(with pedal)
Verse:
G C G
bon - nie lies o - ver the o - cean. My
blow the winds o'er the o - cean. And
Em7 A7 Am7 D7
bon - nie lies o - ver the sea. My
blow the winds o'er the sea. Oh,
G C G Em
bon - nie lies o - ver the o - cean, so
blow the winds o'er the o - cean and

Am7
D7
G
C/G
G
17
bring back my bon - nie to me.
bring back my bon - nie to me.
Chorus:
G
C
A7
21
Bring back, bring back, oh,
mf
D
D7
G
25
bring back my bon - nie to me.
C
A7
29
Bring back, bring back, oh

33
D
D7
1.
G
C/G
G
bring back my bon - nie to me.
2. Oh,
dim.
mp
37
2.
G
C/G
G
G
C
me.
dim.
mp
41
G/D
D7
G
rit. e dim.
p

Oats, Peas, Beans and Barley Grow

Traditional

F
C7
Gm
Moderately (♩. = 108)
mf
Chorus:
Oats, peas, beans and bar - ley grow. Oats, peas, beans and bar - ley grow. Can you or I or an - y - one know how oats, peas, beans and bar - ley grow.
Verse:
1. First the far - mer sows his seed, stands e - rect and takes his ease. He
2–4. See additional lyrics

F C7 F
19
stamps his foot and claps his hands, and turns a - round to view his lands.
Chorus:
Gm C7
23
Oats, peas, beans and bar - ley grow. Oats, peas, beans and bar - ley grow. Can
F C7 F
27
you or I or an - y - one know how oats, peas, beans and bar - ley grow.
1.–3. 4.
C7 F F
31

Verse 2:
Next the farmer waters the seed,
Stands erect and takes his ease.
He stamps his foot and claps his hands,
And turns around to view his lands.
(To Chorus:)

Verse 3:
Next the farmer hoes the weeds,
Stands erect and takes his ease.
He stamps his foot and claps his hands,
And turns around to view his lands.
(To Chorus:)

Verse 4:
Last the farmer harvests his seed,
Stands erect and takes his ease.
He stamps his foot and claps his hands,
And turns around to view his lands.
(To Chorus:)

Oh Dear, What Can the Matter Be?

C Cmaj7 C6 Dm7 G7
Moderate waltz (♩ = 144)
Traditional
mf
(with pedal)
Chorus:
Oh, dear! What can the mat - ter be?
Oh, dear! What can the mat - ter be?
Oh, dear! What can the mat - ter be?
Johnny's so long at the fair.
To Coda
1. He
2. He

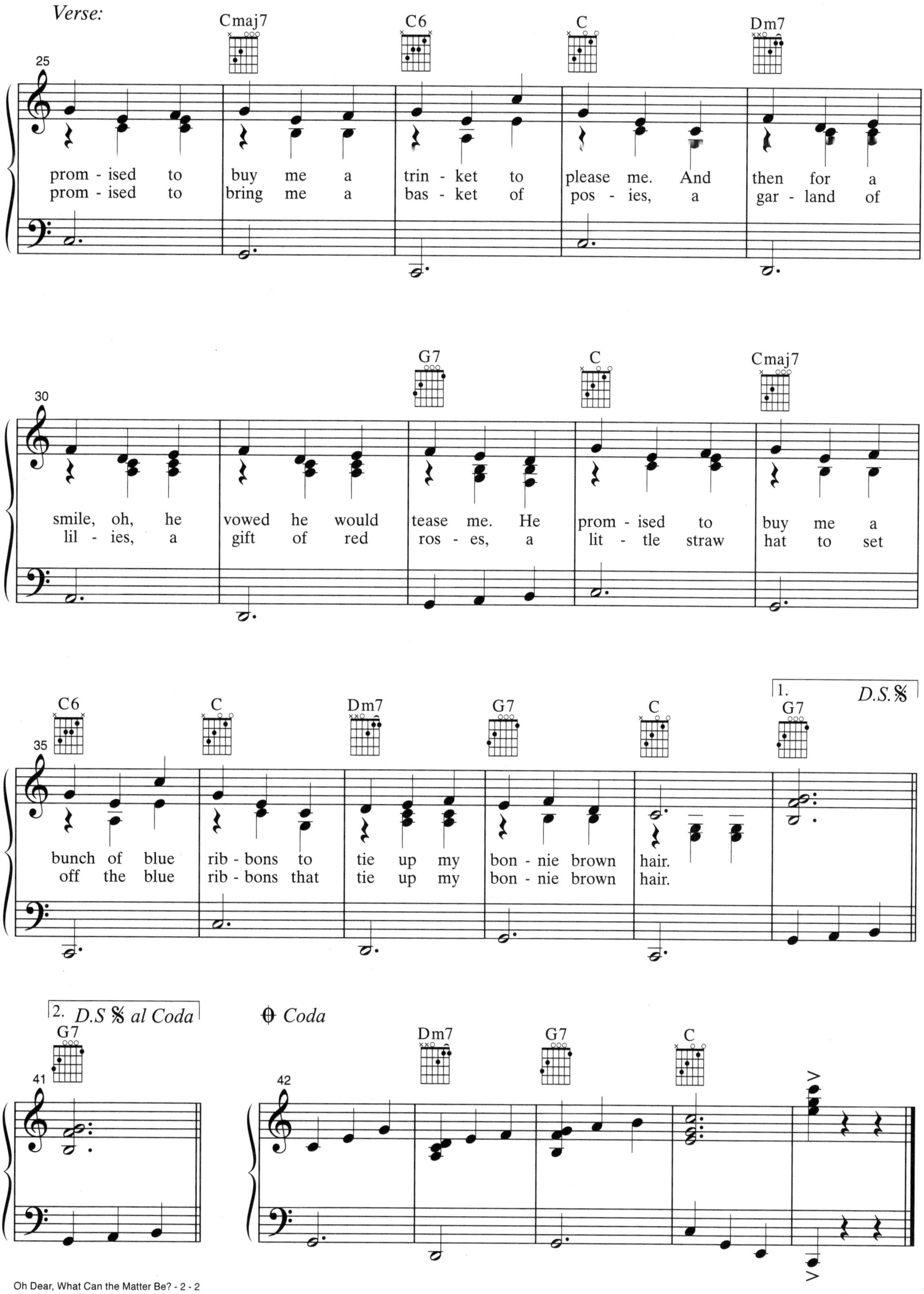
Verse:
Cmaj7 C6 C Dm7
25
prom - ised to buy me a trin - ket to please me. And then for a
prom - ised to bring me a bas - ket of pos - ies, a gar - land of
G7 C Cmaj7
30
smile, oh, he vowed he would tease me. He prom - ised to buy me a
lil - ies, a gift of red ros - es, a lit - tle straw hat to set
C6 C Dm7 G7 C
1. D.S. 𝄋
G7
35
bunch of blue rib - bons to tie up my bon - nie brown hair.
off the blue rib - bons that tie up my bon - nie brown hair.
2. D.S 𝄋 al Coda
G7
41
Coda
Dm7 G7 C
42

Oh Where, Oh Where Has My Little Dog Gone?

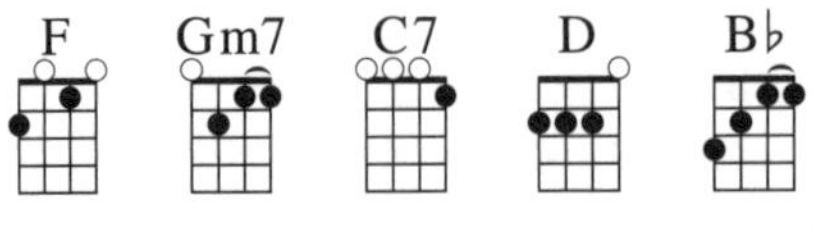
F
Gm7
C7
D
B♭

Moderate waltz tempo (in one) (𝅗𝅥. = 52)

Traditional

F
Gm7
C7
mf
Oh
(with pedal)
F
C7
where, oh where has my lit - tle dog gone? Oh
F
D
Gm7
C7
where, oh where can he be? With his

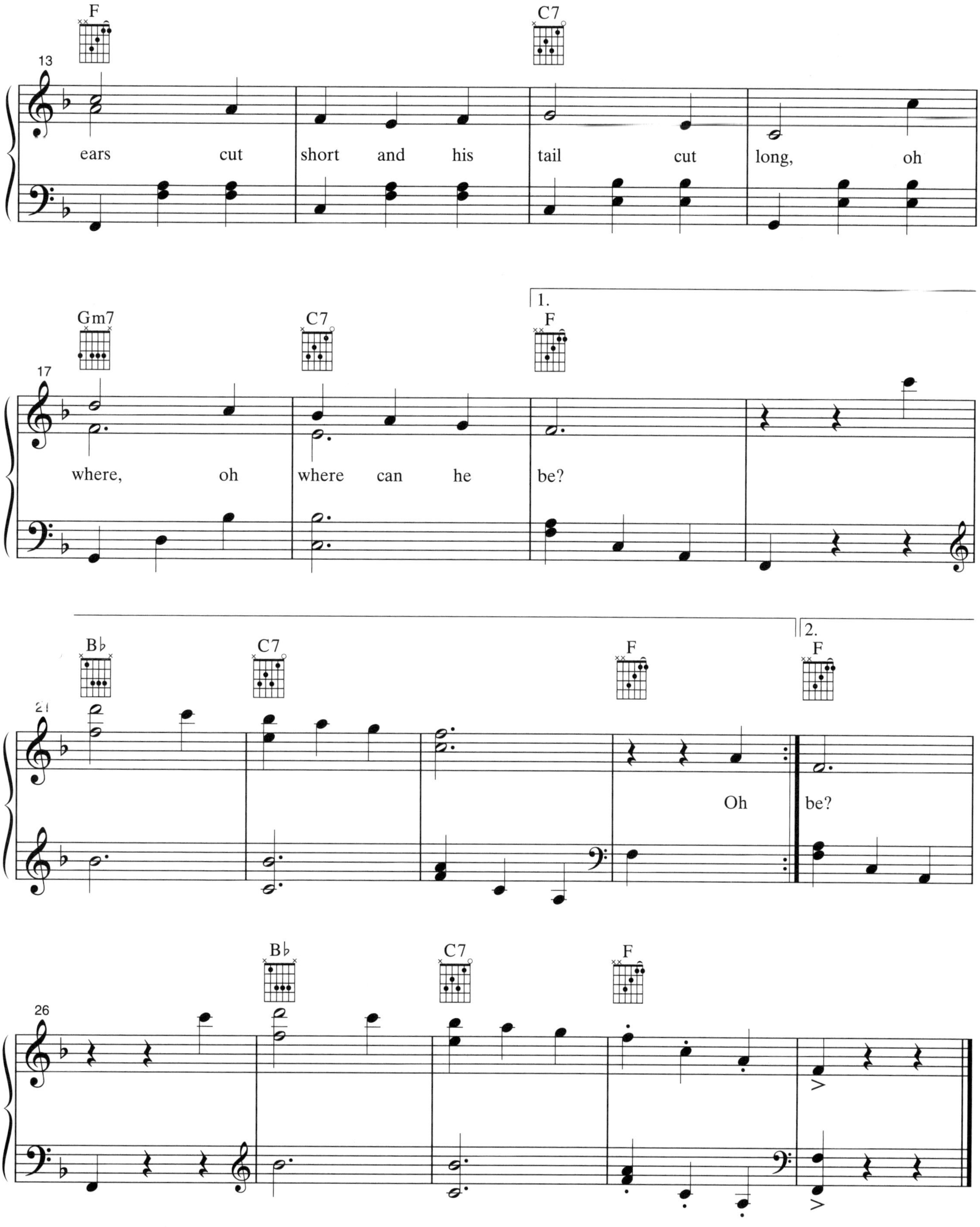
F
C7
13
ears cut short and his tail cut long, oh
Gm7
C7
1.
F
17
where, oh where can he be?
B♭
C7
F
2.
F
21
Oh be?
B♭
C7
F
26

The Old Grey Mare

D Bm7 Em7 A7 G

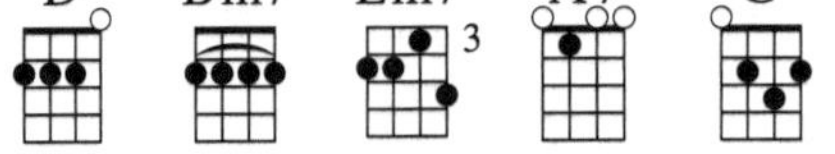

Written by
Thomas Francis McNulty

Moderately (♩ = 112)

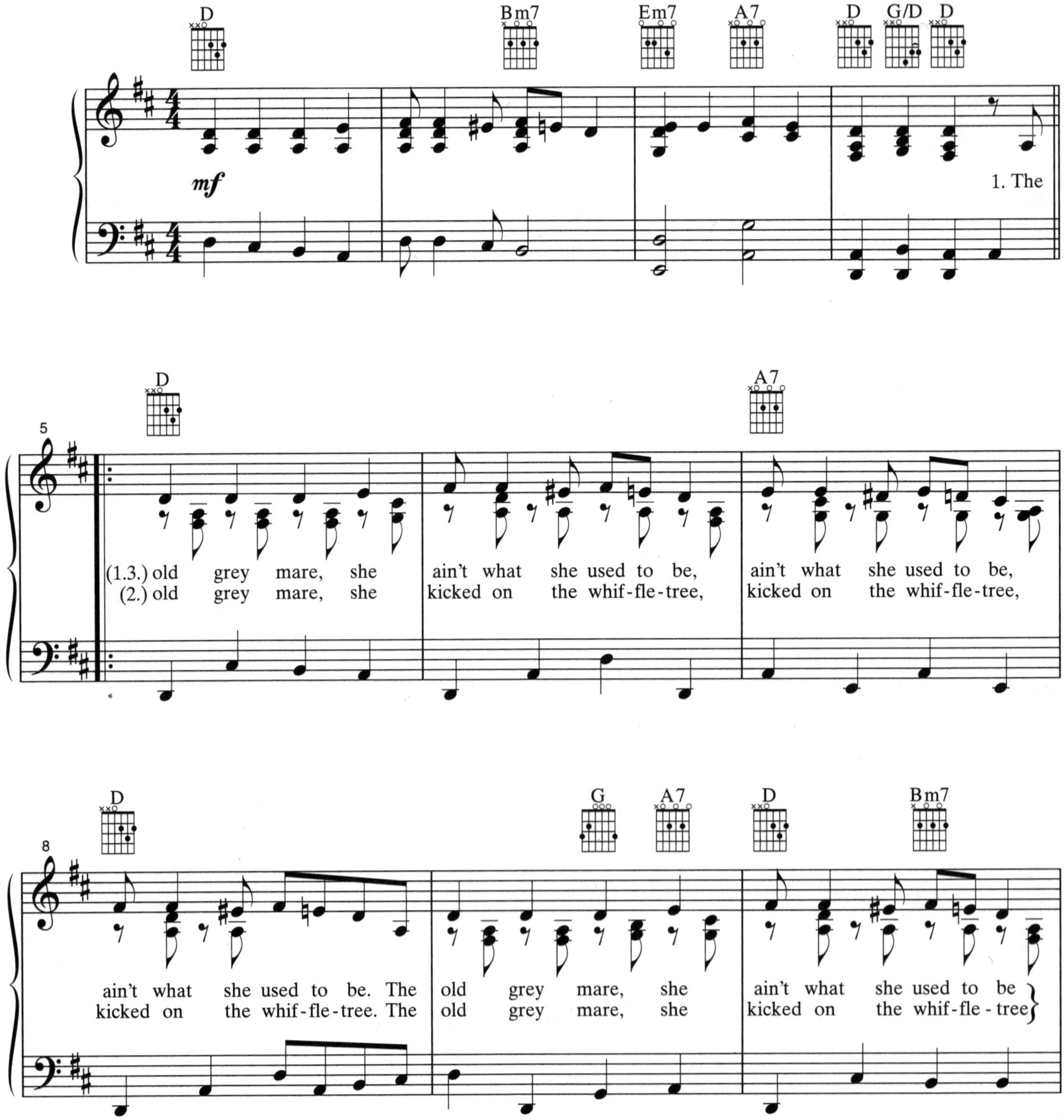
D
Bm7
Em7
A7
D G/D D
mf
1. The
5
D
A7
(1.3.) old grey mare, she ain't what she used to be, ain't what she used to be,
(2.) old grey mare, she kicked on the whif-fle-tree, kicked on the whif-fle-tree,
8
D
G A7
D
Bm7
ain't what she used to be. The old grey mare, she ain't what she used to be
kicked on the whif-fle-tree. The old grey mare, she kicked on the whif-fle-tree

Em7 A7 D G D G
11
man - y long years a - go. Man - y long years a -
D G D
14
go, man - y long years a - go. The
G A7 D Bm7 Em7 A7
17
old grey mare, she ain't what she used to be
she kicked on the whif - fle - tree
man - y long years a -
1.2. 3.
D G D D G D Em7 A7 D
20
go. 2. The
3. The
go.

Old MacDonald Had a Farm

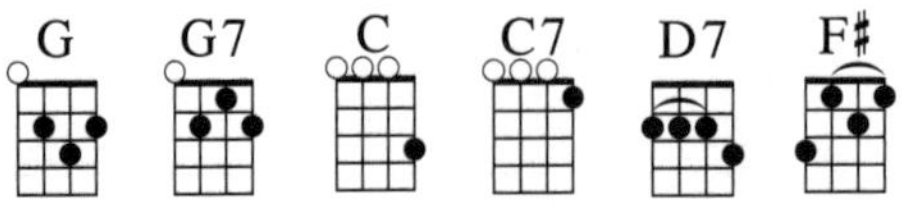
G
G7
C
C7
D7
F♯

Moderately fast (♩ = 144)

Traditional

G
G7
C
C7
G/D
D7
G
mf
5
C
G
D7
G
Old Mac - Don - ald had a farm, e - i - e - i - o. And
9
C
G
D7
G
on that farm he had some cows, chickens, sheep, pigs, ducks, e - i - e - i - o.
With a
With a
With a
With an
With a

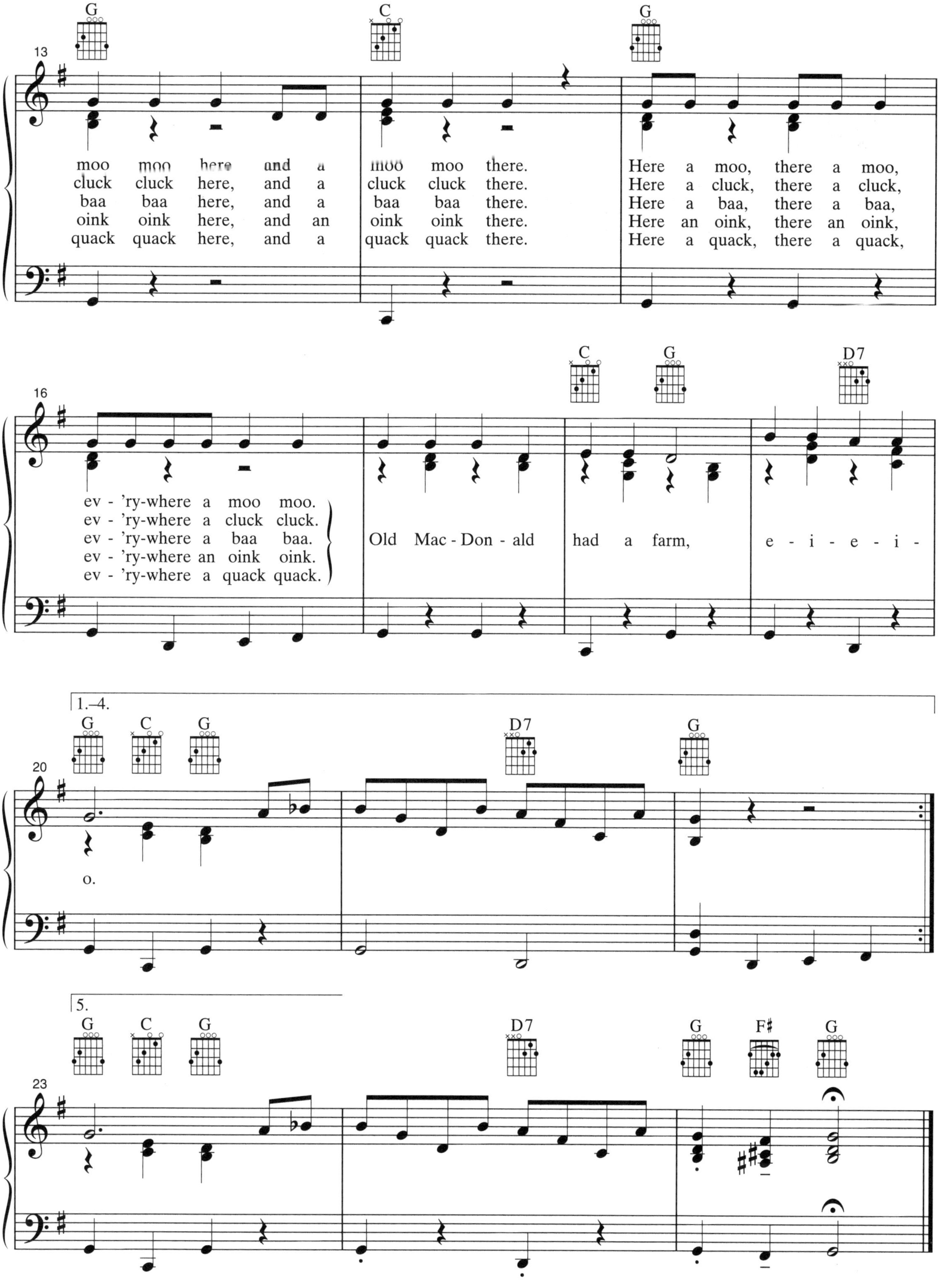
G C G
13
moo moo here and a moo moo there. Here a moo, there a moo,
cluck cluck here, and a cluck cluck there. Here a cluck, there a cluck,
baa baa here, and a baa baa there. Here a baa, there a baa,
oink oink here, and an oink oink there. Here an oink, there an oink,
quack quack here, and a quack quack there. Here a quack, there a quack,
C G D7
16
ev - 'ry-where a moo moo.
ev - 'ry-where a cluck cluck.
ev - 'ry-where a baa baa.
ev - 'ry-where an oink oink.
ev - 'ry-where a quack quack.
Old Mac - Don - ald had a farm, e - i - e - i -
1.–4.
G C G D7 G
20
o.
5.
G C G D7 G F♯ G
23

On the Bridge of Avignon

F
C
B♭
C7

Moderately (♩ = 98)

Traditional

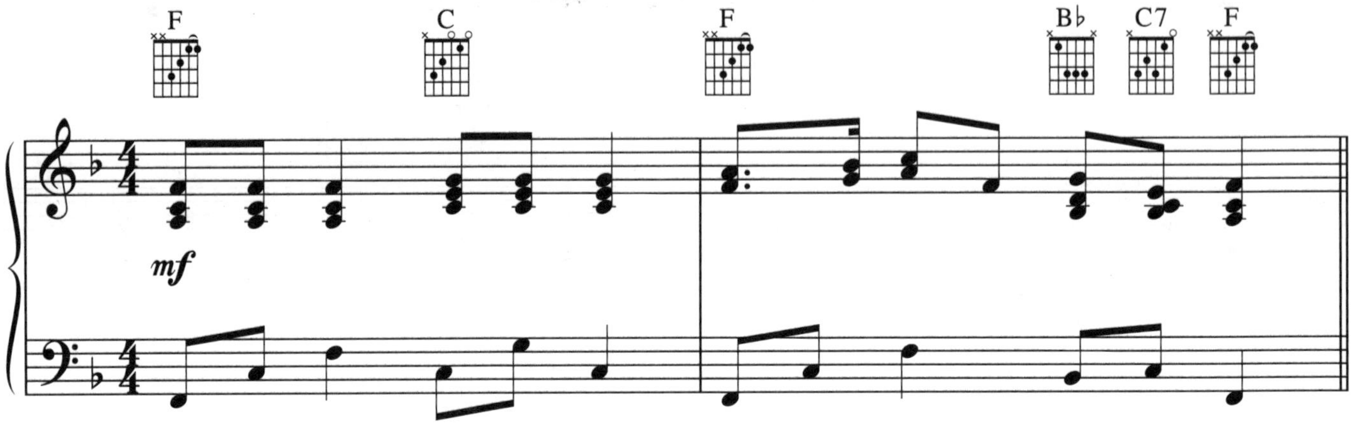
F
C
F
B♭
C7
F
mf

Chorus:

C
F
C7
On the bridge of A - vig - non, they're all danc - ing, they're all danc - ing.
Sur le pont d'A - vig - non, l'on y dan - se l'on y dan - se.
F
C
F
B♭
C7
F
On the bridge of A - vig - non, they're all danc - ing in a ring.
Sur le pont d'A - vig - non, l'on y dan - se tout en rond.

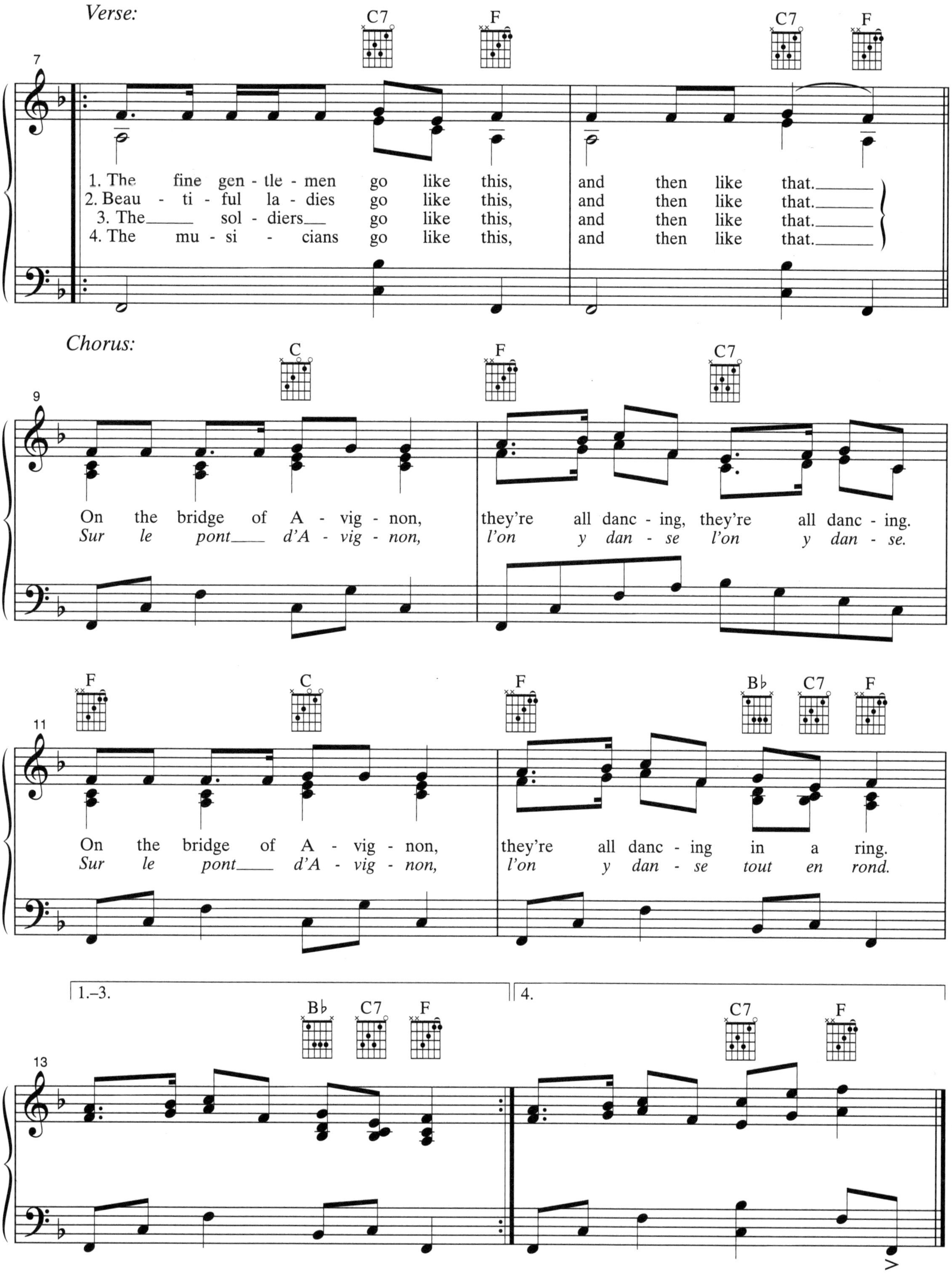
Verse:
C7
F
C7
F
1. The fine gen - tle - men go like this, and then like that.
2. Beau - ti - ful la - dies go like this, and then like that.
3. The sol - diers go like this, and then like that.
4. The mu - si - cians go like this, and then like that.
Chorus:
C
F
C7
On the bridge of A - vig - non, they're all danc - ing, they're all danc - ing.
Sur le pont d'A - vig - non, l'on y dan - se l'on y dan - se.
F
C
F
B♭
C7
F
On the bridge of A - vig - non, they're all danc - ing in a ring.
Sur le pont d'A - vig - non, l'on y dan - se tout en rond.
1.–3.
4.
B♭
C7
F
C7
F

On Top of Old Smokey

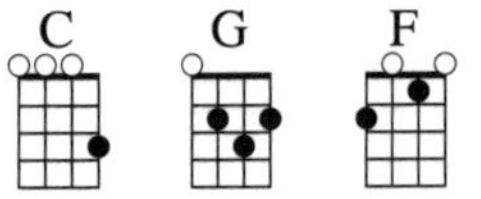
C
G
F

Moderate country waltz (♩ = 144)

Traditional

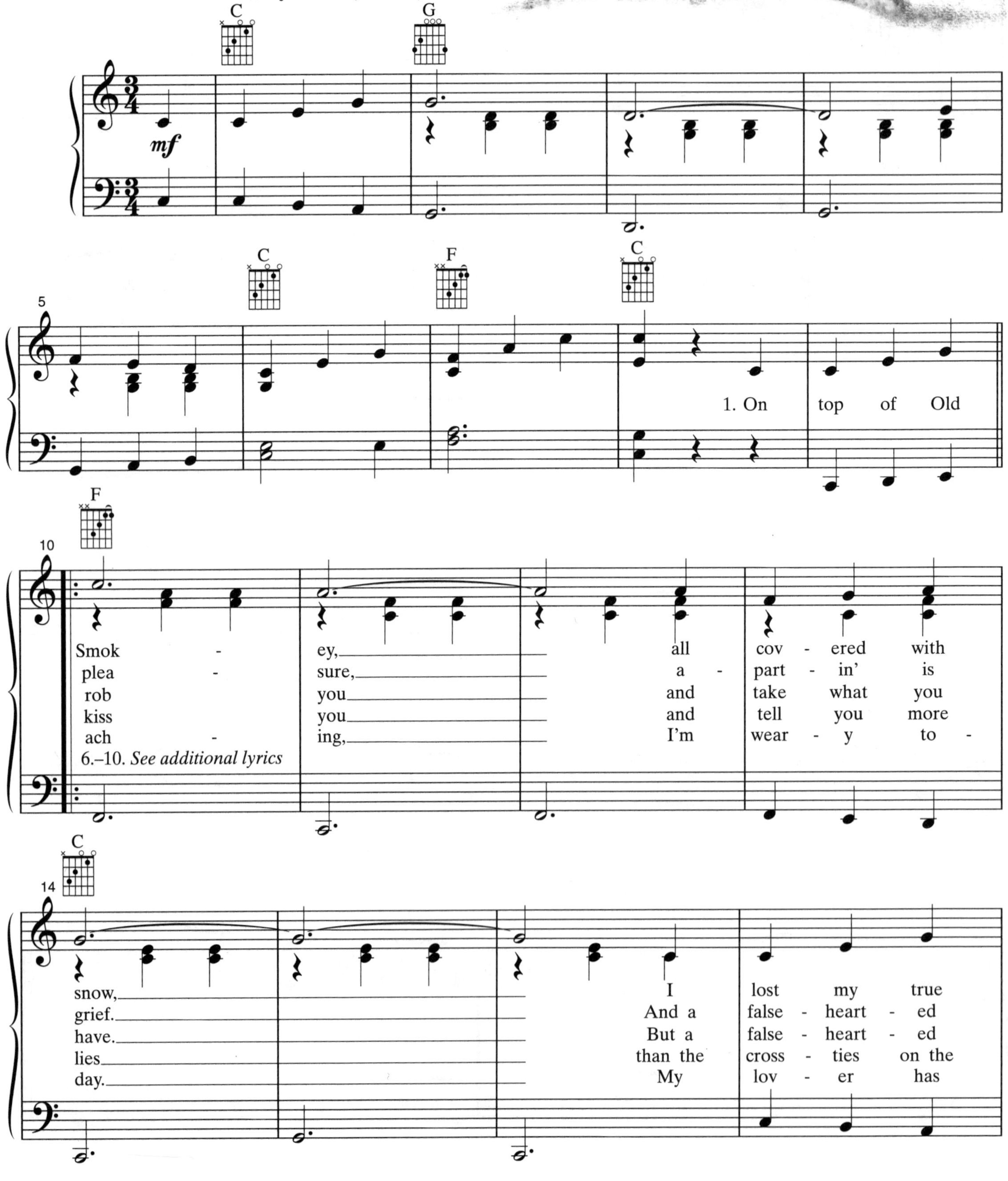
C
G
mf
C
F
C
1. On
top of Old
F
Smok - ey, all cov - ered with
plea - sure, a - part - in' is
rob you and take what you
kiss you and tell you more
ach - ing, I'm wear - y to -
6.–10. See additional lyrics
C
snow, I lost my true
grief. And a false - heart - ed
have. But a false - heart - ed
lies than the cross - ties on the
day. My lov - er has

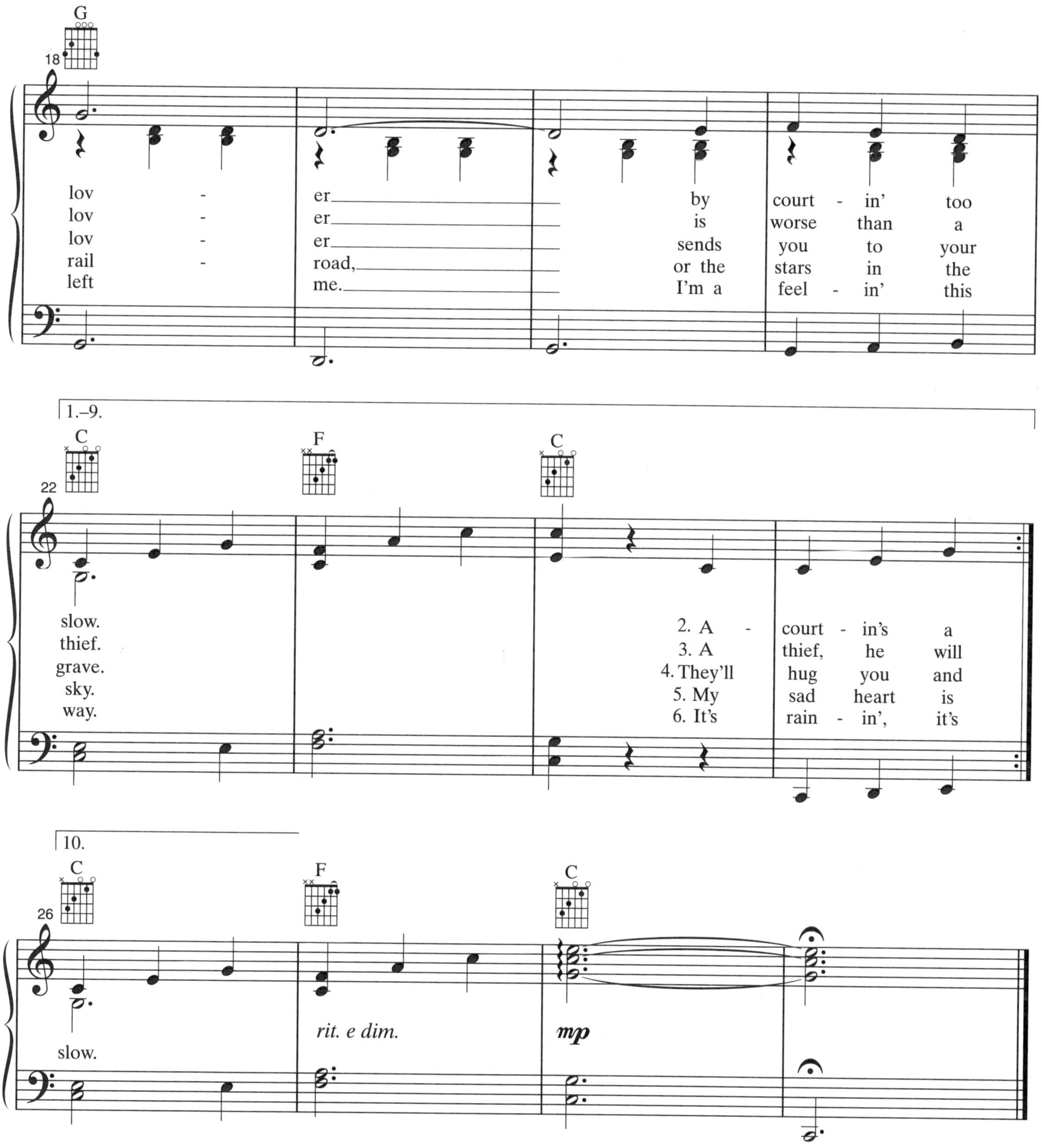
G
18
lov - er by court - in' too
lov - er is worse than a
lov - er sends you to your
rail - road, or the stars in the
left me. I'm a feel - in' this
1.–9.
C
F
C
22
slow. 2. A - court - in's a
thief. 3. A thief, he will
grave. 4. They'll hug you and
sky. 5. My sad heart is
way. 6. It's rain - in', it's
10.
C
F
C
26
slow.
rit. e dim.
mp

Verse 6:
It's rainin', it's pourin'.
The moon gives no light.
My horse, he won't travel
This dark lonesome night.

Verse 7:
I'm goin' away, dear.
I'll write you my mind.
My mind is to marry,
And to leave you behind.

Verse 8:
Come all you young people
And listen to me.
Don't place your affection
On a green willow tree.

Verse 9:
The leaves, they will wither,
The roots, they will die.
You will be forsaken
And never know why.

Verse 10:
On top of Old Smokey,
All covered with snow,
I lost my true lover
A-courtin' too slow.

Over the River and Through the Woods

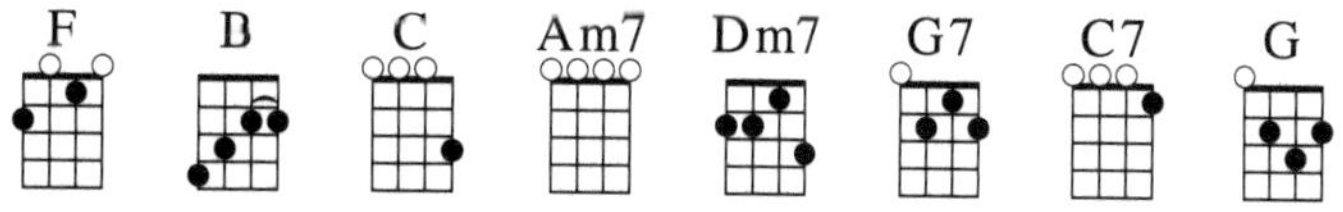
F
B
C
Am7
Dm7
G7
C7
G

Moderately bright, with spirit (in one) (𝅗𝅥. = 80)

Words by Lydia Marie Child

F
B/F♯
C
Am7
mf
(with pedal)
Dm7
G7
C
5
9
C7
F
1. O - ver the riv - er and through the woods to Grand - moth - er's
2. O - ver the riv - er and through the woods to have a full
3. O - ver the riv - er and through the woods, and straight through the
14
C
Dm7
G7
house we go. The horse knows the way to
day of play. Oh, hear the bells ring - ing
barn - yard gate. It seems that we go so

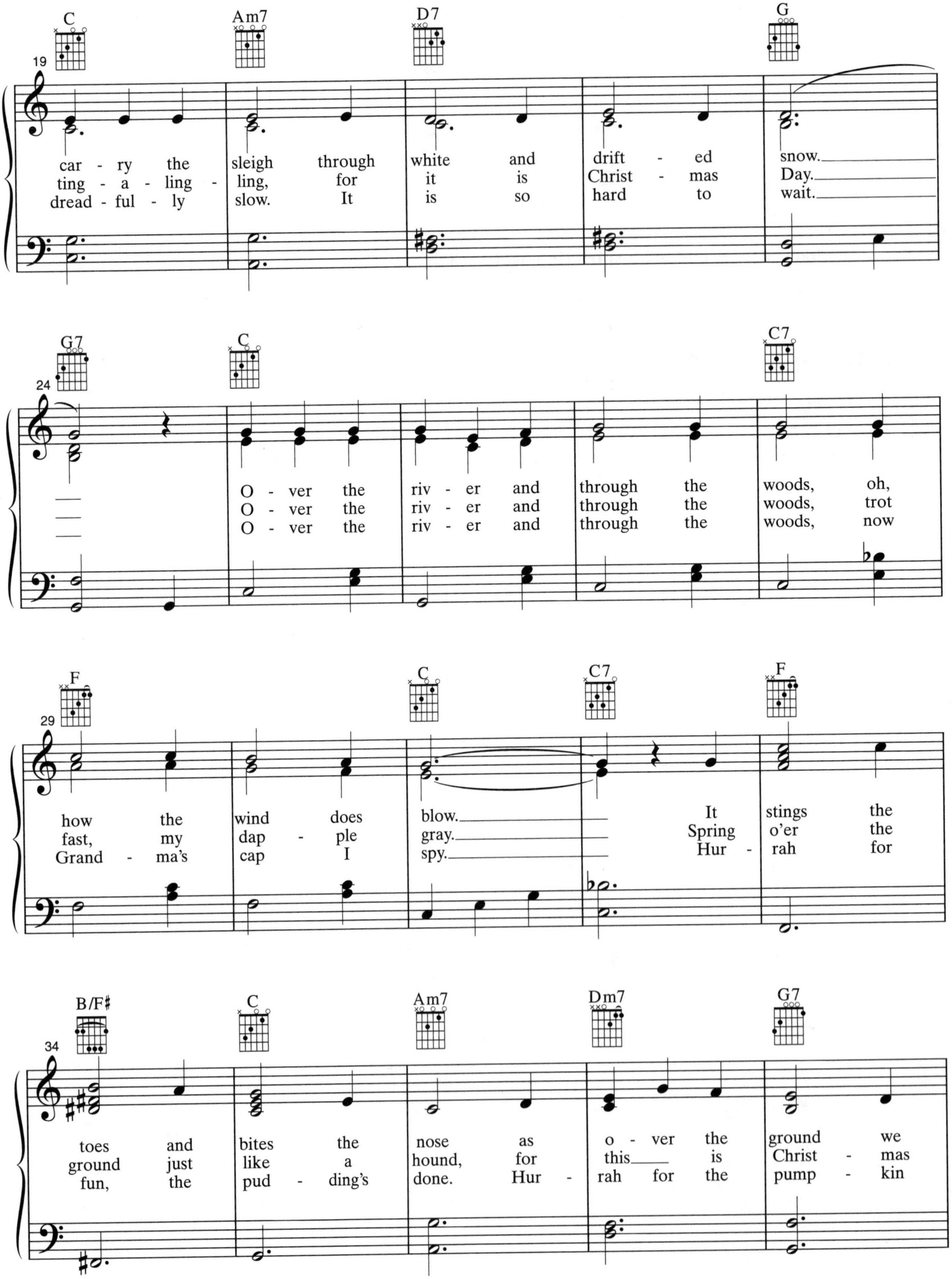
C Am7 D7 G
19
car - ry the sleigh through white and drift - ed snow.
ting - a - ling - ling, for it is Christ - mas Day.
dread - ful - ly slow. It is so hard to wait.
G7 C C7
24
O - ver the riv - er and through the woods, oh,
O - ver the riv - er and through the woods, trot
O - ver the riv - er and through the woods, now
F C C7 F
29
how the wind does blow. It stings the
fast, my dap - ple gray. Spring o'er the
Grand - ma's cap I spy. Hur - rah for the
B/F♯ C Am7 Dm7 G7
34
toes and bites the nose as o - ver the ground we
ground just like a hound, for this is Christ - mas
fun, the pud - ding's done. Hur - rah for the pump - kin

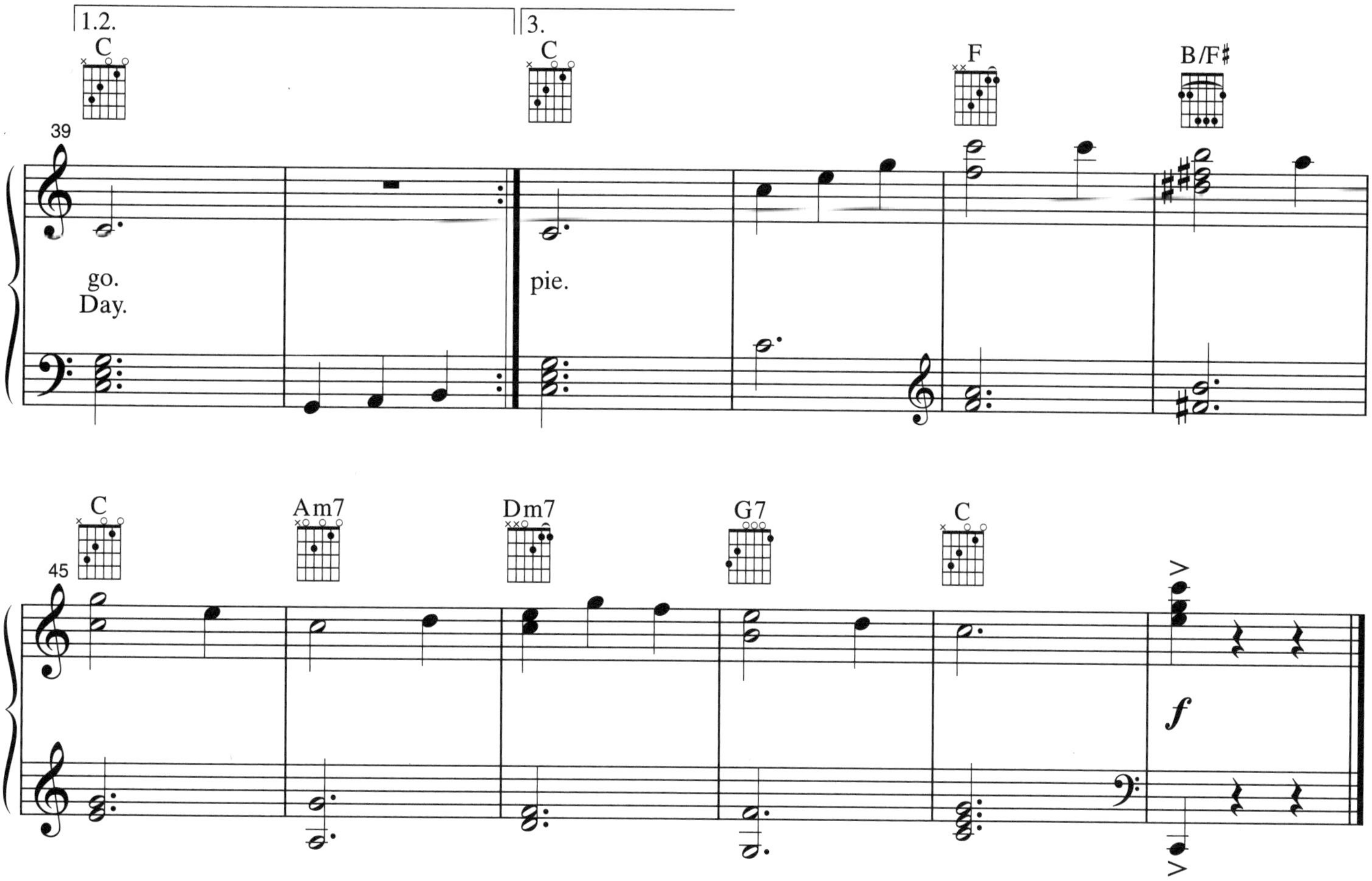
1.2.
3.
C
C
F
B/F♯
39
go.
Day.
pie.
C
Am7
Dm7
G7
C
45
f

Alternate Lyrics

Verse 1:
Over the river and through the woods
To Grandfather's house we go.
The horse knows the way to carry the sleigh
Through the white and drifted snow.
Over the river and through the woods,
To Granfather's house away.
We would not stop for doll or top,
For 'tis Thanksgiving Day.

Verse 2:
Over the river and through the woods
Oh, how the wind does blow.
It stings the toes, and bites the nose,
As over the ground we go.
Over the river and through the woods,
With a clear blue winter sky.
The dogs do bark, and children hark,
As we go jingling by.

Verse 3:
Over the river and through the woods
To have a first-rate play.
Hear the bells ring, ting a ling ding.
Hurrah for Thanksgiving Day.
Over the river and through the woods,
No matter the winds that blow,
Or if we get the sleigh upset
Into a bank of snow.

Verse 4:
Over the river and through the woods
To see little John and Ann.
We will kiss them all and play snowball,
And stay as long as we can.
Over the river and through the woods,
Trot fast, my dapple gray!
Spring over the ground like a hunting-hound,
For 'tis Thanksgiving Day.

Verse 5:
Over the river and through the woods
And straight through the barnyard gate.
We seem to go extremely slow.
It is so hard to wait.
Over the river and through the woods,
Old Jowler hears our bells.
He shakes his paw with a loud bow-wow.
And thus the news he tells.

Verse 6:
Over the river and through the woods.
When Grandmother sees us come,
She will say, "Oh dear, the children are here,"
Bring a pie for everyone.
Over the river and through the woods.
Now Grandmother's cap I spy!
Hurrah for the fun! Is the pudding done?
Hurrah for the pumpkin pie!

PAT-A-CAKE

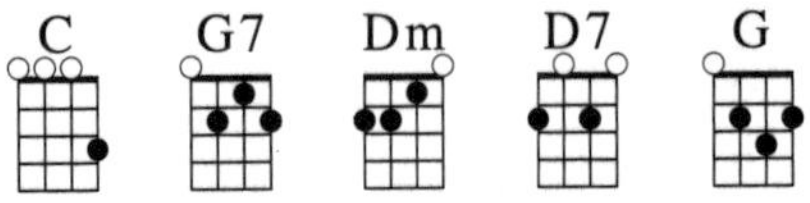
C
G7
Dm
D7
G

Moderately (♩. = 72)

Traditional

C
G7
C
mf
Pat - a - cake, pat - a - cake,

Dm
G7
C
4
bak - er's man.
Bake me a cake__ as
fast as you can.

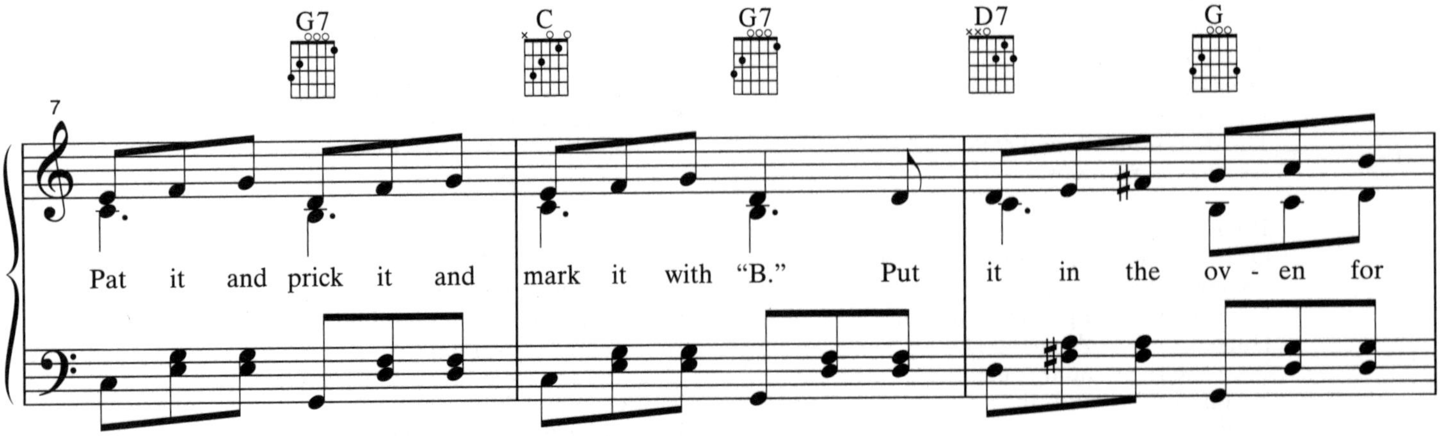
G7
C
G7
D7
G
7
Pat it and prick it and
mark it with "B." Put
it in the ov - en for

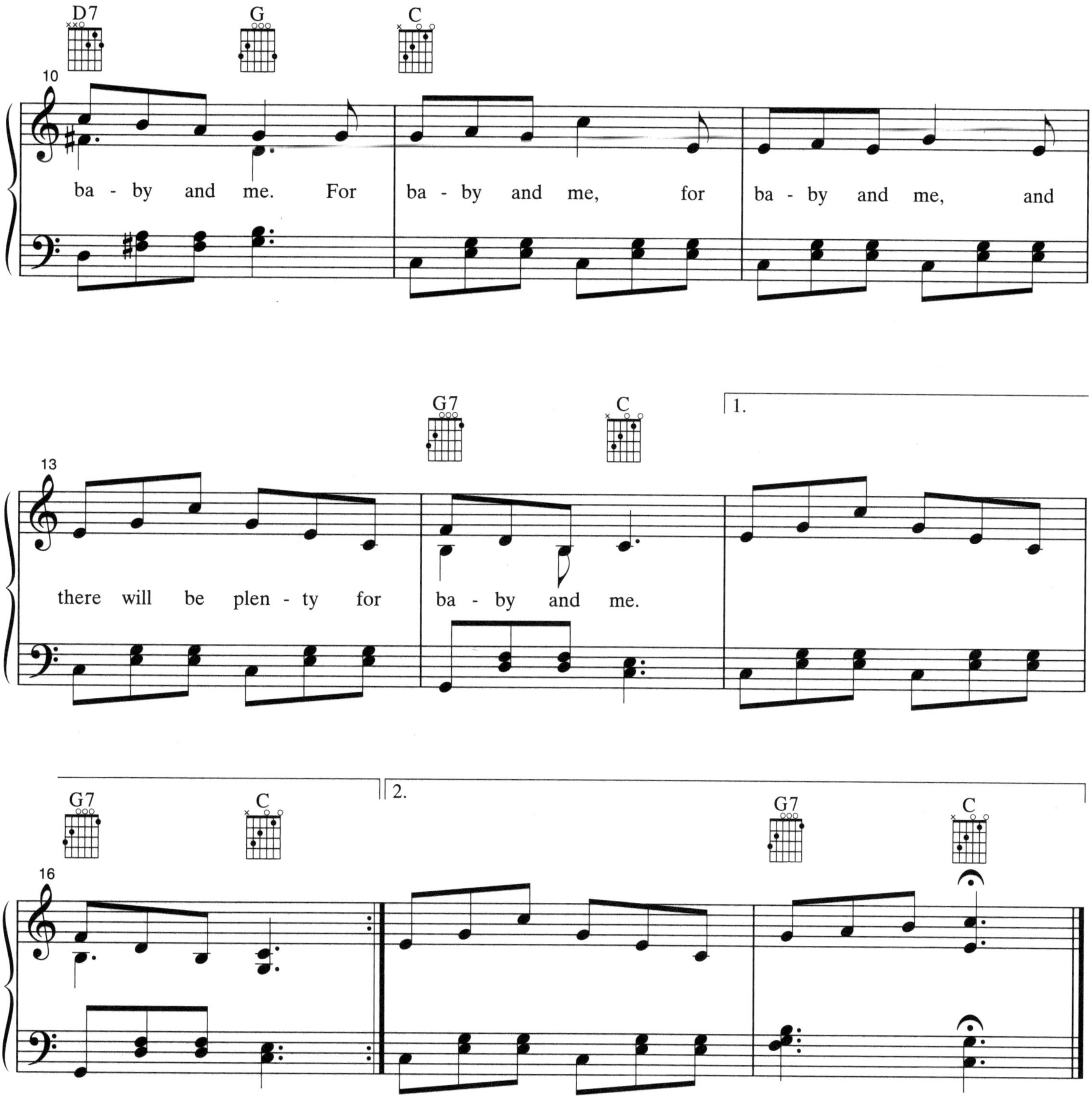
D7
G
C
10
ba - by and me. For
ba - by and me, for
ba - by and me, and
G7
C
1.
13
there will be plen - ty for
ba - by and me.
G7
C
2.
G7
C
16

Peas Pudding

C F Dm7 G7
Moderately (♩ = 120)
Traditional
C F C Dm7 C G7 C
mf
5
F C G7 C G7 C
Peas pud-ding hot, peas pud-ding cold, peas pud-ding in the pot, nine days old.
9
F C G7 C G7 C
Some like it hot, some like it cold, some like it in the pot, nine days old.
13
G7 C
1.
G7 C
2.
G7 C

Polly Wolly Doodle

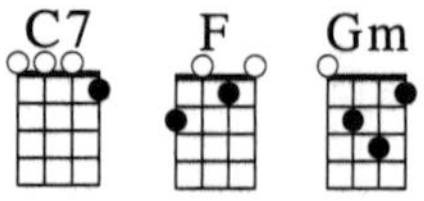
C7
F
Gm

Moderately (𝅗𝅥 = 84)

By Daniel Decatur Emmett

C7
F
mf
1. Oh, I
Verse:
went down South for to see my Sal. Sing Pol - ly wol - ly doo - dle all the
Sal, she is a ___ maid - en fair. Sing Pol - ly wol - ly doo - dle all the
3.–5. See additional lyrics
day. My ___ Sal, she is a spunk - y gal. Sing
day. With ___ cur - ly eyes and laugh - ing hair. Sing
Pol - ly wol - ly doo - dle all the day.
Pol - ly wol - ly doo - dle all the day.
Chorus:
Fare thee well, fare thee

Gm C7
well, fare thee well, my fair - y fay, for I'm
Gm C7 Gm C7
goin' to Lou'-si-an-a for to see my Su-sy-an-na. Sing Pol-ly wol-ly doo-dle all the
1.–4.
F C7 F
day. 2. Oh, my
5.
F C7 F
day.
8va

Verse 3:
Down behind the barn on my hands and knees,
Sing Polly wolly doodle all the day,
I thought I heard a chicken sneeze,
Sing Polly wolly doodle all the day.
(To Chorus:)

Verse 4:
He sneezed so hard with the whooping cough,
Sing Polly wolly doodle all the day,
He sneezed his head and tail right off,
Sing Polly wolly doodle all the day.
(To Chorus:)

Verse 5:
Oh, a grasshopper sitting on a railroad track,
Sing Polly wolly doodle all the day,
A-picking his teeth with a carpet tack,
Sing Polly wolly doodle all the day.
(To Chorus:)

Polly, Put the Kettle On

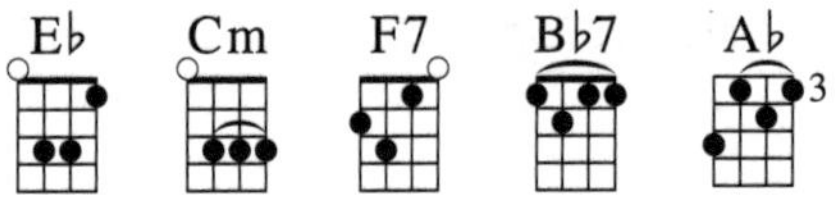
E♭
Cm
F7
B♭7
A♭
3

Moderately fast (in two) (𝅗𝅥 = 84)

Traditional

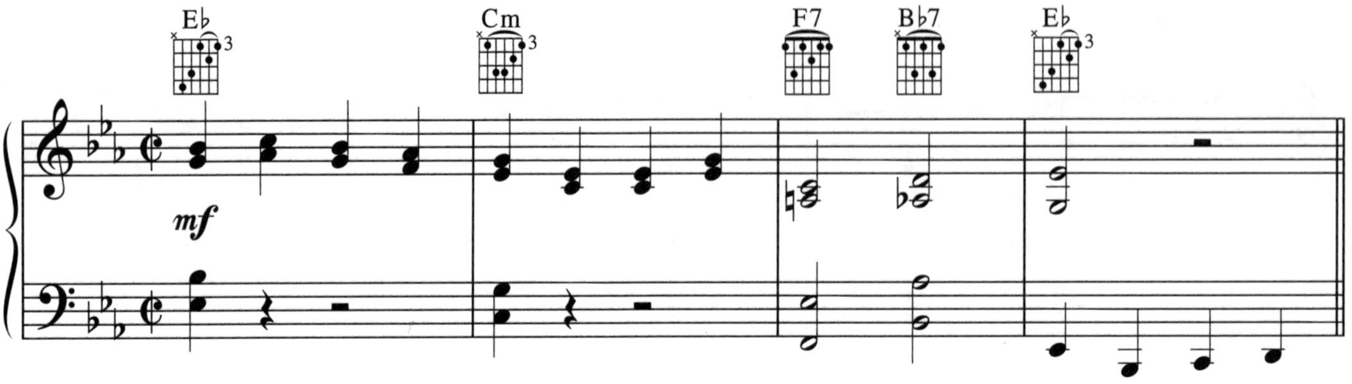
E♭
Cm
F7
B♭7
E♭
mf

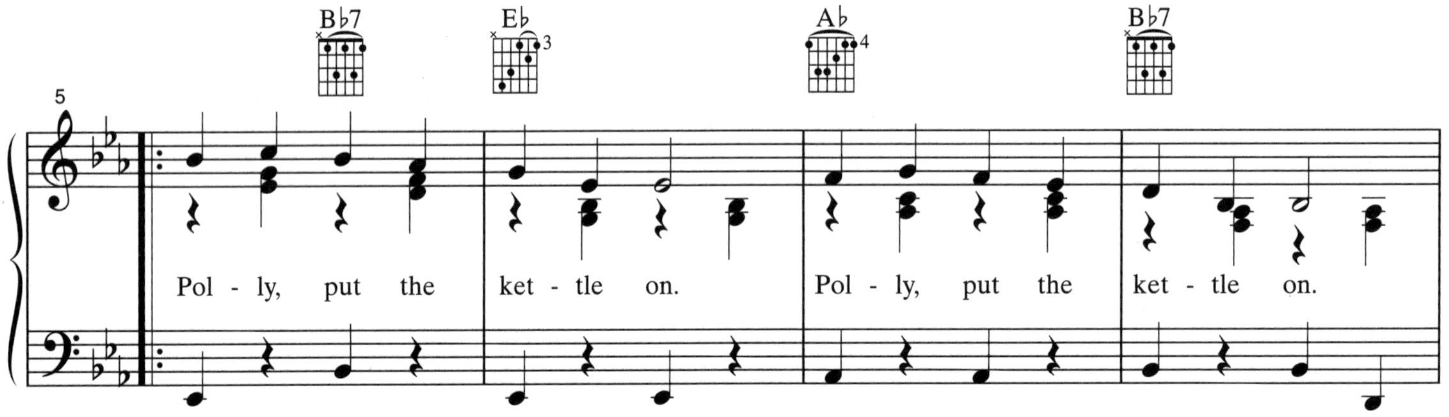
5
B♭7
E♭
A♭
B♭7
Pol - ly, put the ket - tle on. Pol - ly, put the ket - tle on.

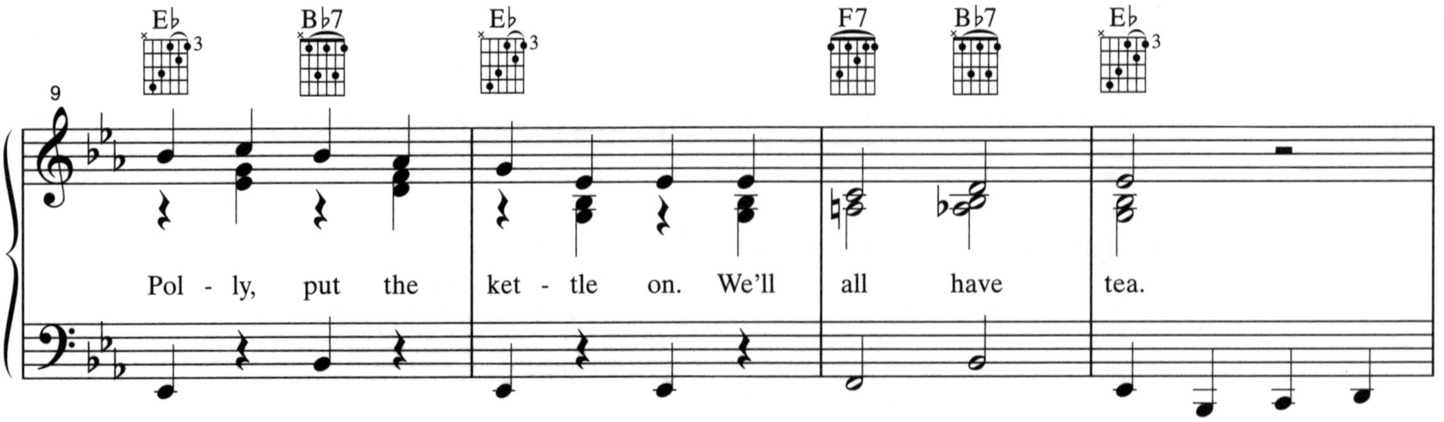
9
E♭
B♭7
E♭
F7
B♭7
E♭
Pol - ly, put the ket - tle on. We'll all have tea.

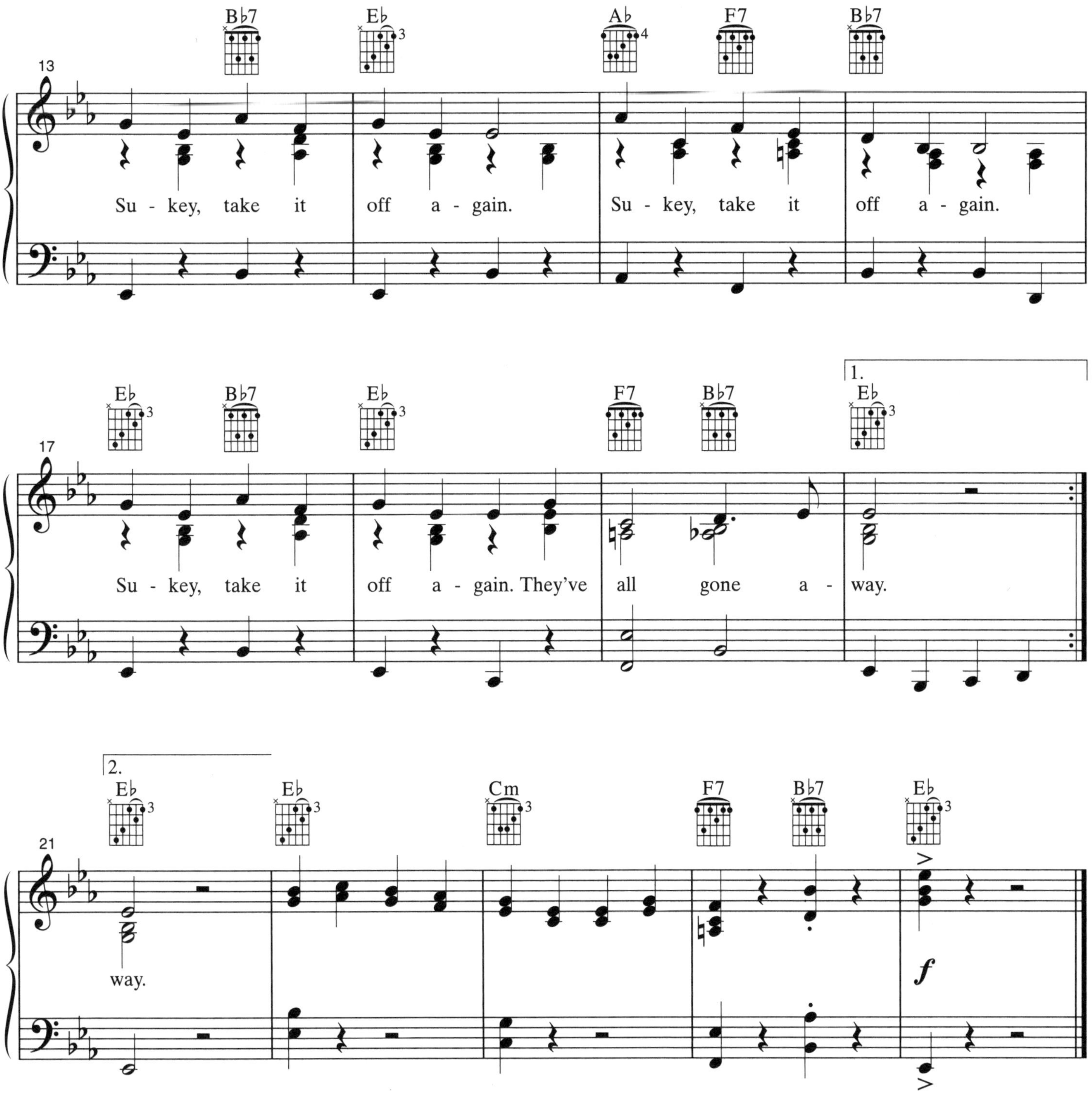
13
B♭7
E♭
A♭
F7
B♭7
Su - key, take it off a - gain. Su - key, take it off a - gain.
17
E♭
B♭7
E♭
F7
B♭7
1.
E♭
Su - key, take it off a - gain. They've all gone a - way.
2.
E♭
E♭
Cm
F7
B♭7
E♭
21
way.
f

Pop! Goes the Weasel

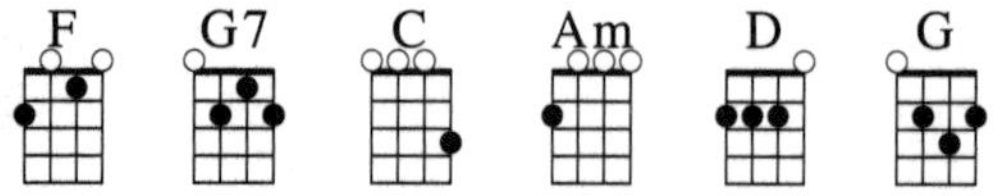
F G7 C Am D G

Moderately bright (♩. = 100)

Traditional

F G7 C
mf
G7 C G7 C
All a - round the mul - ber - ry bush the mon - key chased the wea - sel. The
G7 C F G7 C
mon - key thought 'twas all in fun. Pop goes the wea - sel. A
Am D G Am D G
pen - ny for a spool of thread, a pen - ny for a nee - dle.

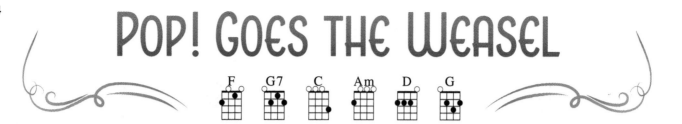

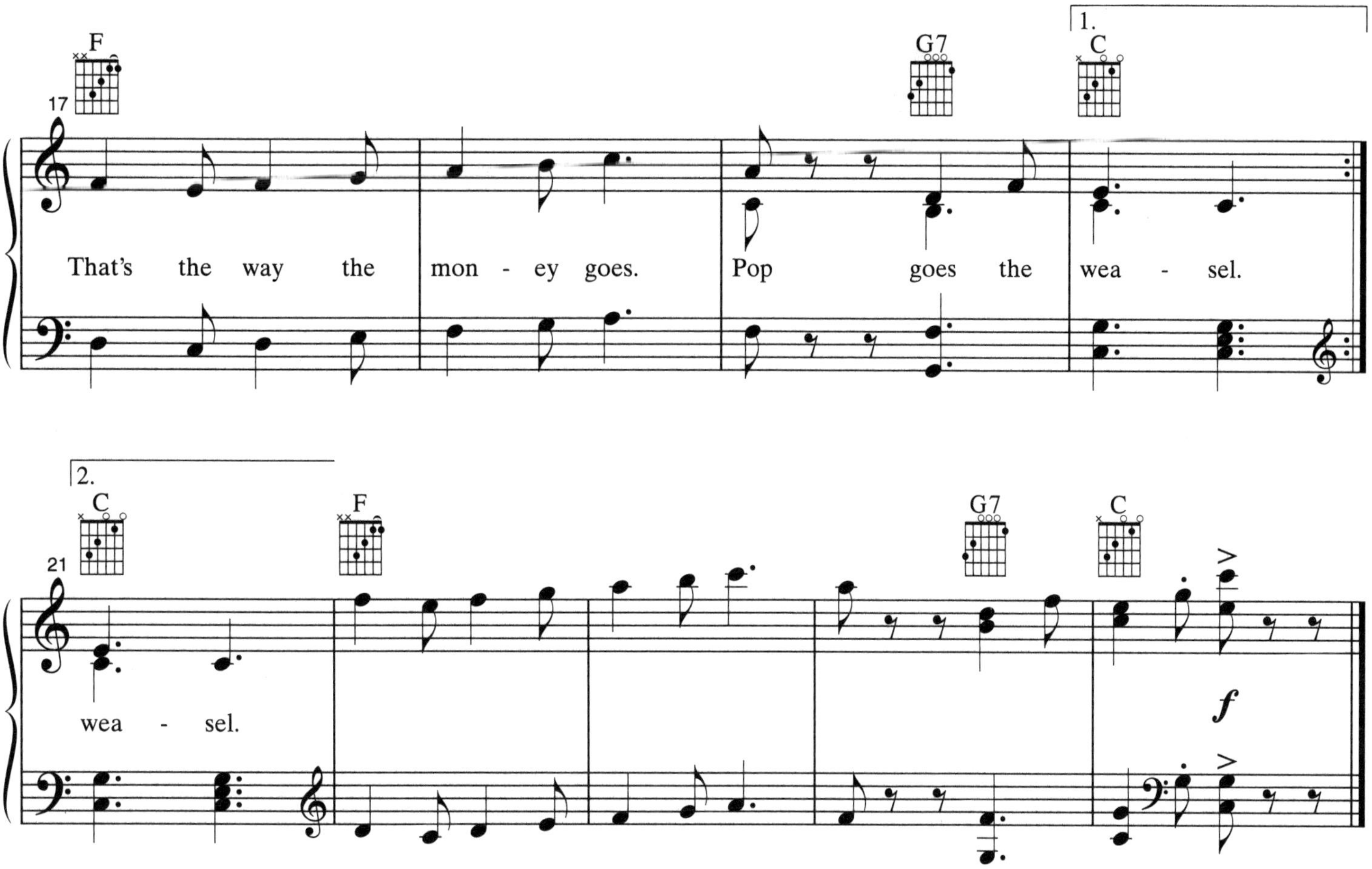
F
17
G7
1.
C
That's the way the mon - ey goes. Pop goes the wea - sel.
2.
C
21
F
G7
C
wea - sel.
f

RAISINS AND ALMONDS

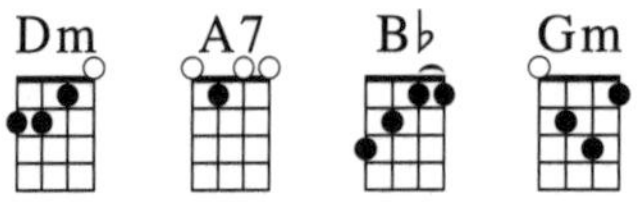
Dm
A7
B♭
Gm

Moderately (♩ = 132)

Traditional

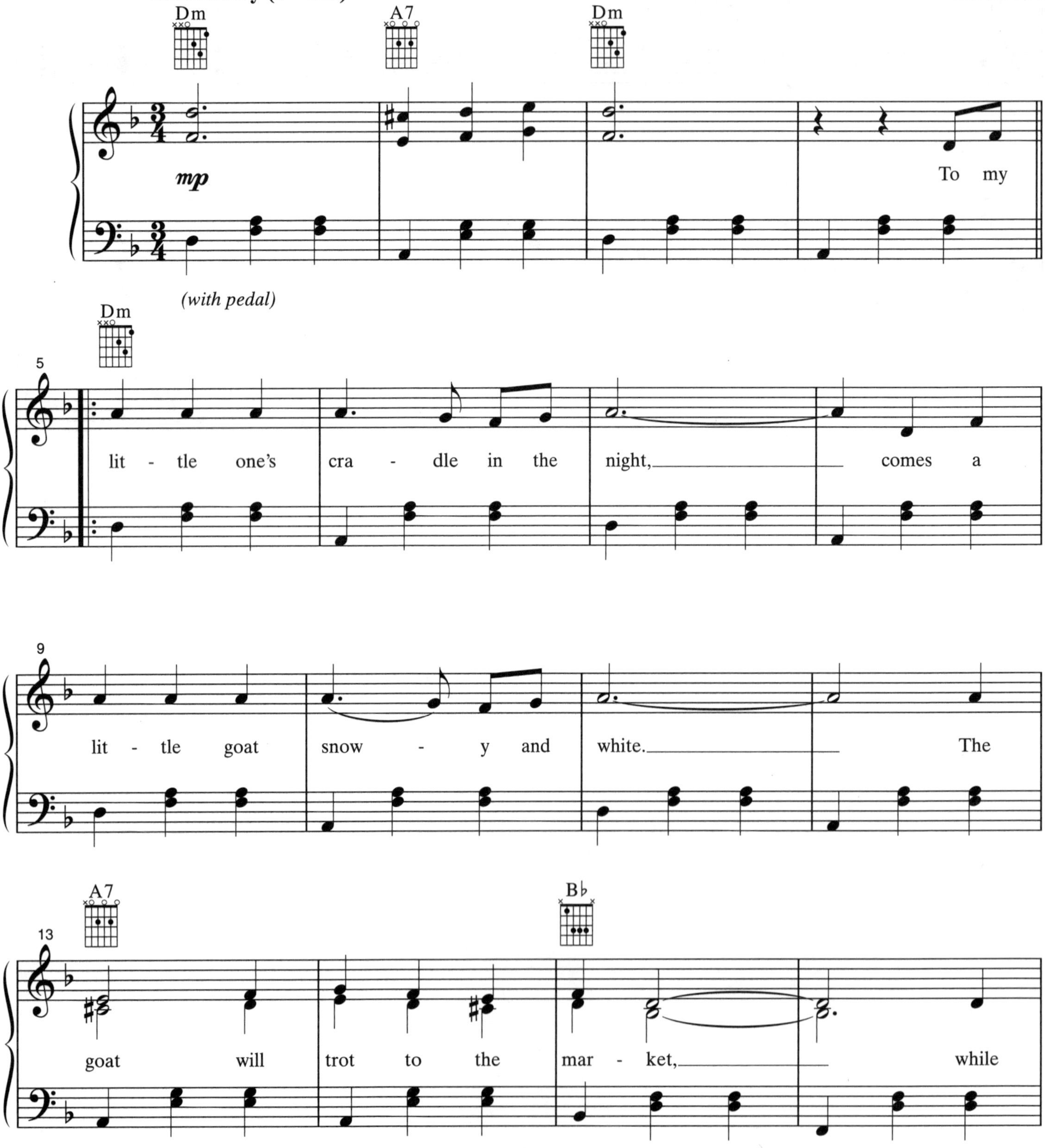
Dm
A7
Dm
mp
To my
(with pedal)
Dm
5
lit - tle one's cra - dle in the night, comes a
9
lit - tle goat snow - y and white. The
A7
B♭
13
goat will trot to the mar - ket, while

Gm
Dm
17
mother her
father his
watch does keep.
A7
B♭
21
bring - ing back rais - ins and al - monds.
A7
1.
Dm
25
Sleep, my lit - tle one, sleep.
2.
Dm
29
To my sleep.
rit.

RIG-A-JIG-JIG

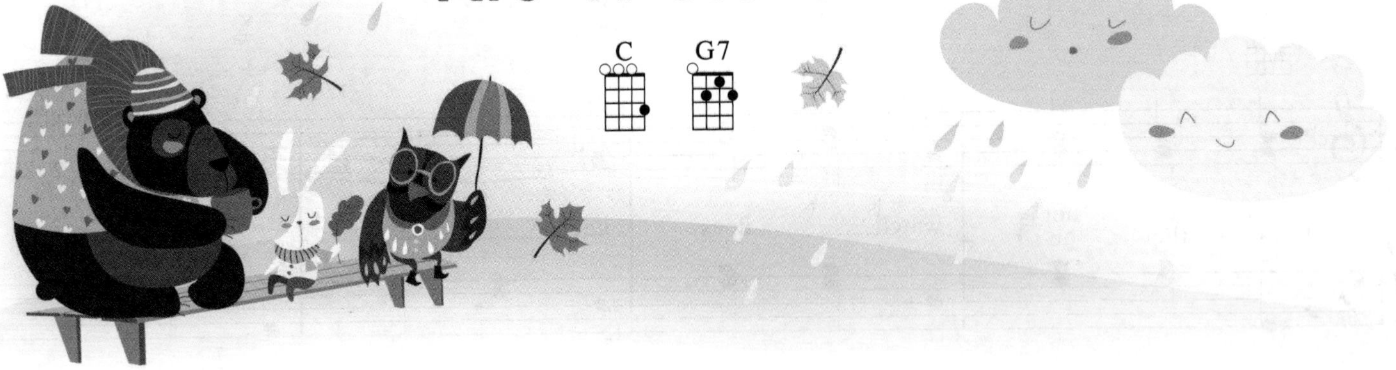
C
G7

Moderately bright, with spirit (♩. = 92)

Traditional

C
G7
C
G7
mf
As
(with pedal)
Verse:
C
G7
C
I was walk - ing down the street, down the street, down the street, a
G7
C
G7
friend of mine I chanced to meet, hi - ho, hi - ho, hi - ho! A -

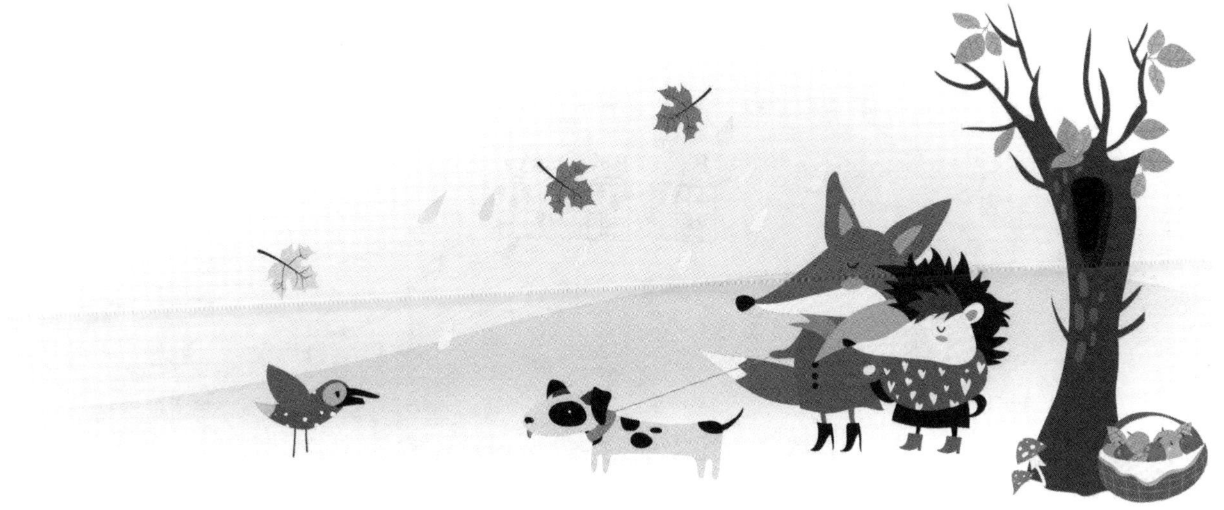

Chorus:
C
G7
C
13
rig - a - jig - jig and a - way we go, a - way we go, a - way we go. A -
f
G7
1.
C
D.C.
17
rig - a - jig - jig and a - way we go, hi - ho, hi - ho, hi - ho!
2.
C
C
G7
C
21
ho!
mf
f

Ring Around the Rosie

E♭
B♭7
A♭
3

Moderately (♩. = 84)

Traditional

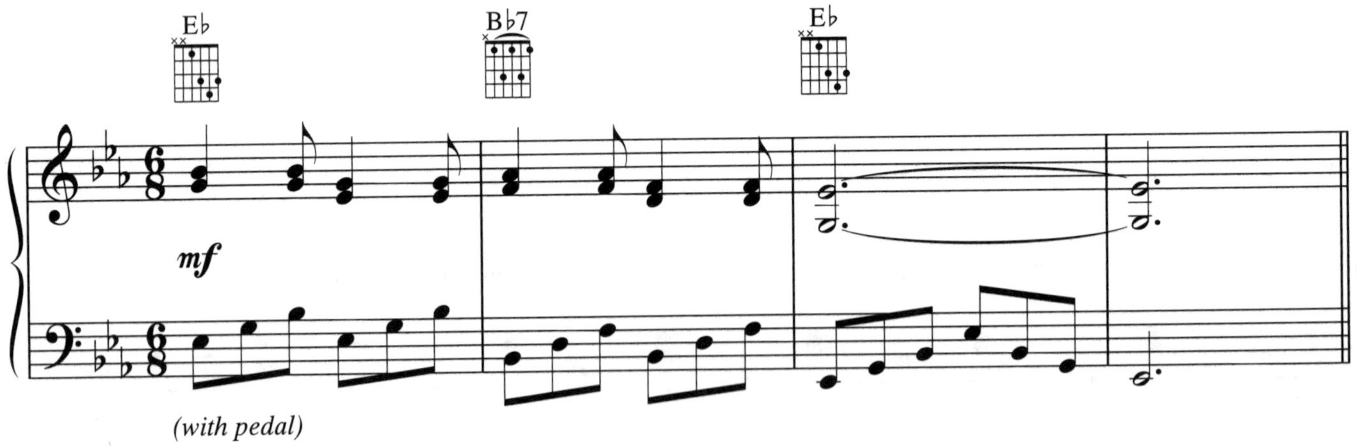
E♭
B♭7
E♭
mf
(with pedal)

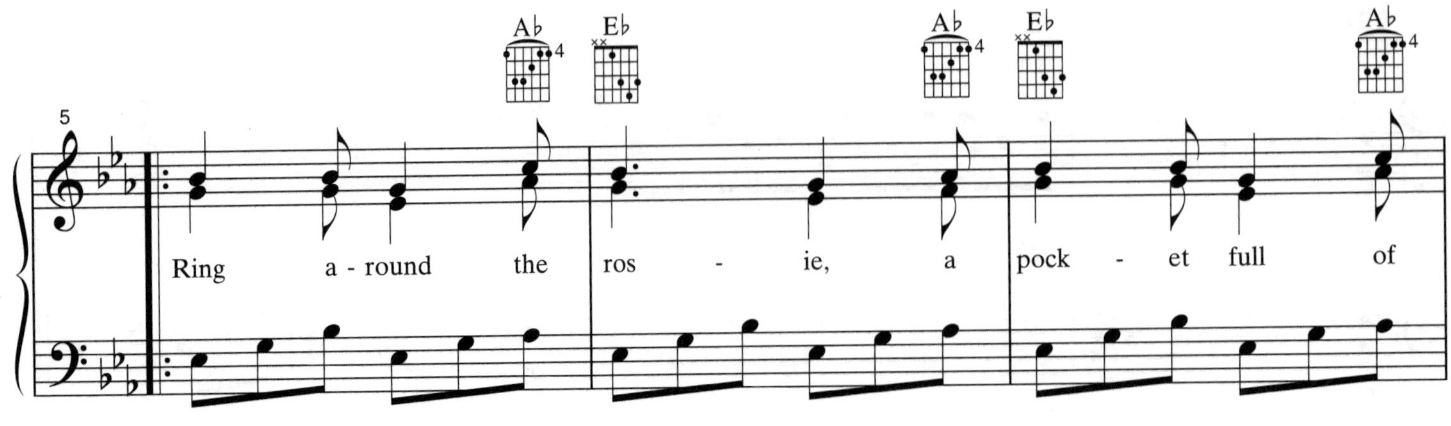
5
A♭
E♭
A♭
E♭
A♭
Ring a - round the ros - ie, a pock - et full of

E♭
B♭7
8
pos - ies. Ash - es! Ash - es! We all fall
E♭
B♭7
12
down.
1.
2.
E♭
E♭
15

Rock-a-Bye Baby

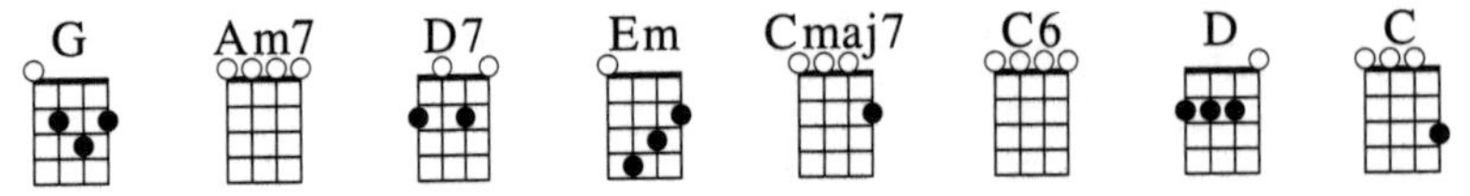
G
Am7
D7
Em
Cmaj7
C6
D
C

Gentle lullaby (♩ = 92)

Traditional

G
Am7
D7
Em
p
(with pedal)
5
Cmaj7
C6
D7
G
9
G
D
Rock - a - bye ba - by on the tree top.
13
Am7
D7
C/G
G
When the wind blows, the cra - dle will rock.

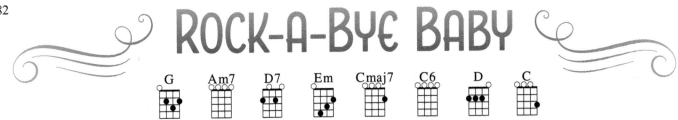

17
D
C
When the bough breaks, the cra - dle will fall, and
21
G/B
C
G/D
Am7
D7
1.
G
down will come ba - by, cra - dle and all.
25
C
G/B
Am7
D7
G
p
29
2.
G
C
G/B
Am7
D7
G
all.
p
rit. e dim.
pp

Row, Row, Row Your Boat

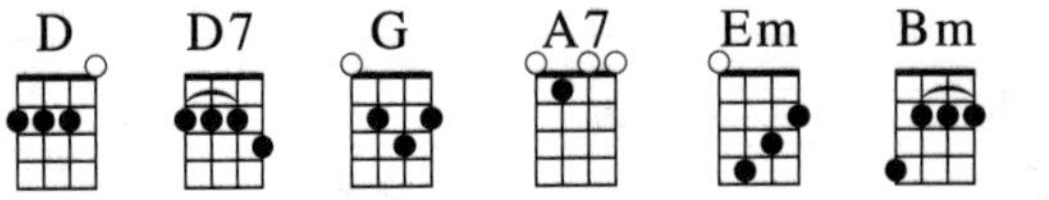
D
D7
G
A7
Em
Bm

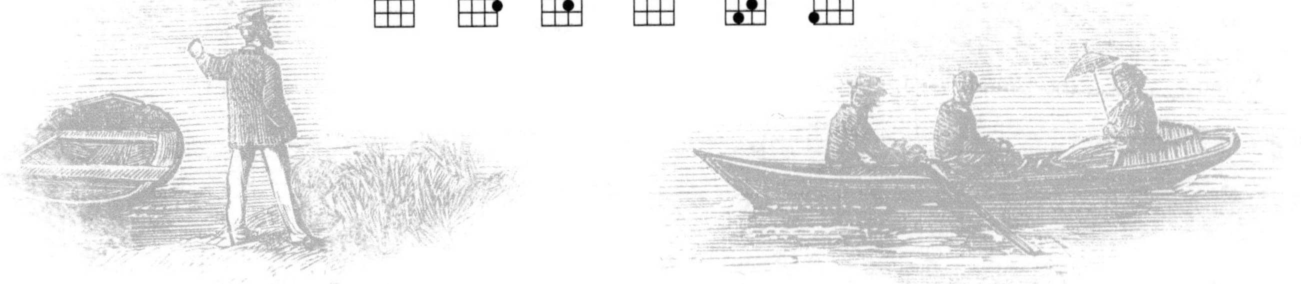

Moderately (♩. = 88)

Traditional

D
D7
G
A7
mf
(with pedal)
D
A7
D
Em
D
4
Row, row, row your boat
*For round part 2 start here
*For round part 3 start here
Bm
A7
D
7
gent - ly down the stream.
Mer - ri - ly, mer - ri - ly,

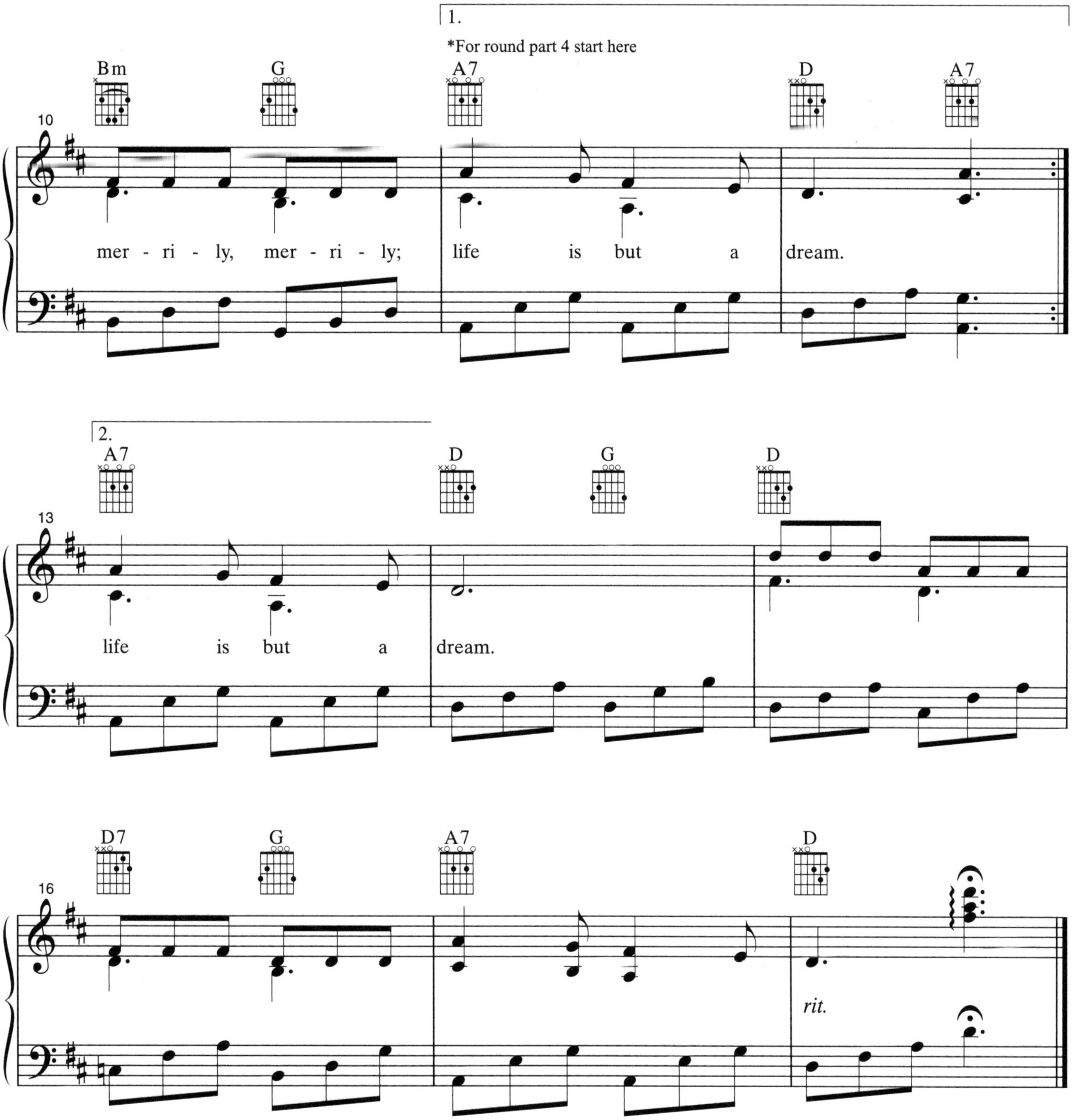
1.
*For round part 4 start here
Bm
G
A7
D
A7
10
mer - ri - ly, mer - ri - ly; life is but a dream.
2.
A7
D
G
D
13
life is but a dream.
D7
G
A7
D
16
rit.

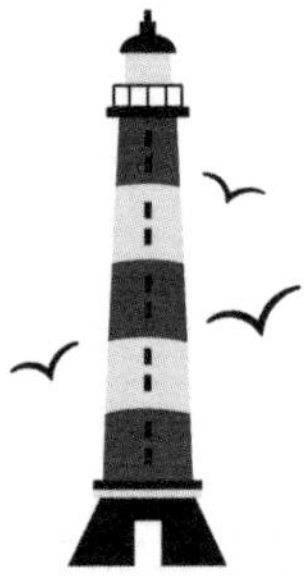

SAILING, SAILING

N
W
E
S

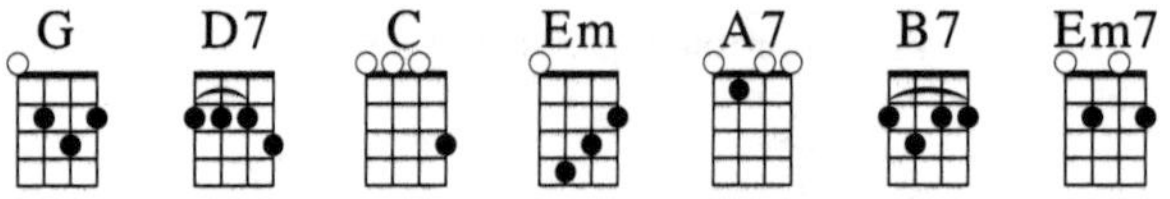
G
D7
C
Em
A7
B7
Em7

Moderately bright (♩. = 96)

Traditional

G
D7
G
mf
G
C
G
5
Sail - ing, sail - ing, o - ver the bound - ing main, where
D7
G
Em
A7
D7
9
man - y a storm - y wind shall blow 'ere Jack comes home a - gain.
G
C
B7
13
Sail - ing, sail - ing, o - ver the bound - ing main, where

Em B7 Em A7 G D7
17
many - y a storm - y wind shall blow 'ere Jack comes home a -
G Em B7 Em7 A7
20
gain.
1. 2.
G D7 G G D7 G
23

She'll Be Coming 'Round the Mountain

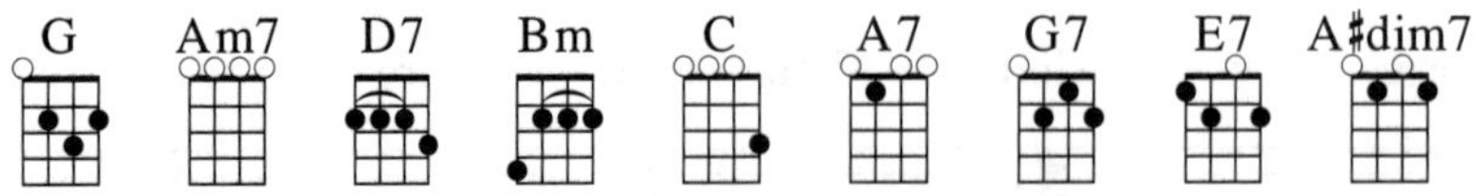
G
Am7
D7
Bm
C
A7
G7
E7
A♯dim7

Moderately bright (𝅗𝅥 = 110)

Traditional

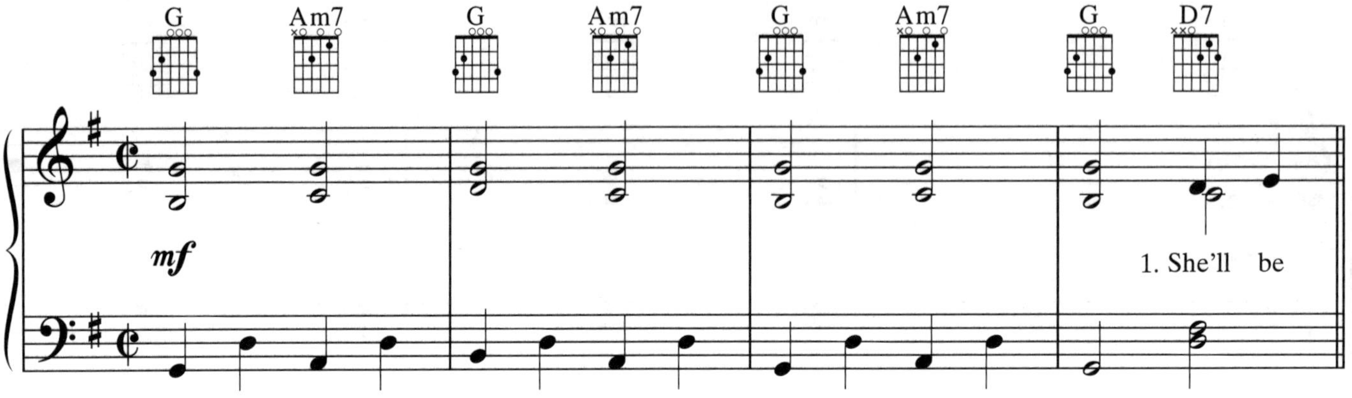
G Am7 G Am7 G Am7 G D7
mf
1. She'll be

Verse:

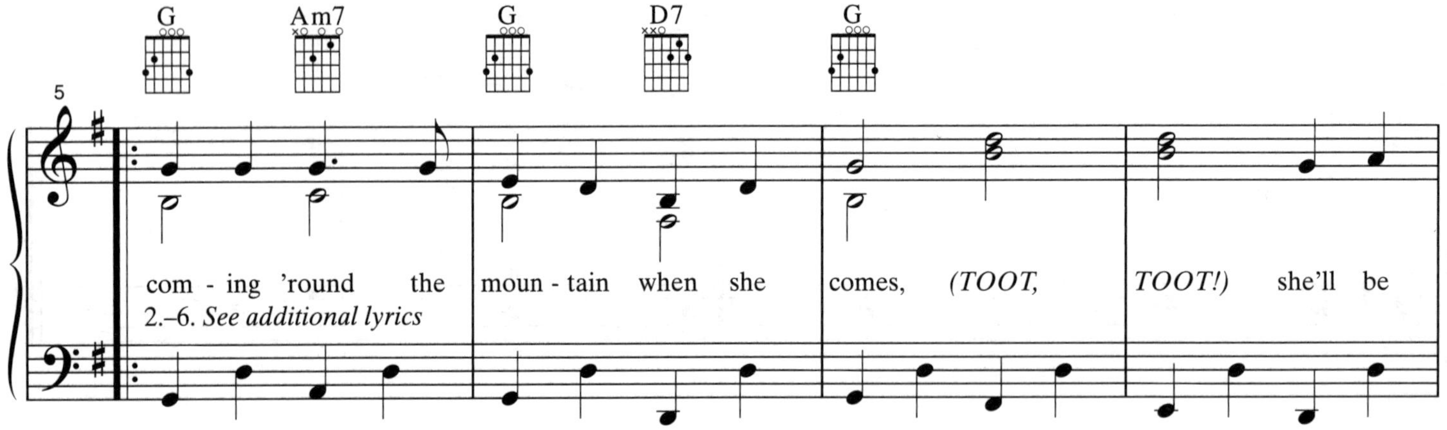
G Am7 G D7 G
5
com - ing 'round the moun - tain when she comes, (TOOT, TOOT!) she'll be
2.–6. See additional lyrics

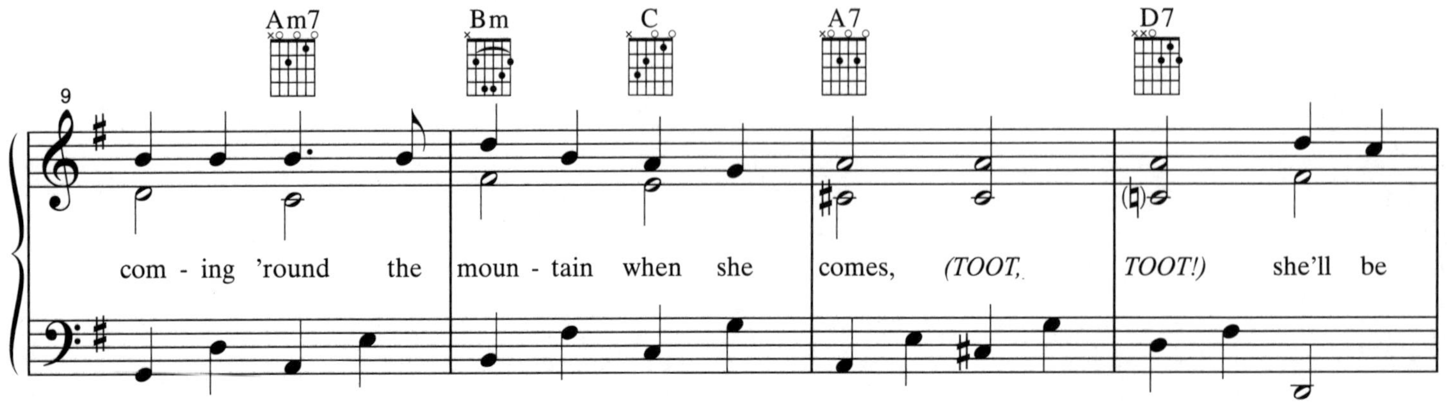
Am7 Bm C A7 D7
9
com - ing 'round the moun - tain when she comes, (TOOT, TOOT!) she'll be

G Am7 G G7 C E7 Am7 A♯dim7
13
com - ing 'round the moun - tain, she'll be com - ing 'round the moun - tain, she'll be
G A7 D7
1.
G Am7 G D7
17
com - ing 'round the moun - tain when she comes. (TOOT, TOOT!) 2. She'll be
2.
G Am7 G D7 G D7
3.
G Am7
21
comes. (WHOA, BACK! TOOT, TOOT!) 3. We'll comes. (HI,
G D7 G D7 G D7
4.
G Am7
25
BABE! WHOA, BACK! TOOT, TOOT!) 4. Oh, we'll comes. (YUM,

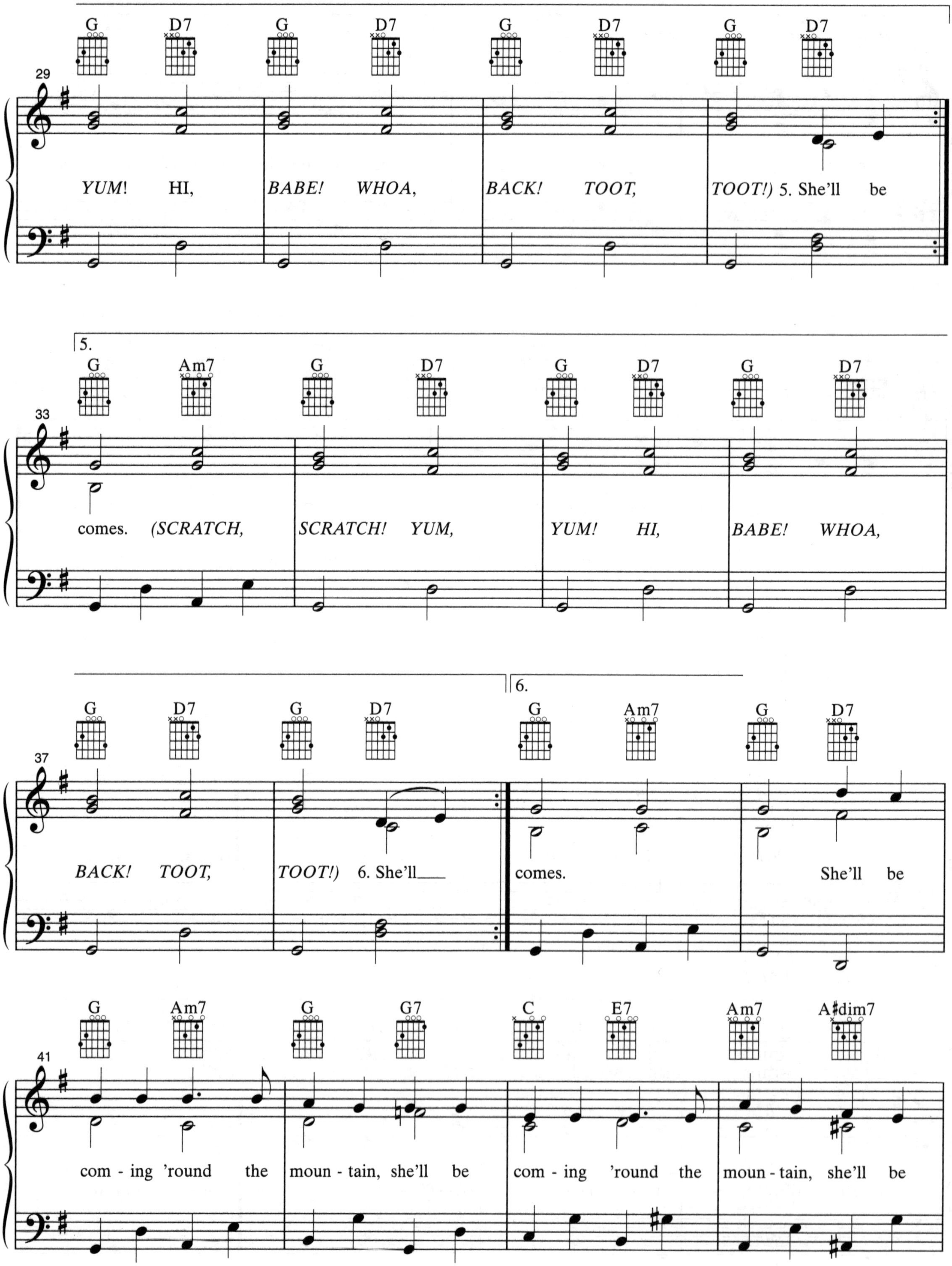
G D7 G D7 G D7 G D7
29
YUM! HI, BABE! WHOA, BACK! TOOT, TOOT!) 5. She'll be
5.
G Am7 G D7 G D7 G D7
33
comes. (SCRATCH, SCRATCH! YUM, YUM! HI, BABE! WHOA,
6.
G D7 G D7 G Am7 G D7
37
BACK! TOOT, TOOT!) 6. She'll comes. She'll be
G Am7 G G7 C E7 Am7 A♯dim7
41
com - ing 'round the moun - tain, she'll be com - ing 'round the moun - tain, she'll be

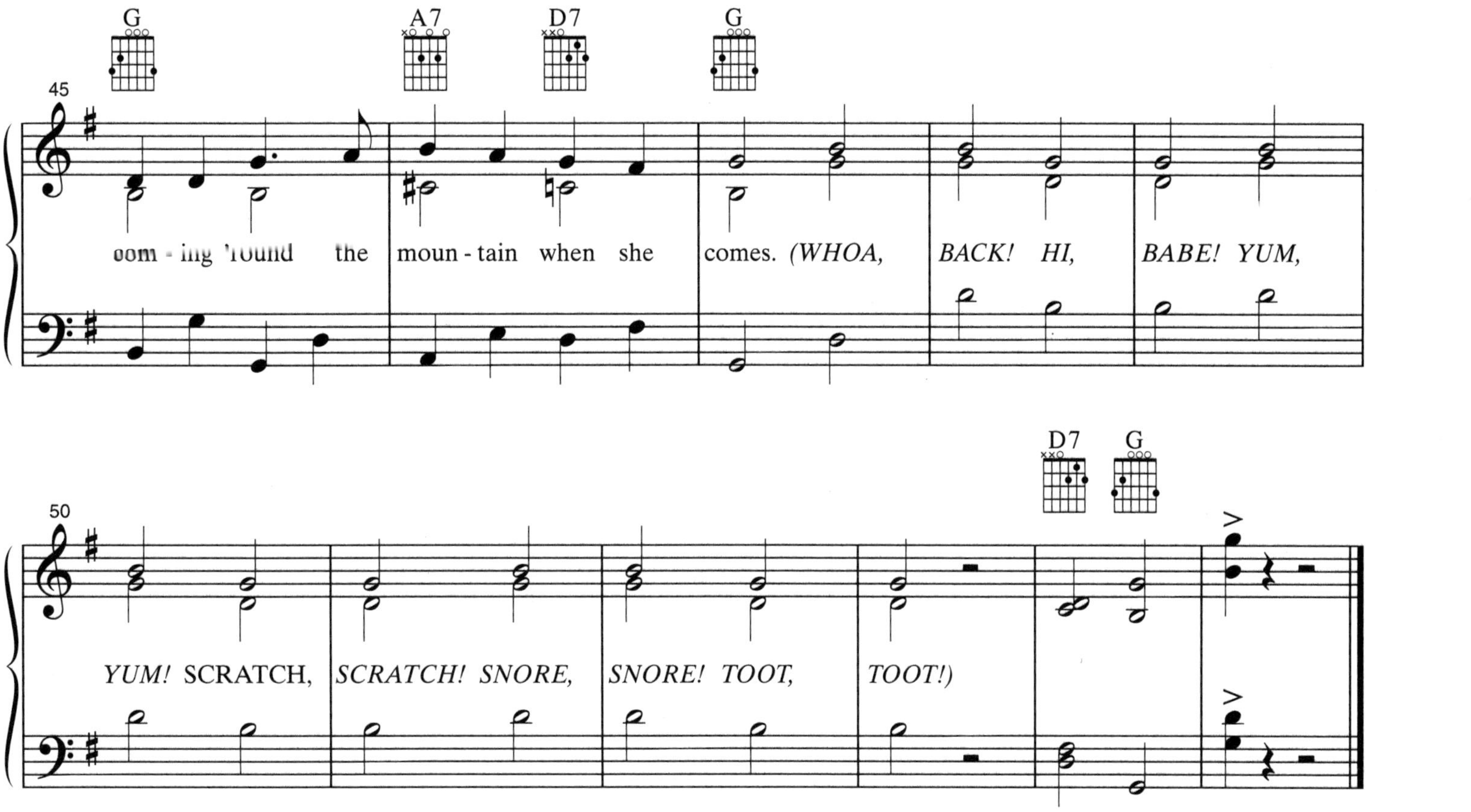
G
A7
D7
G
45
com - ing 'round the moun - tain when she comes. (WHOA, BACK! HI, BABE! YUM,
50
YUM! SCRATCH, SCRATCH! SNORE, SNORE! TOOT, TOOT!)
D7
G

Verse 2:
She'll be drivin' six white horses when she comes, *(WHOA, BACK!)*
She'll be drivin' six white horses when she comes,*(WHOA, BACK!)*
She'll be drivin' six white horses, she'll be drivin' six white horses,
She'll be drivin' six white horses when she comes.
(WHOA, BACK! TOOT, TOOT!)

Verse 3:
We'll all come out to meet her when she comes, (*HI, BABE!*)
We'll all come out to meet her when she comes, (*HI, BABE!*)
We'll all come out to meet her, we'll all come out to meet her,
We'll all come out to meet her when she comes.
(*HI, BABE! WHOA, BACK! TOOT, TOOT!)*

Verse 4:
Oh, we'll all have chicken and dumplings when she comes, (*YUM, YUM!*)
Oh, we'll all have chicken and dumplings when she comes, (*YUM, YUM!*)
Oh, we'll all have chicken and dumplings, we'll all have chicken and dumplings,
Oh, we'll all have chicken and dumplings when she comes.
(*YUM, YUM! HI, BABE! WHOA, BACK! TOOT, TOOT!)*

Verse 5:
She'll be wearing wool pajamas when she comes, (*SCRATCH, SCRATCH!*)
She'll be wearing wool pajamas when she comes, (*SCRATCH, SCRATCH!*)
She'll be wearing wool pajamas, she'll be wearing wool pajamas,
She'll be wearing wool pajamas when she comes.
(*SCRATCH, SCRATCH! YUM, YUM! HI, BABE! WHOA, BACK! TOOT, TOOT!)*

Verse 6:
She'll have to sleep with Grandma when she comes, (*SNORE, SNORE!*)
She'll have to sleep with Grandma when she comes, (*SNORE, SNORE!*)
She'll have to sleep with Grandma, she'll have to sleep with Grandma,
She'll have to sleep with Grandma when she comes.
(SNORE, SNORE! SCRATCH, SCRATCH! YUM, YUM! HI, BABE! WHOA, BACK! TOOT, TOOT!)

Shoo Fly

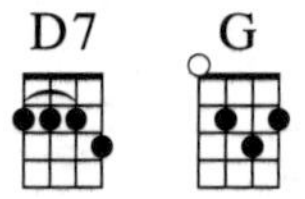
D7
G

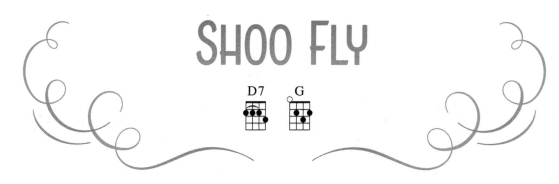

Moderately bright (𝅗𝅥 = 92)

Traditional

D7
G
D7
mf
Shoo - fly, don't both - er me.
5
G
D7
Shoo - fly, don't both - er me. Shoo - fly, don't both - er me, for
9
G
I be - long to some - bod - y. I feel, I feel, I

D7
13
feel like a morn - ing star. I feel, I feel, I
1.
2.
G
G
D7
17
feel like a morn - ing star. star. I feel like a
G
21
morn - ing star.

Roll Over (Six in the Bed)

Traditional

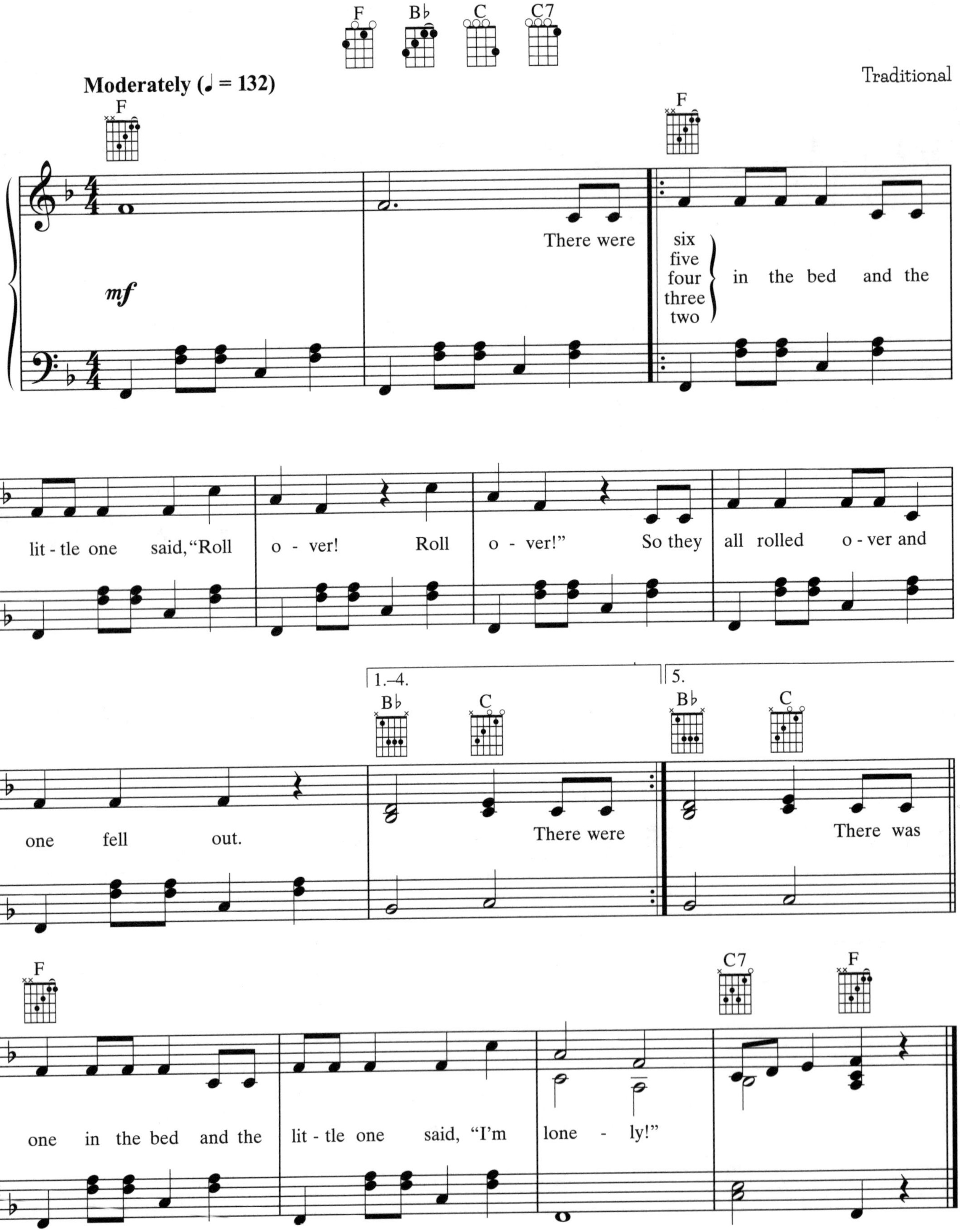
F B♭ C C7
Moderately (♩ = 132)
F
mf
There were
F
six five four three two in the bed and the
lit - tle one said, "Roll o - ver! Roll o - ver!" So they all rolled o - ver and
one fell out.
1.–4.
B♭ C
There were
5.
B♭ C
There was
F
one in the bed and the lit - tle one said, "I'm lone - ly!"
C7 F

Shortnin' Bread

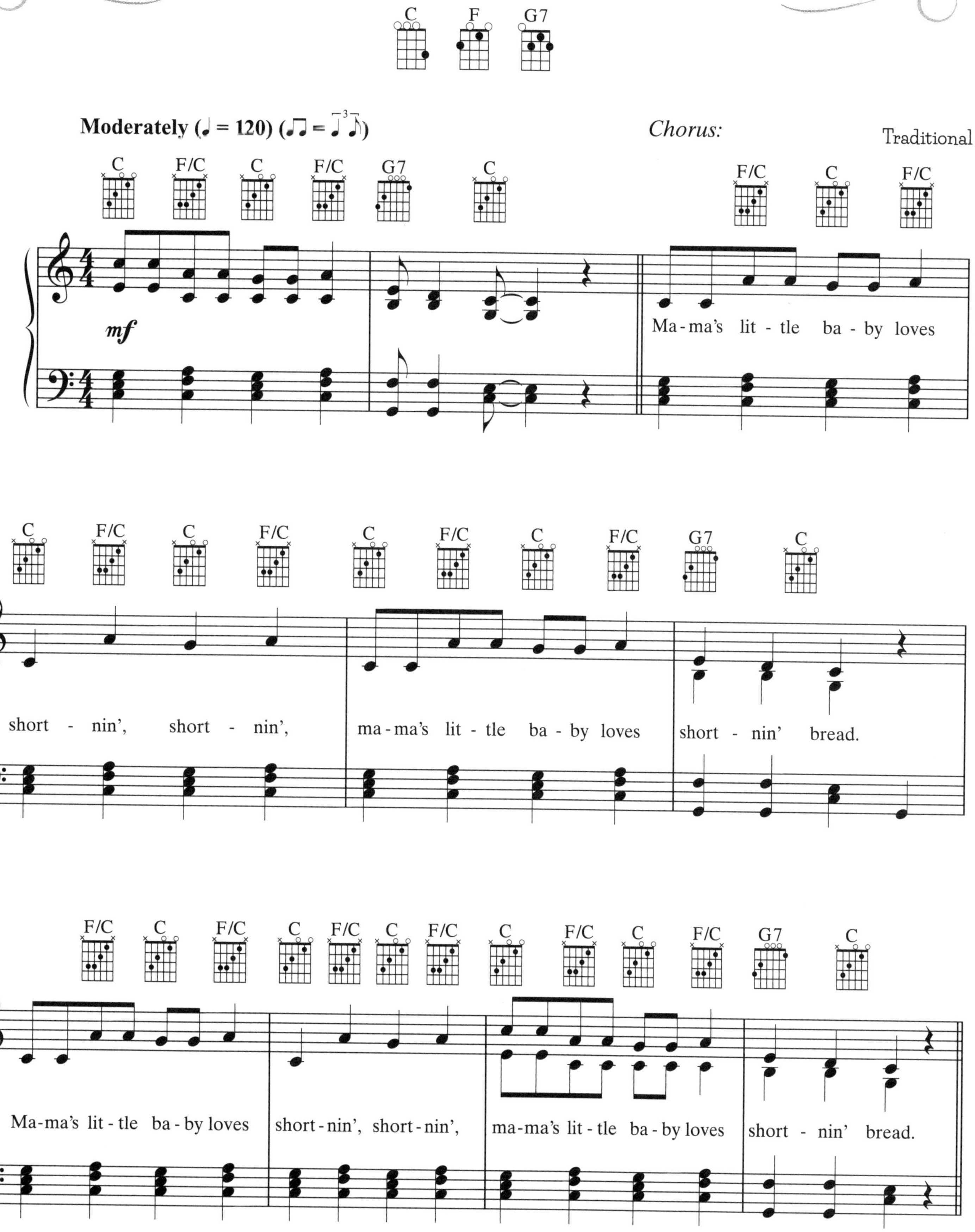
C F G7
Moderately (♩ = 120)
Chorus:
Traditional
C F/C C F/C G7 C F/C C F/C
mf
Ma-ma's lit - tle ba - by loves
C F/C C F/C C F/C C F/C G7 C
short - nin', short - nin', ma-ma's lit - tle ba - by loves short - nin' bread.
F/C C F/C C F/C C F/C C F/C C F/C G7 C
Ma-ma's lit-tle ba-by loves short-nin', short-nin', ma-ma's lit-tle ba-by loves short - nin' bread.

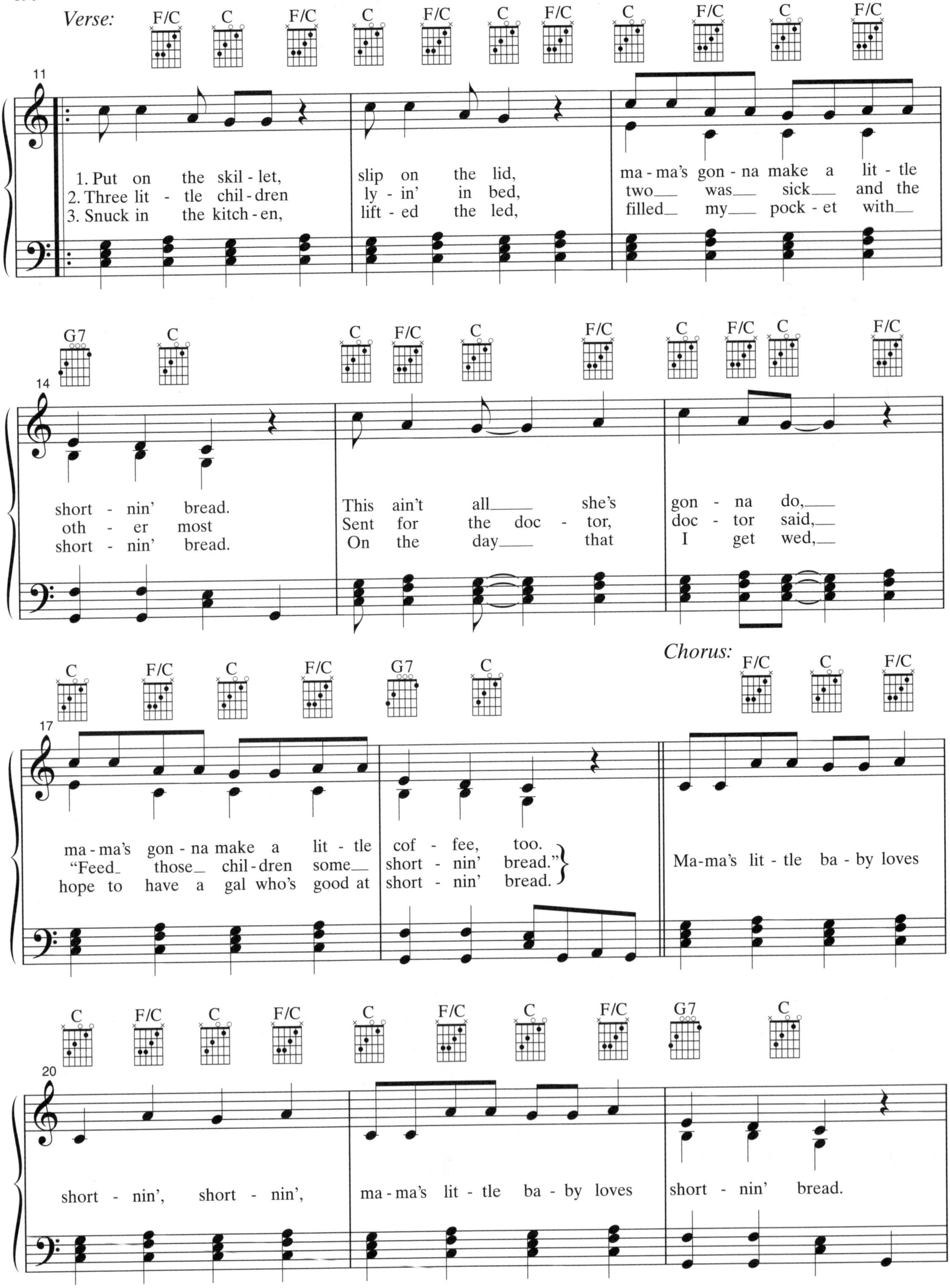
Verse:
F/C C F/C C F/C C F/C C F/C C F/C
1. Put on the skil - let, slip on the lid, ma - ma's gon - na make a lit - tle
2. Three lit - tle chil - dren ly - in' in bed, two was sick and the
3. Snuck in the kitch - en, lift - ed the led, filled my pock - et with
G7 C C F/C C F/C C F/C C F/C
short - nin' bread. This ain't all she's gon - na do,
oth - er most Sent for the doc - tor, doc - tor said,
short - nin' bread. On the day that I get wed,
C F/C C F/C G7 C
ma - ma's gon - na make a lit - tle cof - fee, too.
"Feed those chil - dren some short - nin' bread."
hope to have a gal who's good at short - nin' bread.
Chorus:
F/C C F/C
Ma - ma's lit - tle ba - by loves
C F/C C F/C C F/C C F/C G7 C
short - nin', short - nin', ma - ma's lit - tle ba - by loves short - nin' bread.

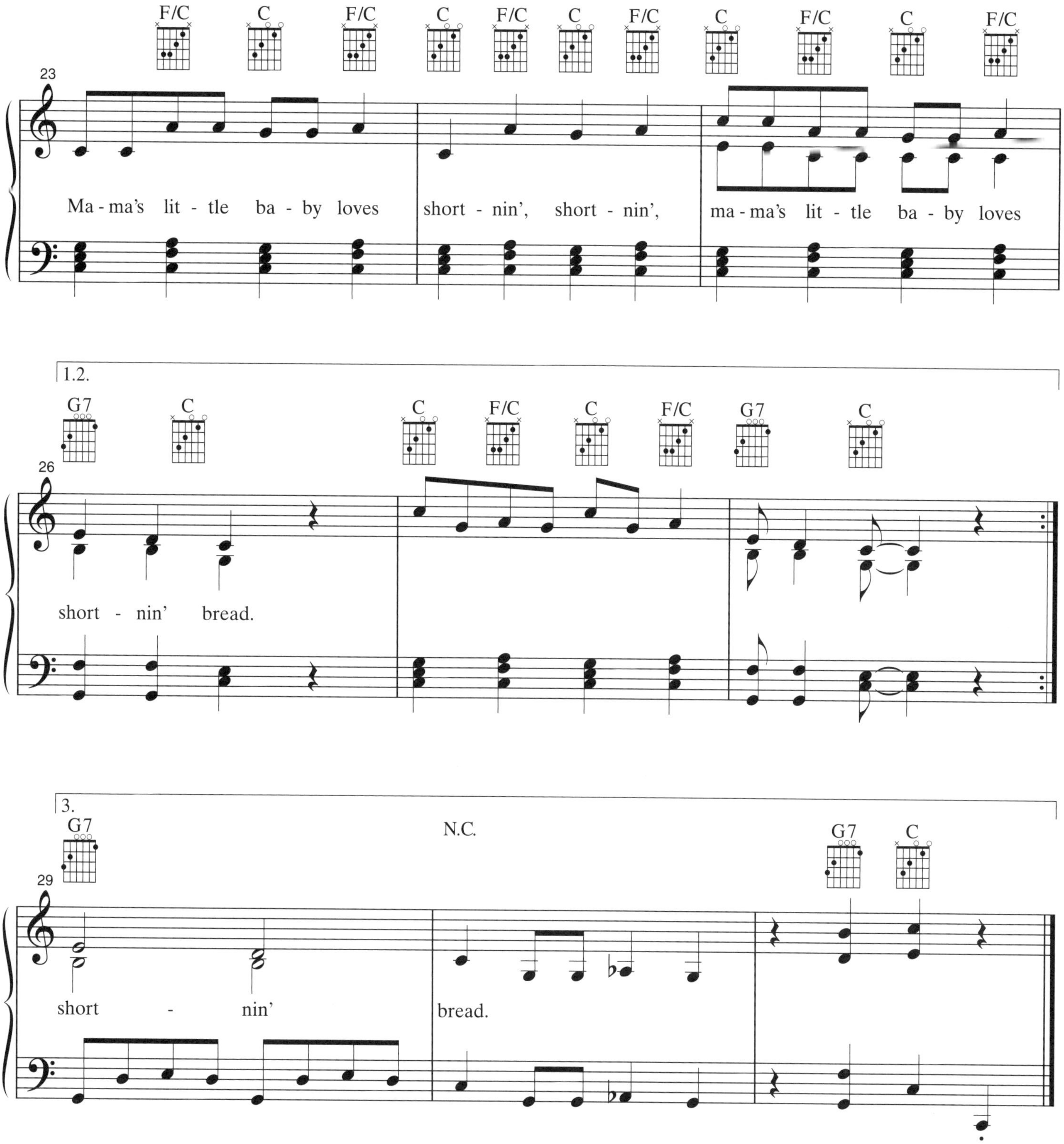
F/C C F/C C F/C C F/C C F/C C F/C
23
Ma - ma's lit - tle ba - by loves short - nin', short - nin', ma - ma's lit - tle ba - by loves
1.2.
G7 C C F/C C F/C G7 C
26
short - nin' bread.
3.
G7 N.C. G7 C
29
short - nin' bread.

Sing a Song of Sixpence

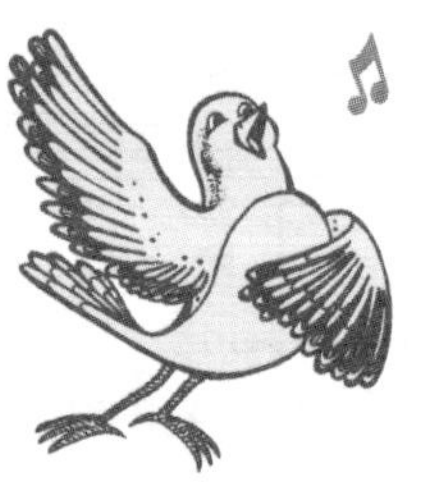

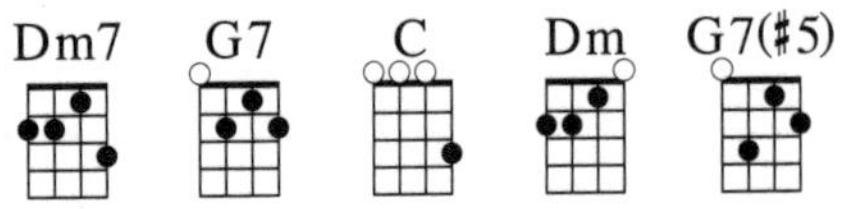
Dm7
G7
C
Dm
G7(♯5)

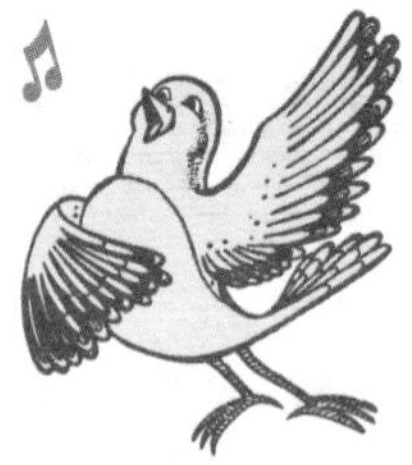

Moderately (♩. = 100)

Traditional

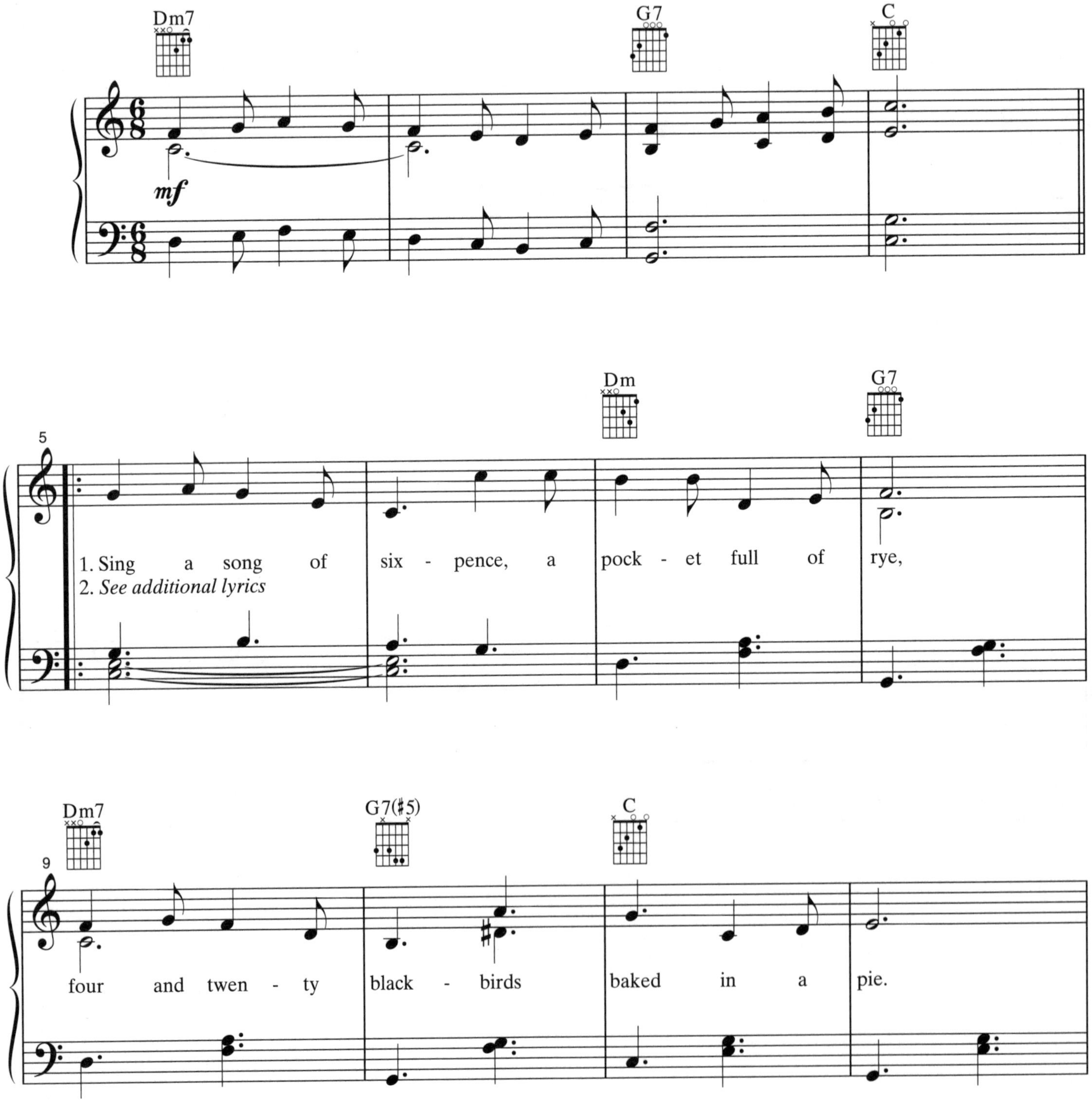
Dm7
G7
C
mf
5
Dm
G7
1. Sing a song of six - pence, a pock - et full of rye,
2. *See additional lyrics*
Dm7
G7(♯5)
C
9
four and twen - ty black - birds baked in a pie.

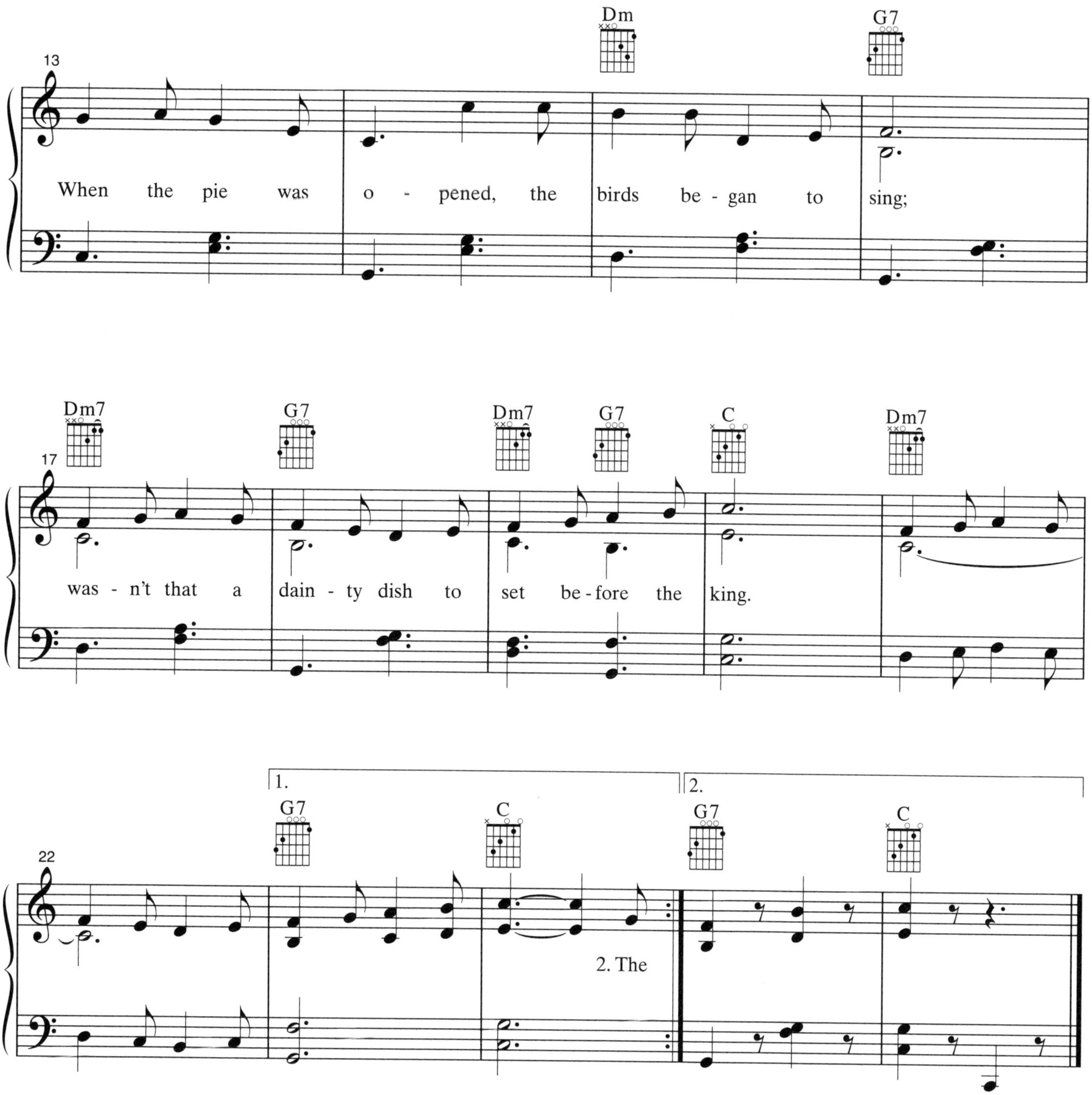
13
Dm
G7
When the pie was o - pened, the birds be - gan to sing;
Dm7
G7
Dm7
G7
C
Dm7
17
was - n't that a dain - ty dish to set be - fore the king.
1.
2.
G7
C
G7
C
22
2. The

Verse 2:
The king was in his counting house, counting out his money,
The queen was in the parlor eating bread and honey.
The maid was in the garden hanging out the clothes,
When down came a blackbird and pecked off her nose.

Six Little Ducks

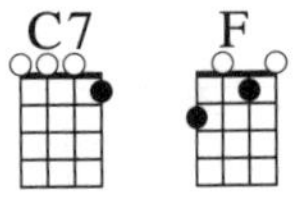
C7
F

Moderately (♩ = 120)

Traditional

C7
F
mf
1. Six lit - tle ducks that I once knew, fat ones, skin - ny ones, fair ones too.
2. Down to the riv - er they would go, wibble, wobble, wib - ble wobble, to and fro.
3. Back from the riv - er they would come, wibble, wobble, wib - ble wobble, ho hum hum.
But the one lit - tle duck with the feath - er on his back, he led the oth - ers with a quack, quack, quack! Quack, quack, quack! Quack, quack, quack!

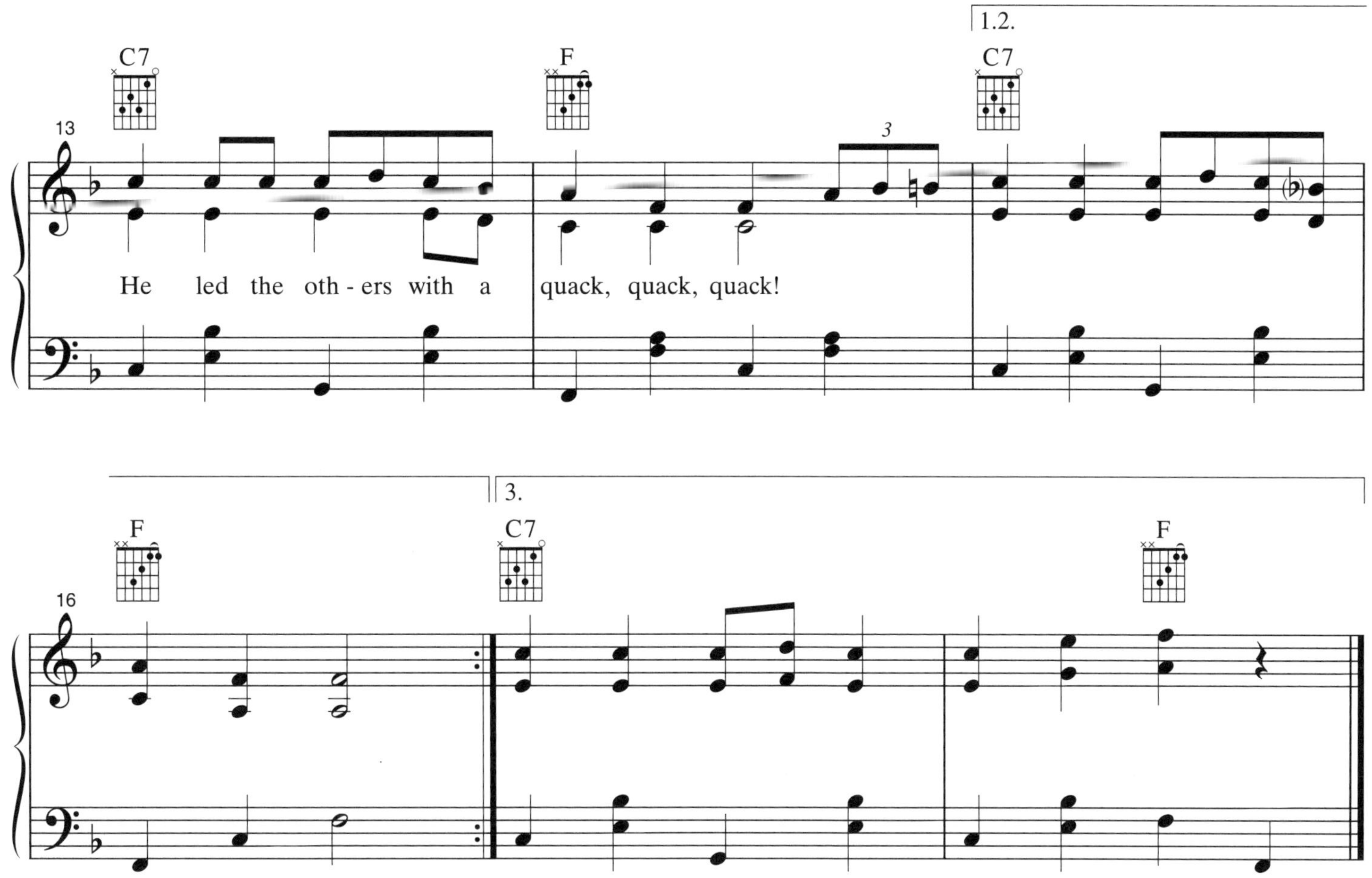
1.2.
C7
F
C7
13
3
He led the oth - ers with a quack, quack, quack!
3.
F
C7
F
16

Skip to My Lou

Gm7
C7
F

Moderately bright (♩ = 154)

Traditional

Chorus:
Gm7
C7
F
mf
Lou, Lou,
skip to my Lou,
Lou, Lou,
skip to my Lou,
Lou, Lou,
skip to my Lou,
skip to my Lou, my
dar - ling.
Verse:
1. Fly in the but-ter-milk,
2.–5. See additional lyrics
shoo fly shoo,
fly in the but-ter-milk,
shoo fly shoo,

F
Gm7
C7
F
15
fly in the but - ter - milk, shoo fly shoo, skip to my Lou, my dar - ling.
Chorus:
C7
19
Lou, Lou, skip to my Lou, Lou, Lou, skip to my Lou,
F
Gm7
C7
1.–4.
F
23
Lou, Lou, skip to my Lou, skip to my Lou, my dar - ling.
Gm7
C7
F
5.
F
27
dar - ling.

Verse 2:
Cows in the pasture two by two,
Cows in the pasture two by two,
Cows in the pasture two by two,
Skip to my Lou, my darling.
(To Chorus:)

Verse 3:
Lost my partner, what'll I do?
Lost my partner, what'll I do?
Lost my partner, what'll I do?
Skip to my Lou, my darling.
(To Chorus:)

Verse 4:
I'll find another one prettier than you,
I'll find another one prettier than you,
I'll find another one prettier than you,
Skip to my Lou, my darling.
(To Chorus:)

Verse 5:
Found my partner, love is true!
Found my partner, love is true!
Found my partner, love is true!
Skip to my Lou, my darling.
(To Chorus:)

Take Me Out to the Ball Game

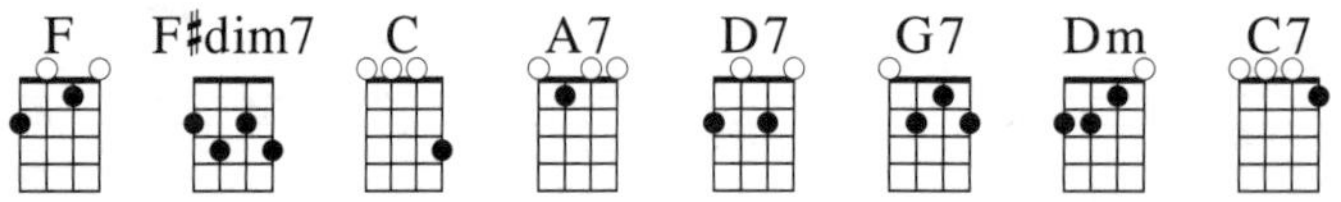
F
F♯dim7
C
A7
D7
G7
Dm
C7

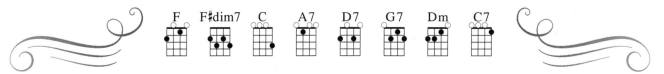

Moderately fast waltz (♩ = 152)

Traditional

F
F♯dim7
C/G
A7
mf
(with pedal)
6
D7
G7
C
G7
C
Take me out to the
12
G7
C
G7
ball game. Take me out to the crowd.
18
A7
Dm
D7
Buy me some pea - nuts and Crack - er Jacks. I don't care if I

G7 C G7
24
nev - er get back. Let me root, root, root for the home team. If
C C7 F F♯dim7
30
they don't win, it's a shame. For it's one, two,
C/G A7 1. D7 G7 C
36
three strikes you're out at the old ball game.
G7 2. D7 G7 C
41
old ball game.

This Is the Way the Ladies Ride

F Gm7 C7
Moderately (♩. = 84)
Traditional
F Gm7 C7 F
mf
5
Gm7 C7 F
1. This is the way the ladies ride. Tri tre tri tree, tri tre tri tree!
2. This is the way the gentle-men ride. Gal-lop-a-trot! Gal-lop-a-trot!
3. This is the way the far-mers ride. Hob-bele-ty-hoy! Hob-bele-ty-hoy!
9
Gm7 C7 1.2. F
This is the way the la-dies ride so ear-ly in the morn-ing.
This is the way the gentle-men ride so ear-ly in the morn-ing.
This is the way the far-mers ride so ear-ly in the
13
Gm7 C7 F 3. F Gm7 C7 F
morn-ing.

There's a Hole in My Bucket

C
G
D7
Am7
A7

Moderately (♩ = 132)

Traditional

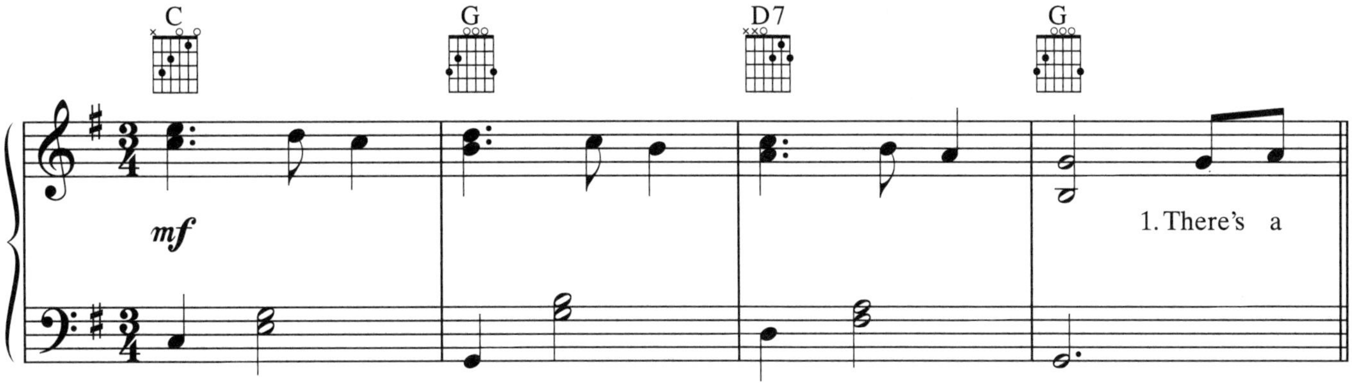
C
G
D7
G
mf
1. There's a

Verses 1–9:

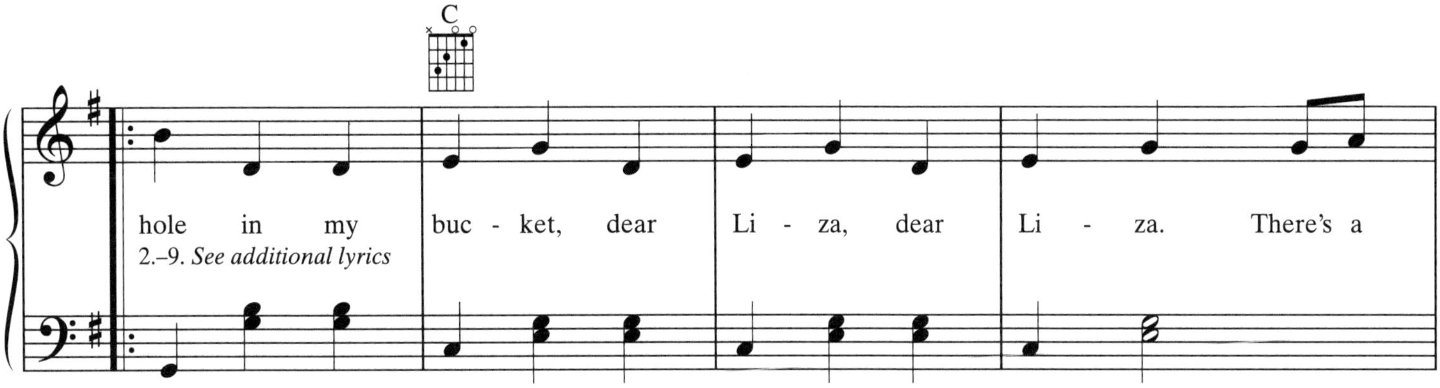
C
hole in my bucket, dear Liza, dear Liza. There's a
2.–9. See additional lyrics

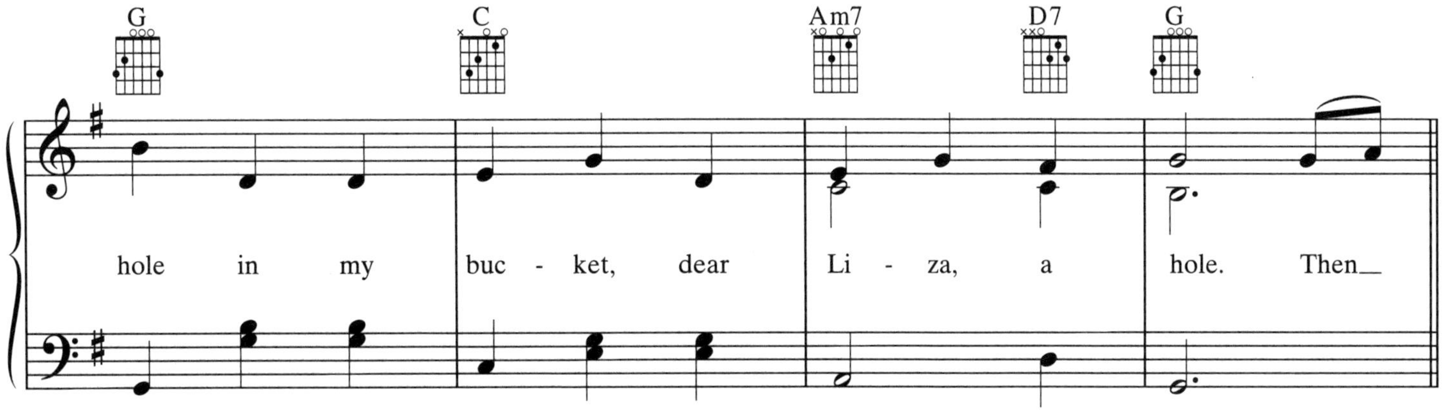
G
C
Am7
D7
G
hole in my bucket, dear Liza, a hole. Then

C
fix it, dear Hen - ry, dear Hen - ry, dear Hen - ry. Then_
G C Am7 D7 G
fix it, dear Hen - ry, dear Hen - ry, fix it.
1.–8. 9.
C G D7 G G
2. With_
10. But, there's a
Slower (♩ = 116)
Verse 10:
G/F C/E A7/C♯
hole in my buc - ket, dear Li - za, dear Li - za. There's a

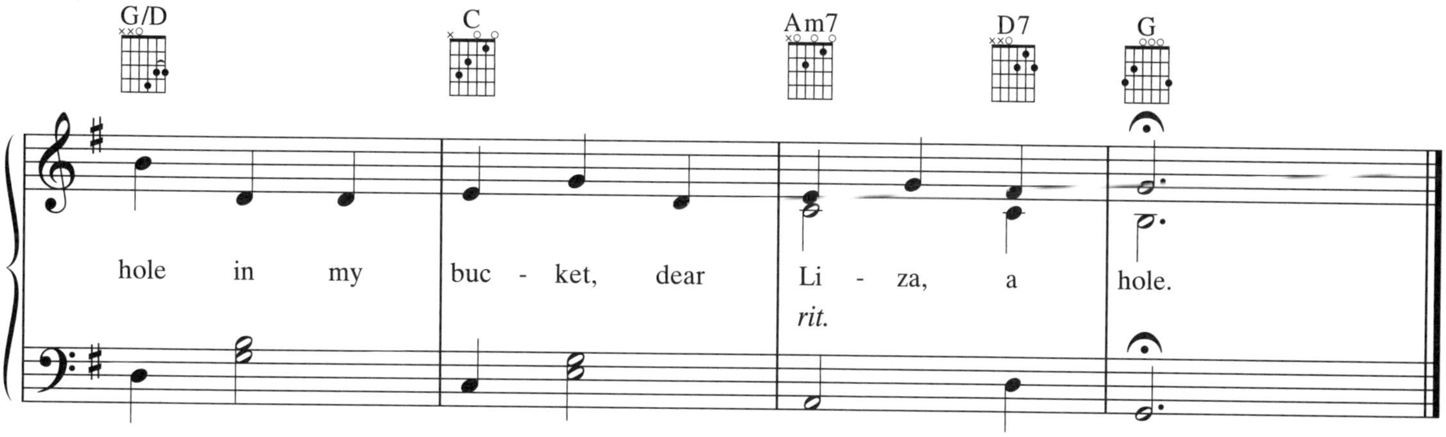
G/D
C
Am7
D7
G
hole in my buc - ket, dear Li - za, a hole.
rit.

Verse 2:
With what shall I fix it,
Dear Liza, dear Liza?
With what shall I fix it,
Dear Liza, with what?
With straw, dear Henry,
Dear Henry, dear Henry.
With straw, dear Henry,
Dear Henry, with straw.

Verse 3:
But the straw is too long,
Dear Liza, dear Liza.
But the straw is too long,
Dear Liza, too long.
Then cut it, dear Henry,
Dear Henry, dear Henry.
Then cut it, dear Henry,
Dear Henry, cut it.

Verse 4:
With what shall I cut it,
Dear Liza, dear Liza?
With what shall I cut it,
Dear Liza, with what?
With a knife, dear Henry,
Dear Henry, dear Henry.
With a knife, dear Henry,
Dear Henry, a knife.

Verse 5:
But the knife is too blunt,
Dear Liza, dear Liza.
But the knife is to blunt,
Dear Liza, too blunt.
Then sharpen it, dear Henry,
Dear Henry, dear Henry.
Then sharpen it, dear Henry,
Dear Henry, sharpen it.

Verse 6:
With what shall I sharpen it,
Dear Liza, dear Liza?
With what shall I sharpen it,
Dear Liza, with what?
With a stone, dear Henry,
Dear Henry, dear Henry.
With a stone, dear Henry,
Dear Henry, a stone.

Verse 7:
But the stone is too dry,
Dear Liza, dear Liza.
But the stone is too dry,
Dear Liza, too dry.
Then wet it, dear Henry,
Dear Henry, dear Henry.
Then wet it, dear Henry,
Dear Henry, wet it.

Verse 8:
With what shall I wet it,
Dear Liza, dear Liza?
With what shall I wet it,
Dear Liza, with what?
With water, dear Henry,
Dear Henry, dear Henry.
With water, dear Henry,
Dear Henry, with water.

Verse 9:
In what should I carry it,
Dear Liza, dear Liza?
In what should I carry it,
Dear Liza, in what?
In a bucket, dear Henry,
Dear Henry, dear Henry.
In a bucket, dear Henry,
Dear Henry, in a bucket.

This Little Light of Mine

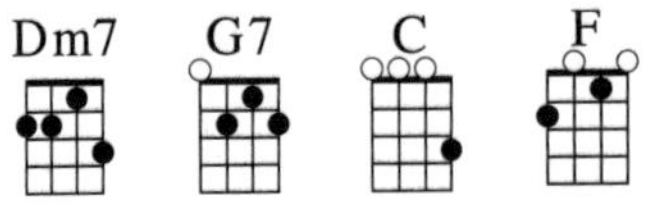
Dm7
G7
C
F

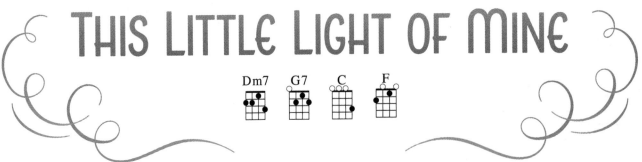

Moderately fast (𝅗𝅥 = 92)

Traditional

Dm7
G7
C
F/C
C
mf
Verses 1 & 5:
1.5. This lit - tle light of mine, I'm gon - na let it shine.
F
This lit - tle light of mine, I'm gon - na let it shine, let it
Dm7
G7
To Coda
shine, let it shine, let it shine.

Verses 2–4:
2. Won't let Sa - tan blow it out.
3. Hide it un - der a bush - el. No!
4. Let it shine 'til Je - sus comes.
I'm gon - na let it shine.
F
C
Won't let Sa - tan blow it out.
Hide it un - der a bush - el. No!
Let it shine 'til Je - sus comes.
I'm gon - na let it shine, let it
Dm7
G7
1.2.
C
F/C
C
3.
D.S 𝄋 al Coda
shine, let it shine, let it shine.
shine.
𝄌 Coda
C
F/C
C
Dm7
G7
C
shine.

THIS OLD MAN

Dm G7 C Cmaj7 C7 F Dm7(♭5) D Dmaj7 D7 G Em7(♭5) A7
Moderately bright (♩ = 160)
Traditional
mf
Dm G7 C Dm G7 C
Cmaj7 C7 F Dm7(♭5)
This old man, he played one. two. three. four. five. He played knick-knack on my thumb. shoe. knee. door. hive. With a
C/G F/A C Dm G7 C
knick-knack pad-dy wack, give the dog a bone. This old man came roll-ing home.
Dm G7 C G7 C D
1.–4.
5.

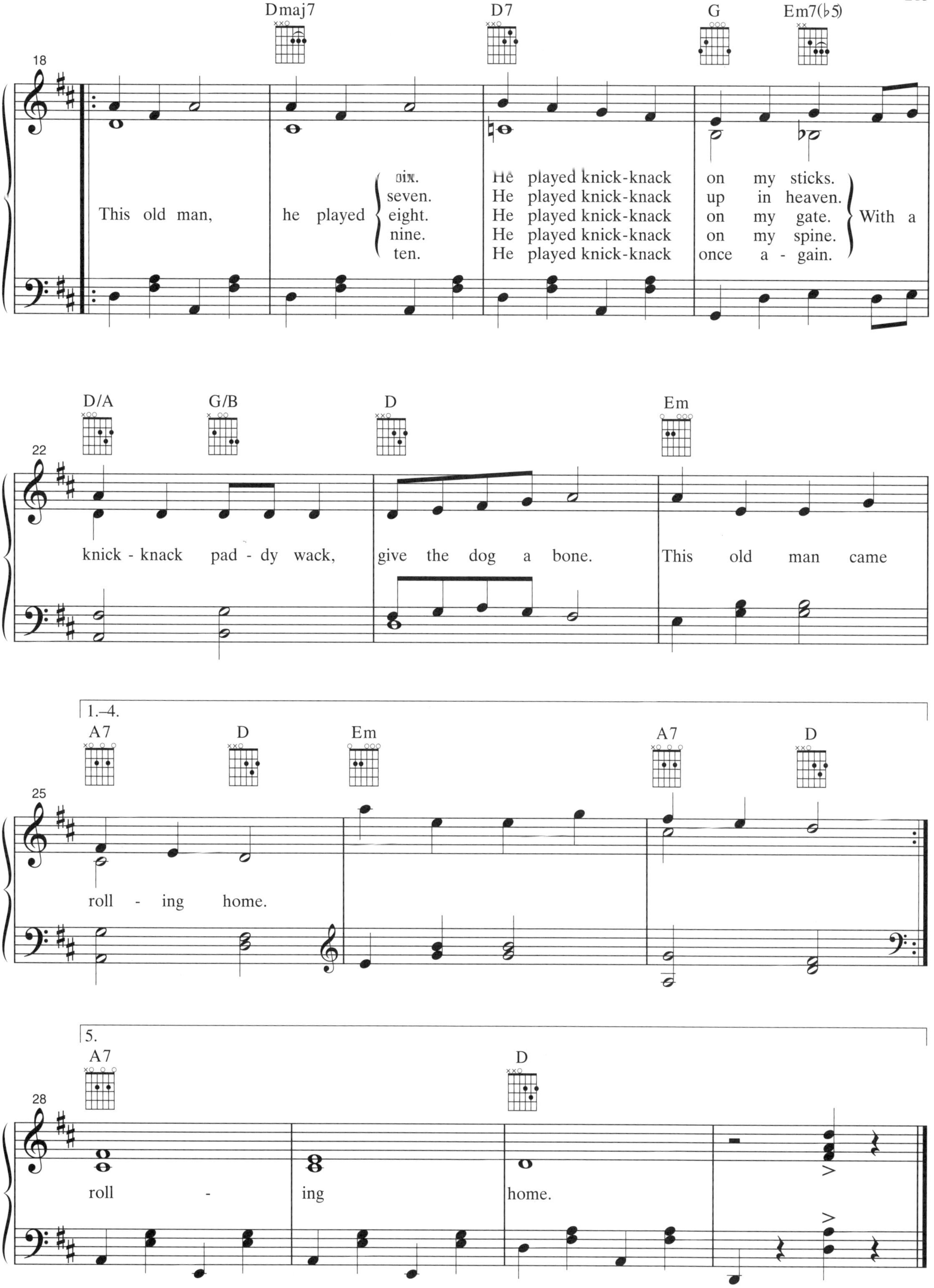
Dmaj7
D7
G
Em7(♭5)
18
This old man, he played six. He played knick-knack on my sticks.
seven. He played knick-knack up in heaven.
eight. He played knick-knack on my gate. With a
nine. He played knick-knack on my spine.
ten. He played knick-knack once a - gain.
D/A
G/B
D
Em
22
knick - knack pad - dy wack, give the dog a bone. This old man came
1.–4.
A7
D
Em
A7
D
25
roll - ing home.
5.
A7
D
28
roll - ing home.

THIS TRAIN IS A-COMIN'

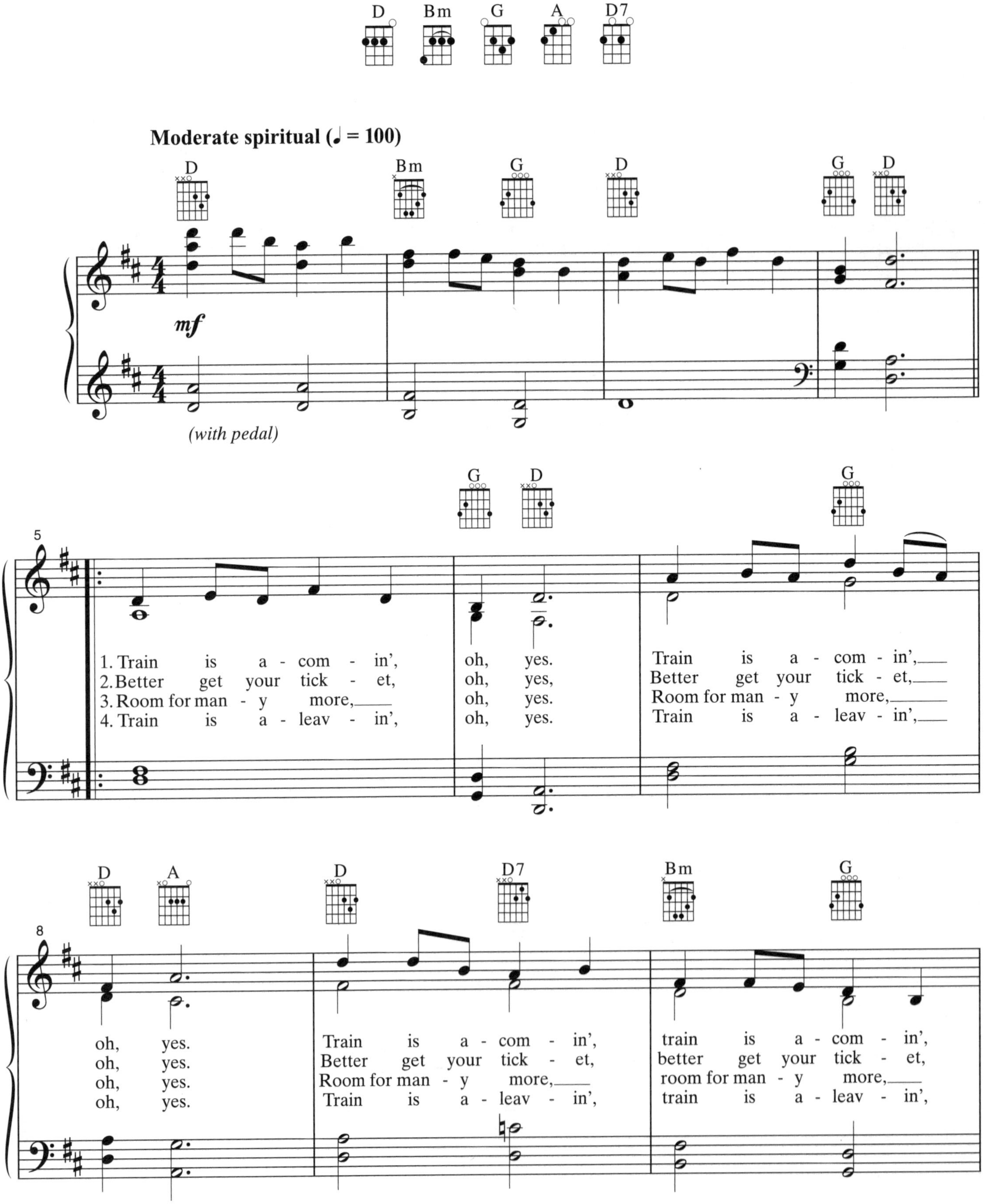
D Bm G A D7
Moderate spiritual (♩ = 100)
D Bm G D G D
mf
(with pedal)
G D G
1. Train is a - com - in', oh, yes. Train is a - com - in',
2. Better get your tick - et, oh, yes, Better get your tick - et,
3. Room for man - y more, oh, yes. Room for man - y more,
4. Train is a - leav - in', oh, yes. Train is a - leav - in',
D A D D7 Bm G
oh, yes. Train is a - com - in', train is a - com - in',
oh, yes. Better get your tick - et, better get your tick - et,
oh, yes. Room for man - y more, room for man - y more,
oh, yes. Train is a - leav - in', train is a - leav - in',

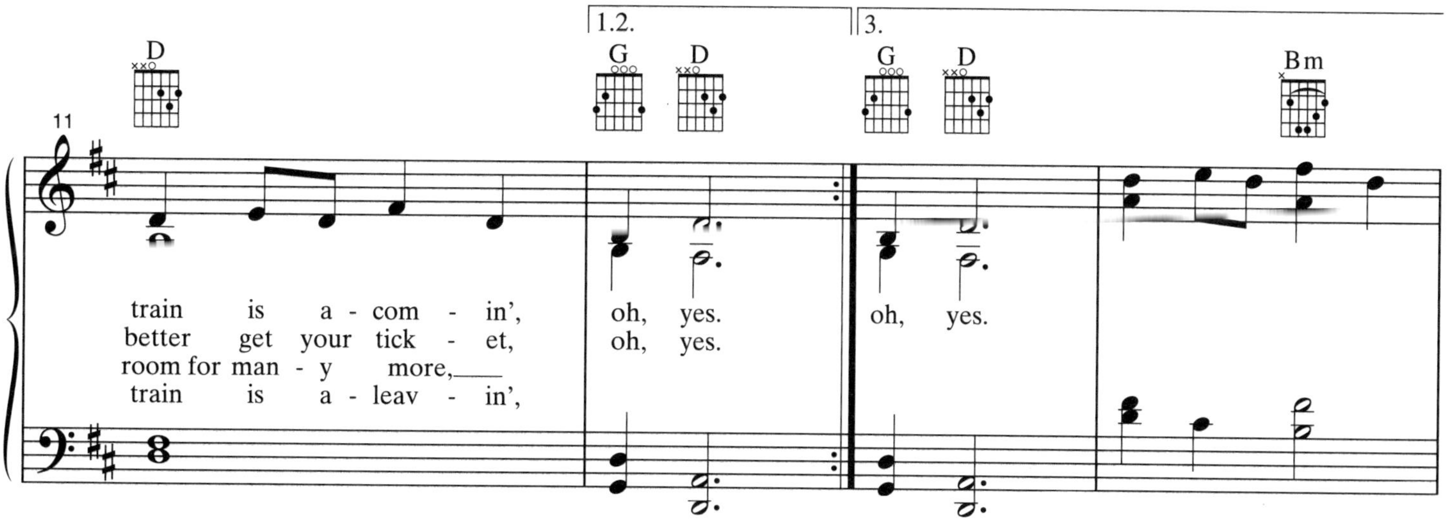
11
1.2.
3.
D
G D
G D
Bm
train is a - com - in', oh, yes. oh, yes.
better get your tick - et, oh, yes.
room for man - y more,
train is a - leav - in',

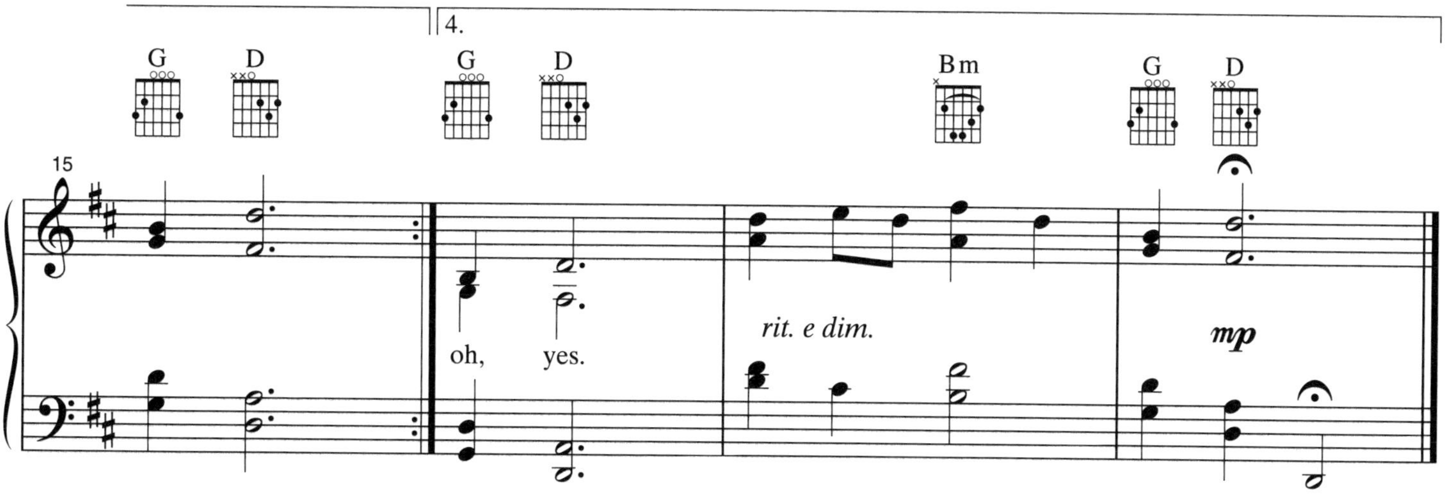
15
4.
G D
G D
Bm
G D
oh, yes.
rit. e dim.
mp

500

Three Blind Mice

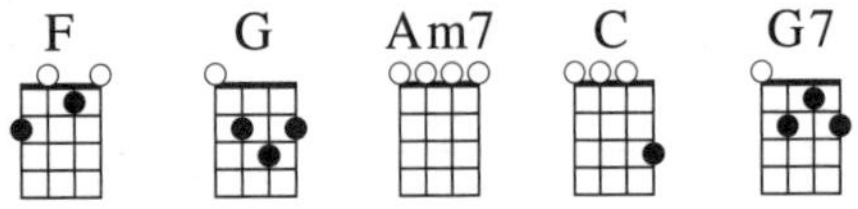
F
G
Am7
C
G7

Moderately (♩. = 84)

Words by Eliza Lee Cabot

F G Am7 C G7 C
mf
5
G7 C G7 C
Three blind mice. Three blind mice.
*For round, part 2 start here
9
G7 C G7 C
See how they run. See how they run. They

*For round, part 3 start here

G7 C G7 C
13
all ran af - ter the far - mer's wife who cut off their tails with a carv - ing knife. Did
G7 C G7 C
17
you ev - er see such a sight in your life as three blind mice?
1.
F G Am7 C G7 C
21
2.
G7 C G7 C
25
Three blind mice. Three blind mice.

Three Little Kittens

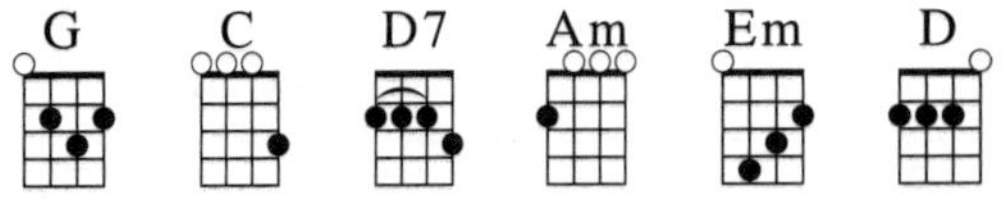
G
C
D7
Am
Em
D

Moderately (♩. = 60)

Words by Eliza Lee Cabot

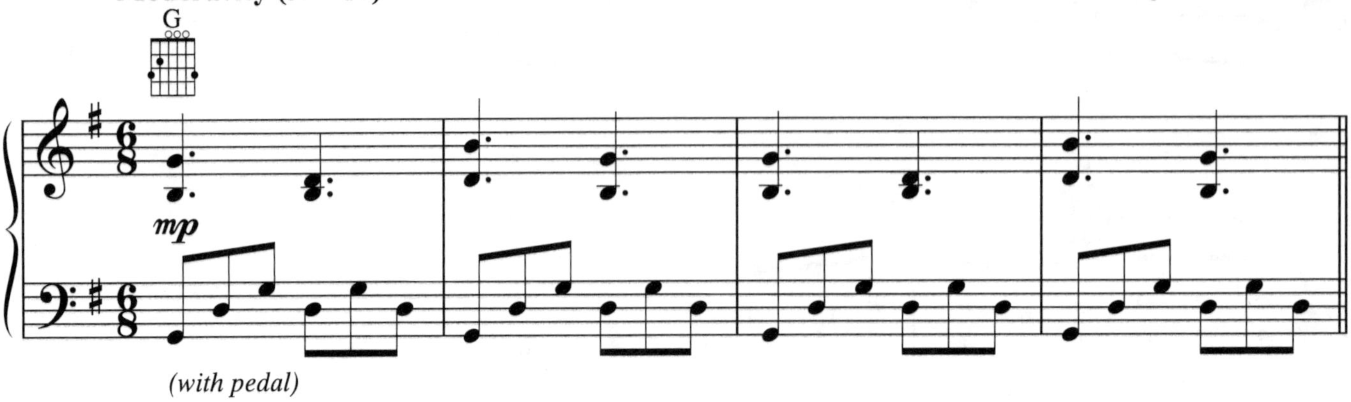
G
mp
(with pedal)

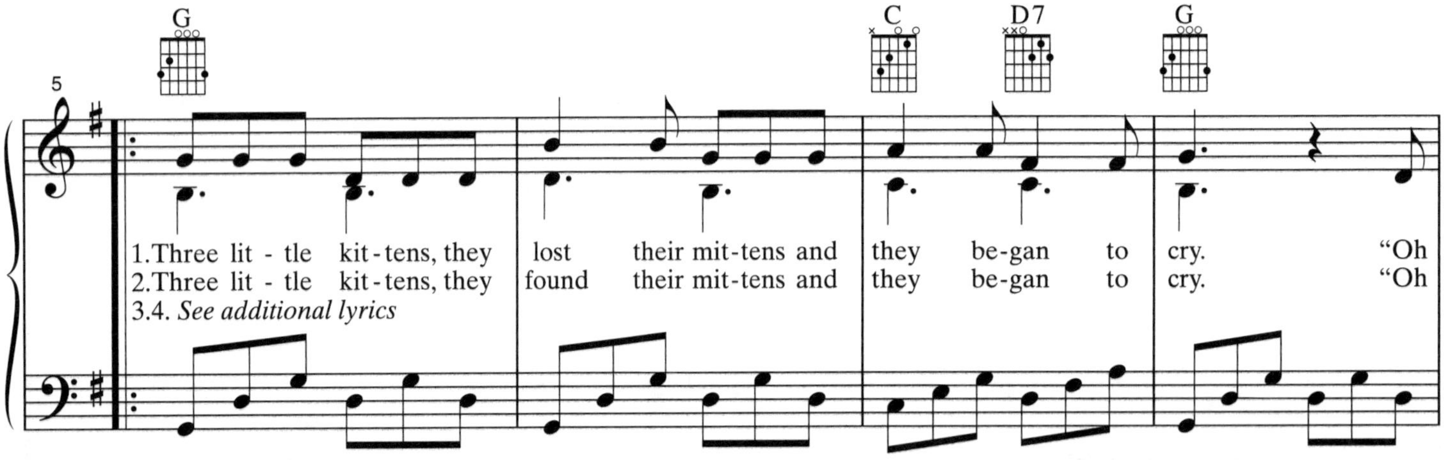
5
G
C
D7
G
1.Three lit - tle kit - tens, they lost their mit - tens and they be - gan to cry. "Oh
2.Three lit - tle kit - tens, they found their mit - tens and they be - gan to cry. "Oh
3.4. See additional lyrics

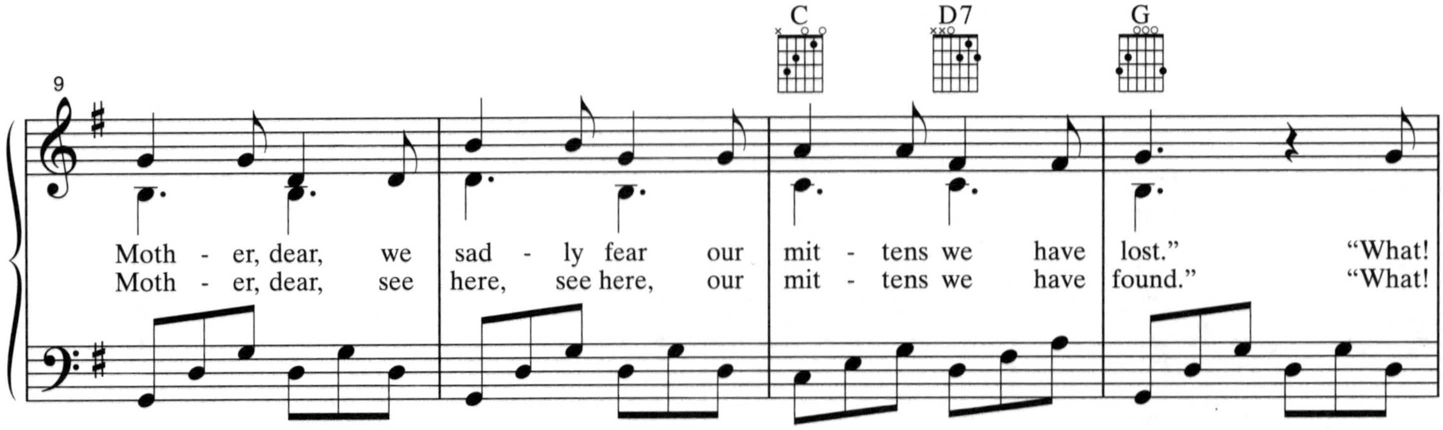
9
C
D7
G
Moth - er, dear, we sad - ly fear our mit - tens we have lost." "What!
Moth - er, dear, see here, see here, our mit - tens we have found." "What!

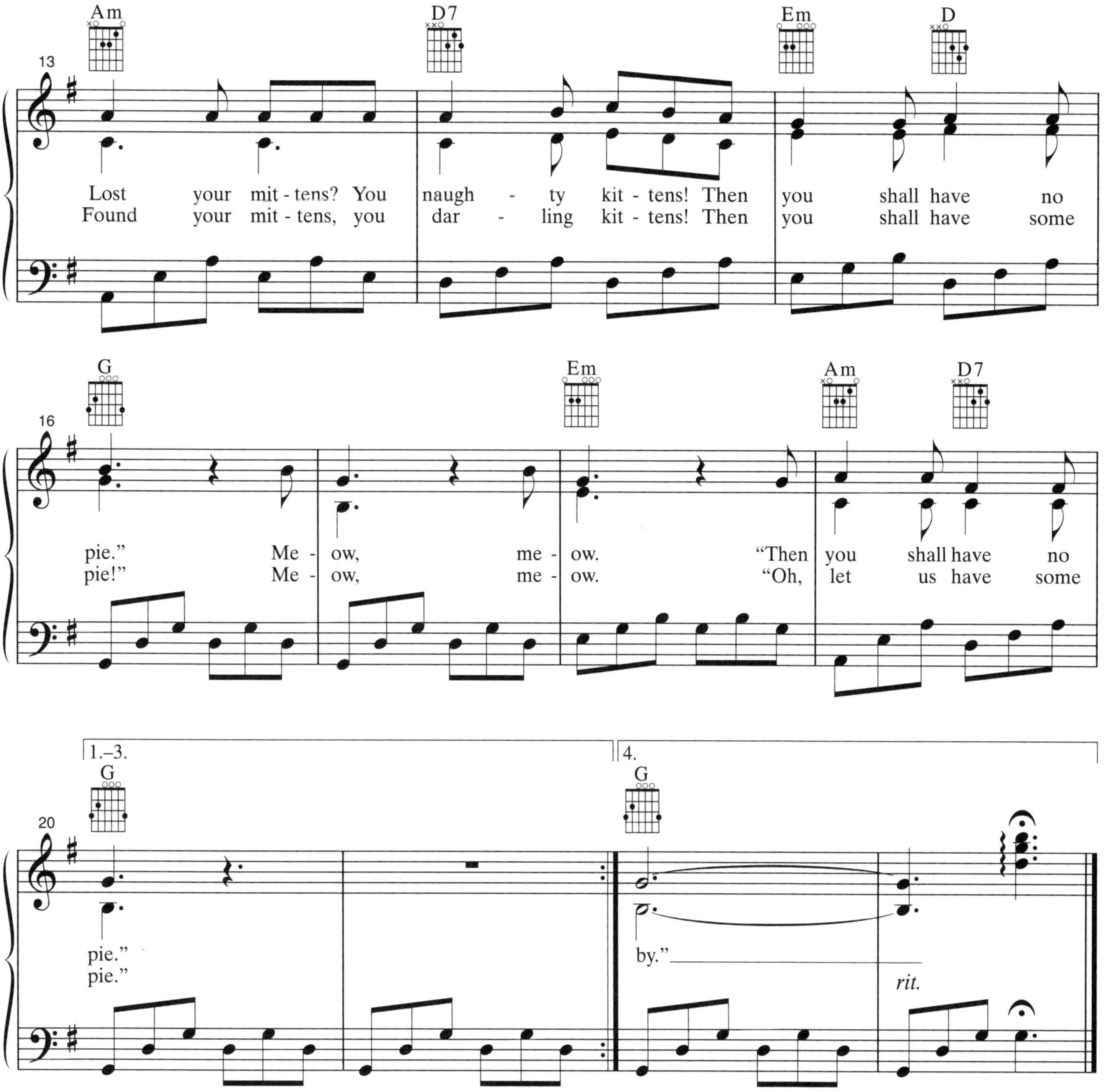
Am
D7
Em
D
13
Lost your mit - tens? You naugh - ty kit - tens! Then you shall have no
Found your mit - tens, you dar - ling kit - tens! Then you shall have some
G
Em
Am
D7
16
pie." Me - ow, me - ow. "Then you shall have no
pie!" Me - ow, me - ow. "Oh, let us have some
1.–3.
4.
G
G
20
pie."
pie."
by."
rit.

Verse 3:
Three little kittens put on their mittens
And soon ate up the pie.
"Oh Mother, dear, we greatly fear
Our mittens we have soiled."
"What? Soiled your mittens?
You naughty kittens!"
Then they began to sigh.
Meow, meow.
Then they began to sigh.

Verse 4:
Three little kittens, they washed their mittens
And hung them out to dry.
"Oh Mother, dear, look here, look here,
Our mittens we have washed."
"What? Washed your mittens?
Then you're good kittens!
But I smell a rat close by."
Meow, meow.
"We smell a rat close by."

A-Tisket, A-Tasket

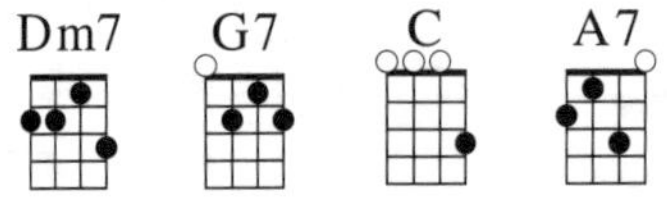
Dm7
G7
C
A7

Moderately (𝅗𝅥 = 84)

Traditional

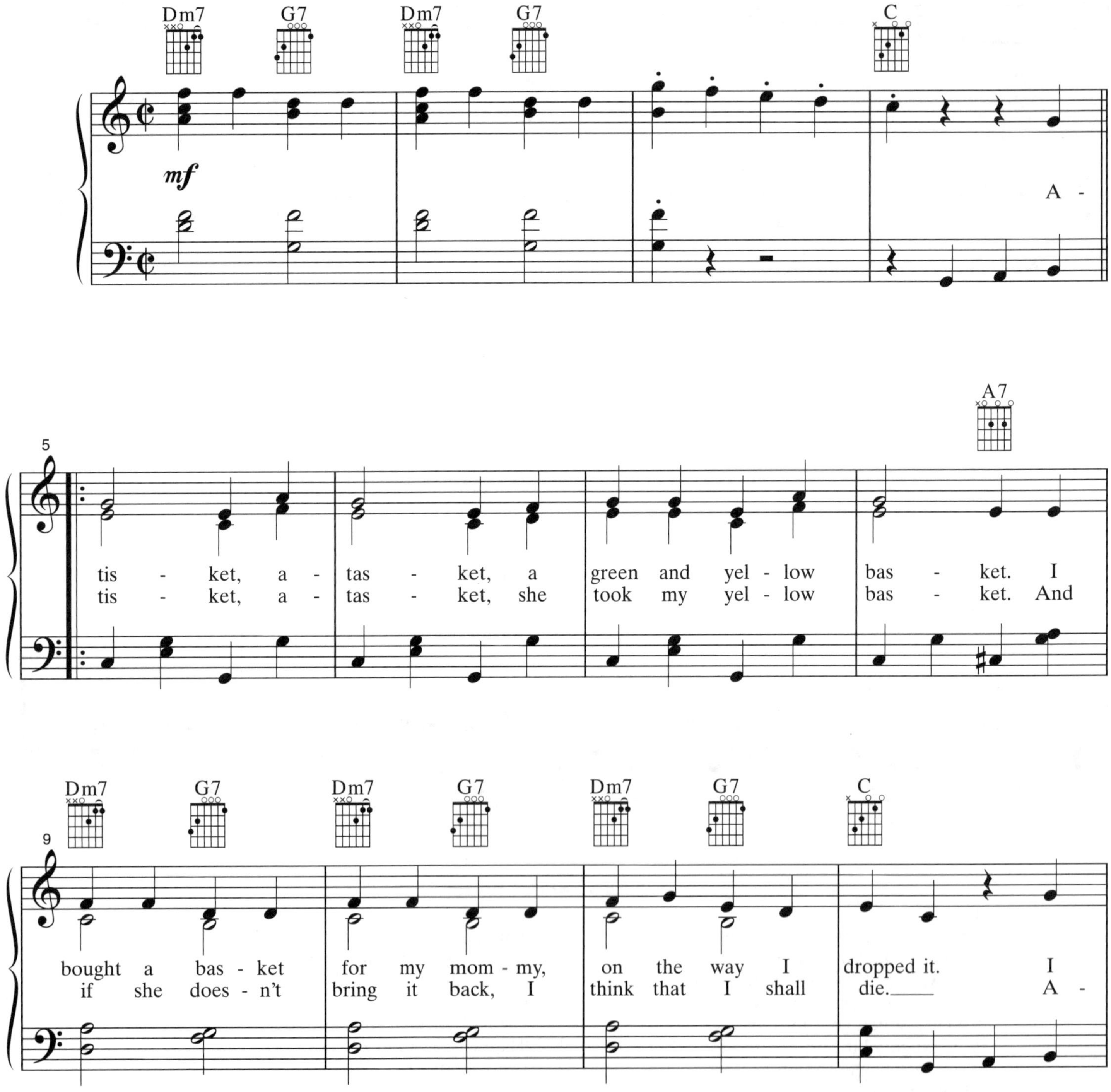
Dm7 G7 Dm7 G7 C
mf
A -
A7
tis - ket, a - tas - ket, a green and yel - low bas - ket. I
tis - ket, a - tas - ket, she took my yel - low bas - ket. And
Dm7 G7 Dm7 G7 Dm7 G7 C
bought a bas - ket for my mom - my, on the way I dropped it. I
if she does - n't bring it back, I think that I shall die.___ A -

13
A7
dropped it, I dropped it. Yes, on the way, I dropped it. A
tis - ket, a - tas - ket, a green and yel - low bas - ket. I
17
Dm7 G7 Dm7 G7 Dm7 G7
1.
C
lit - tle girl - y picked it up and took it to the mar - ket. A -
bought a bas - ket for my mom - my, on the way I
2.
C
21
Dm7 G7 Dm7 G7 C
dropped it.

To Market, to Market

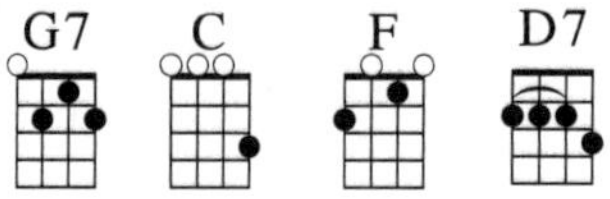
G7
C
F
D7

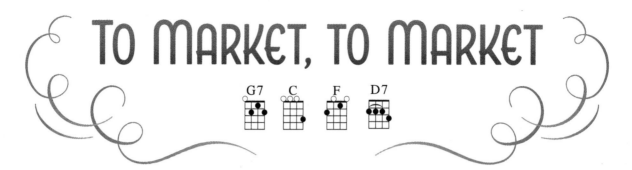

Moderate waltz tempo, in one (𝅗𝅥. = 48) (♩ = 144)
Traditional
G7
C
G7
C
mf
(with pedal)
1. To
mar - ket, to mar - ket to buy a fat pig.
mar - ket, to mar - ket to buy a float cake.
F
C
Home a - gain, home a - gain,
Home a - gain, home a - gain,
D7
G7
C
jig - ge - ty - jig. To mar - ket, to mar - ket to
mar - ket is late. To mar - ket, to mar - ket to

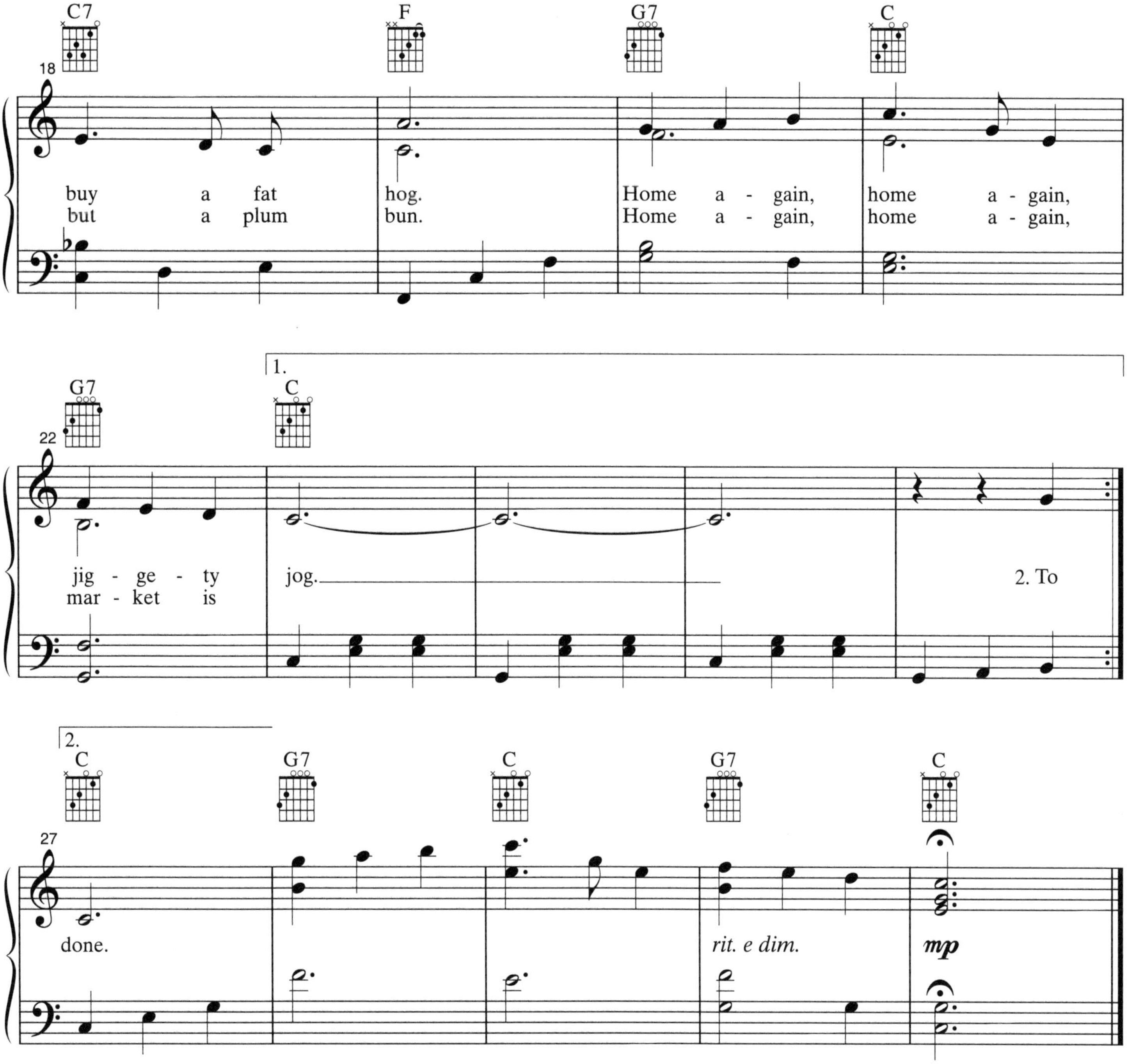
C7 F G7 C
buy a fat hog. Home a - gain, home a - gain,
but a plum bun. Home a - gain, home a - gain,
G7 C
jig - ge - ty jog.
mar - ket is
2. To
C G7 C G7 C
done.
rit. e dim.
mp

The Twelve Days of Christmas

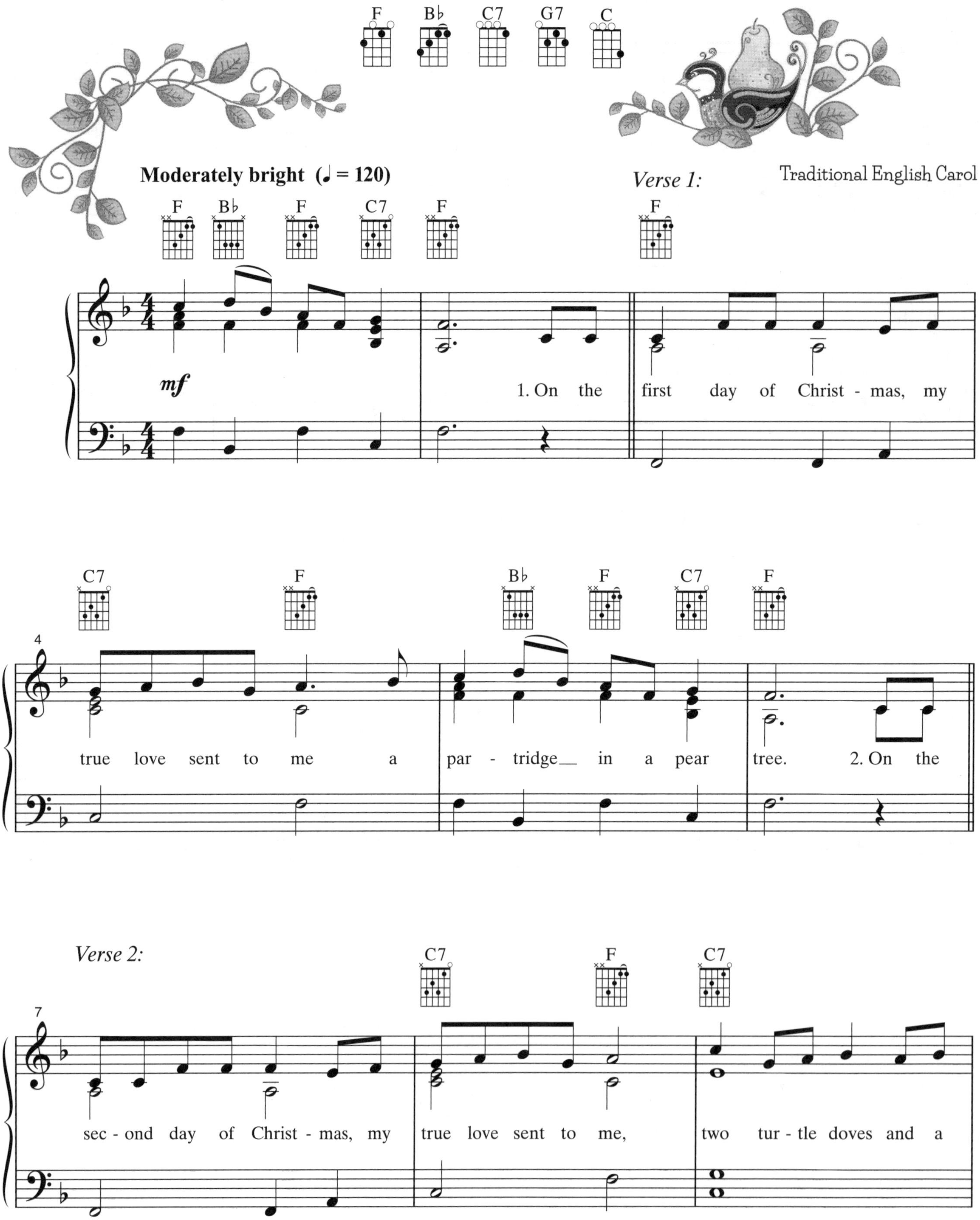
F B♭ C7 G7 C
Moderately bright (♩ = 120)
Verse 1:
Traditional English Carol
F B♭ F C7 F F
mf
1. On the first day of Christ - mas, my
C7 F B♭ F C7 F
4
true love sent to me a par - tridge__ in a pear tree. 2. On the
Verse 2:
C7 F C7
7
sec - ond day of Christ - mas, my true love sent to me, two tur - tle doves and a

F Bb F C7 F
Verse 3:
10
par - tridge__ in a pear tree. 3. On the third day of Christ - mas, my
C7 F C7
13
true love sent to me, three French__ hens, two tur - tle doves and a
F Bb F C7 F
Verse 4:
16
par - tridge__ in a pear tree. 4. On the fourth day of Christ - mas, my
C7 F C7
19
true love sent to me, four call - ing birds, three French__ hens,

F Bb F C7 F
22
two tur - tle doves and a par - tridge in a pear tree. 5. On the
Verse 5:
C7 F G7
25
fifth day of Christ - mas, my true love sent to me, five gold - en
C F Bb
28
rings, four call - ing birds, three French hens,
G7 C7 F Bb F C7 F
31
two tur - tle doves and a par - tridge in a pear tree. 6. On the

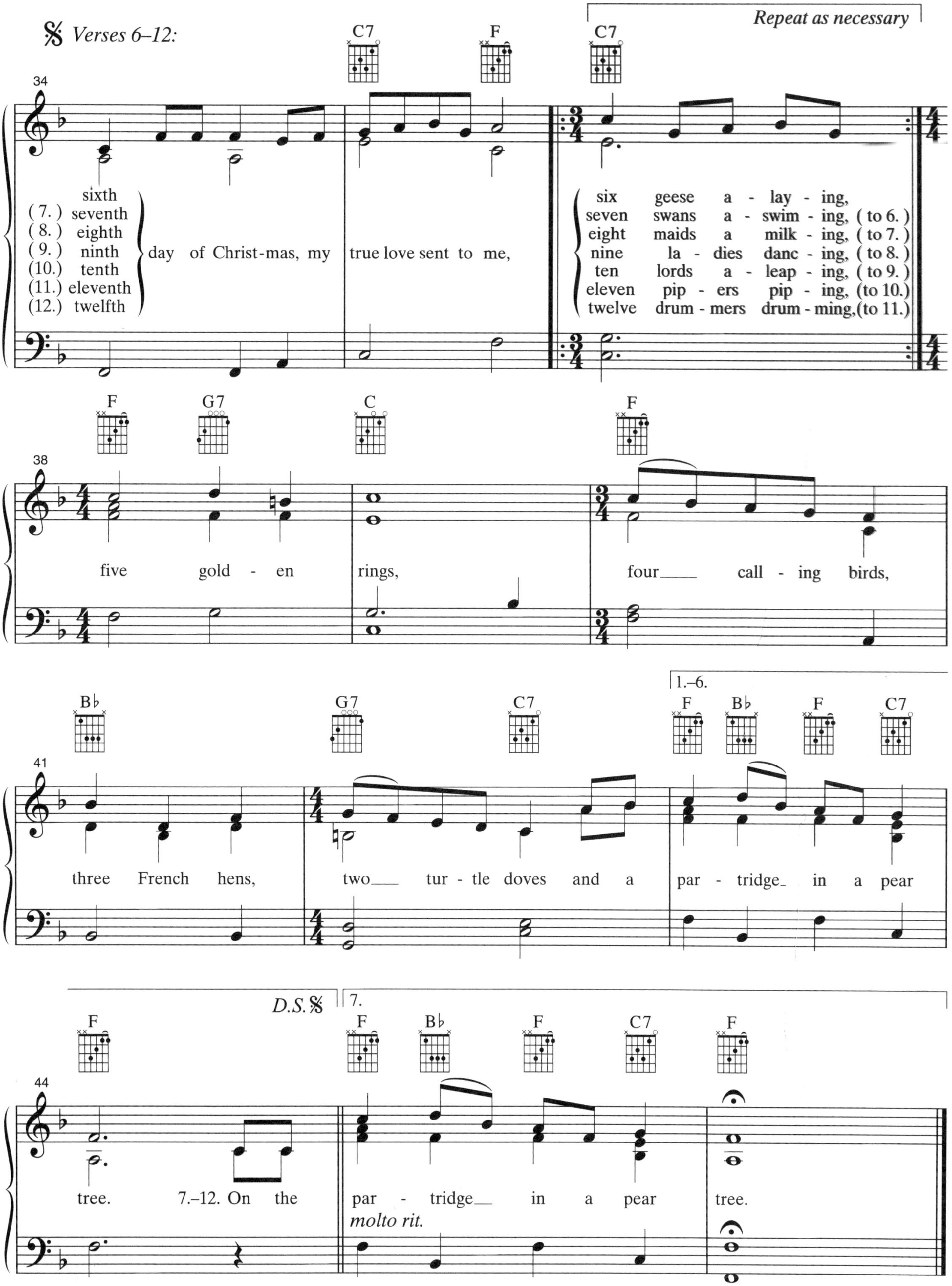
Verses 6–12:
Repeat as necessary
C7 F C7
34
sixth
(7.) seventh
(8.) eighth
(9.) ninth
(10.) tenth
(11.) eleventh
(12.) twelfth
day of Christ-mas, my true love sent to me,
six geese a - lay - ing,
seven swans a - swim - ing, (to 6.)
eight maids a milk - ing, (to 7.)
nine la - dies danc - ing, (to 8.)
ten lords a - leap - ing, (to 9.)
eleven pip - ers pip - ing, (to 10.)
twelve drum - mers drum - ming, (to 11.)
F G7 C F
38
five gold - en rings, four call - ing birds,
B♭ G7 C7
1.–6.
F B♭ F C7
41
three French hens, two tur - tle doves and a par - tridge in a pear
D.S. 𝄋
7.
F F B♭ F C7 F
44
tree. 7.–12. On the par - tridge in a pear tree.
molto rit.

Twinkle, Twinkle, Little Star

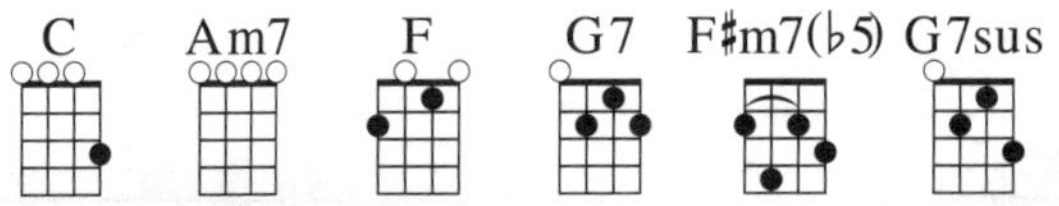
C
Am7
F
G7
F♯m7(♭5)
G7sus

Slowly (♩ = 84)

Words by Jane Taylor

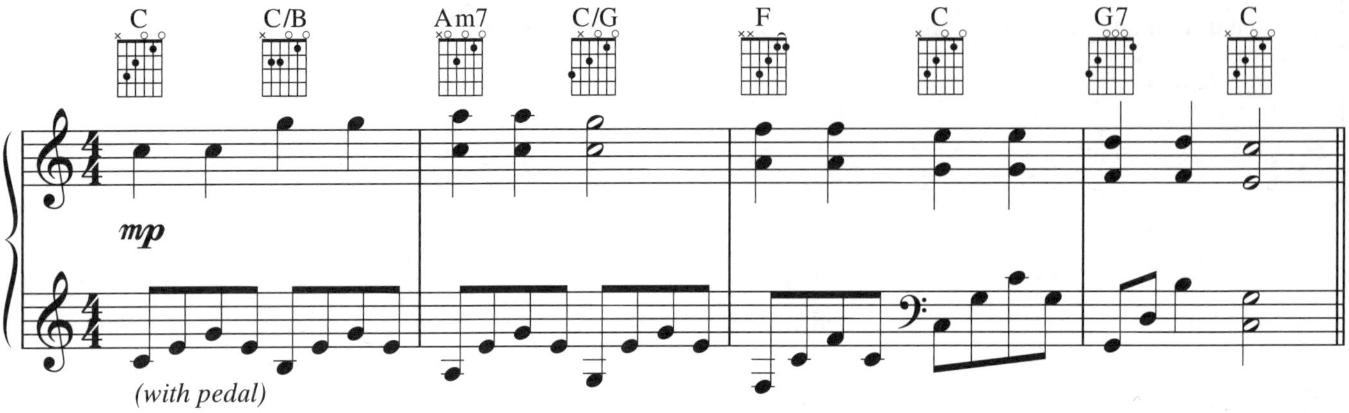
C
C/B
Am7
C/G
F
C
G7
C
mp
(with pedal)

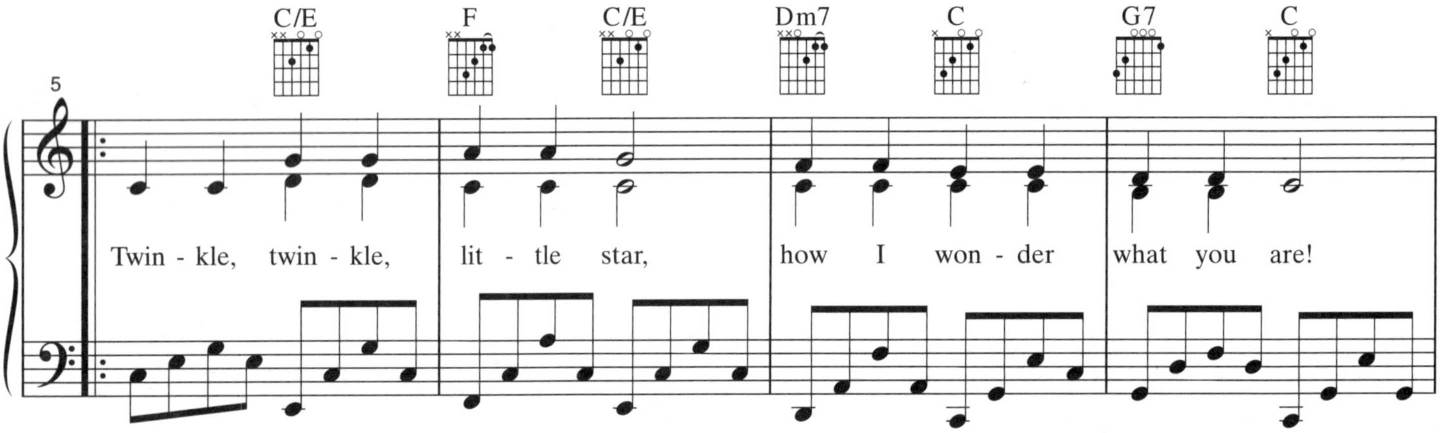
5
C/E
F
C/E
Dm7
C
G7
C
Twin - kle, twin - kle, lit - tle star, how I won - der what you are!

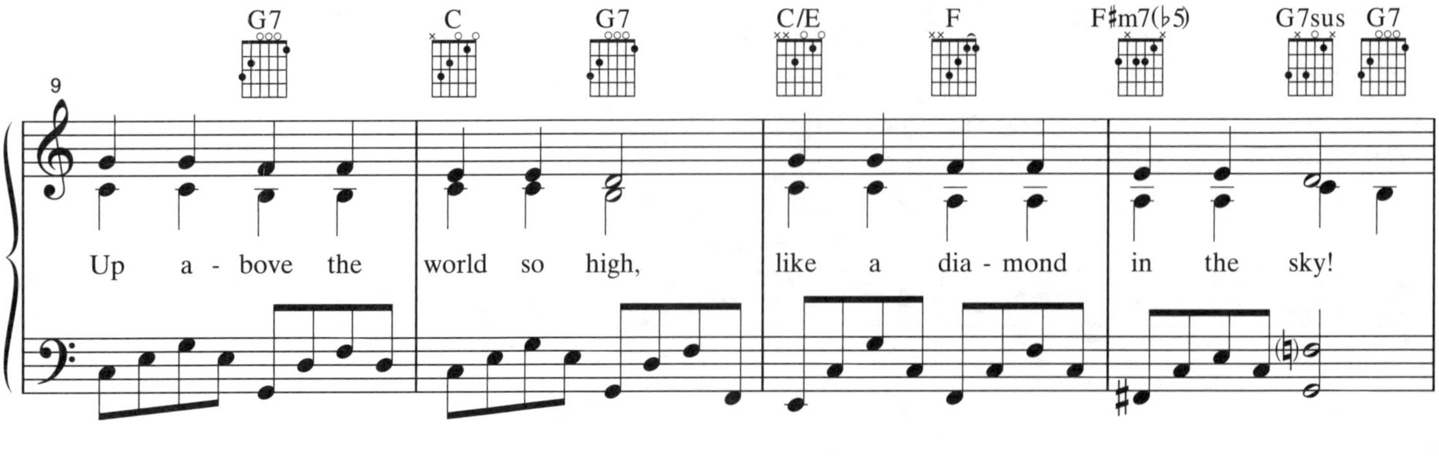
9
G7
C
G7
C/E
F
F♯m7(♭5)
G7sus
G7
Up a - bove the world so high, like a dia - mond in the sky!

C C/E F C/E Dm7 C7 G7 C
13
Twin - kle, twin - kle, lit - tle star, how I won - der what you are!
1.
F C G7 C
17
2.
C/B
Am7 C/G F C G7 C
20
rit.

Waltzing Matilda

D
Bm7
Em7
A7
F#7
Bm
G

Moderately (♩ = 100)
Verse:
Traditional
mf
1. Once a jol - ly swag - man
2.–4. See additional lyrics
camped be - side a bil - la - bong
un - der the shade of a
cool - i - bah tree. And he
sang as he watched and
wait - ed till his bil - ly boiled.
"Who'll come a - waltz - ing, Ma -
til - da, with me."
Chorus:
"Waltz - ing Ma - til - da,
2.–4. See additional lyrics
waltz - ing Ma - til - da,

D
A7
D
F♯7
13
you'll come a-waltz - ing, Ma - til - da, with me." And he sang as he watched and
Bm
G
D
Bm7
1.–3.
Em7
A7
D
Bm7
16
wait-ed till his bil-ly boiled. "You'll come a-waltz - ing, Ma - til - da, with me.
Em7
A7
D
4.
Em7
A7
D
Bm7
Em7
A7
D
20
til - da with me.
rit. e dim.
mp

Verse 2:
Down came a jumbuck to drink at the billabong.
Up jumped the swagman and grabbed him with glee.
And he sang as he shoved that jumbuck in his tucker bag.
"You'll come a-waltzing, Matilda, with me."
(To Chorus 2:)

Chorus 2:
"Waltzing Matilda, waltzing Matilda,
You'll come a-waltzing, Matilda, with me."
And he sang as he shoved that jumbuck in his tucker bag.
"You'll come a-waltzing, Matilda, with me."

Verse 3:
Up rode the squatter, mounted on his thoroughbred.
Down came the troopers, one, two, three.
"Whose is that jumbuck you've got in your tucker bag?
You'll come a-waltzing, Matilda, with me."
(To Chorus 3:)

Chorus 3:
"Waltzing Matilda, waltzing Matilda,
You'll come a-waltzing, Matilda, with me."
"Whose is that jumbuck you've got in your tucker bag?
You'll come a-waltzing, Matilda, with me."

Verse 4:
Up jumped the swagman and sprang into the billabong.
"You'll never take me alive," said he.
And his ghost may be heard as you pass by that billabong.
"Who'll come a-waltzing, Matilda, with me."
(To Chorus 4:)

Chorus 4:
"Waltzing Matilda, waltzing Matilda,
You'll come a-waltzing, Matilda, with me."
And his ghost may be heard as you pass by that billabong.
"You'll come a-waltzing, Matilda, with me."

We Wish You a Merry Christmas

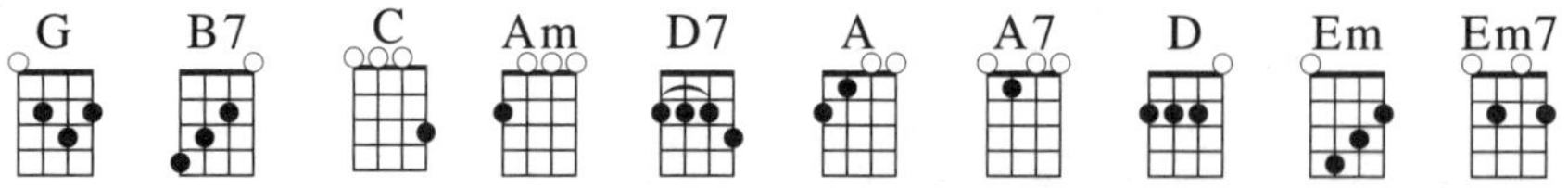
G
B7
C
Am
D7
A
A7
D
Em
Em7

Joyfully (♩ = 122)

Traditional English Folk Song

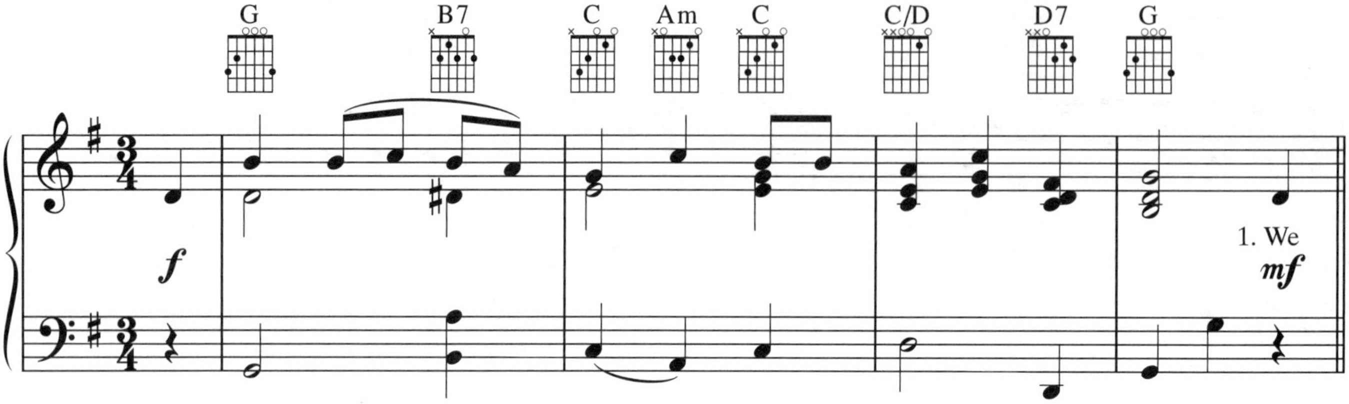
G
B7
C
Am
C
C/D
D7
G
f
1. We
mf

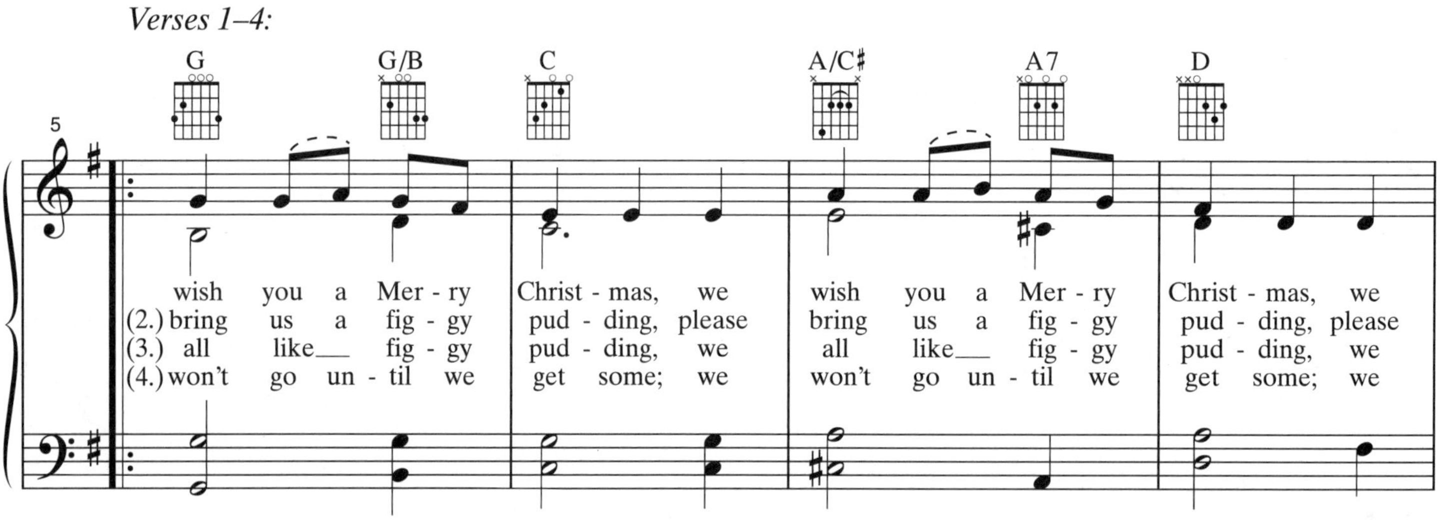
Verses 1–4:
G
G/B
C
A/C♯
A7
D
5
wish you a Mer - ry Christ - mas, we wish you a Mer - ry Christ - mas, we
(2.) bring us a fig - gy pud - ding, please bring us a fig - gy pud - ding, please
(3.) all like___ fig - gy pud - ding, we all like___ fig - gy pud - ding, we
(4.) won't go un - til we get some; we won't go un - til we get some; we

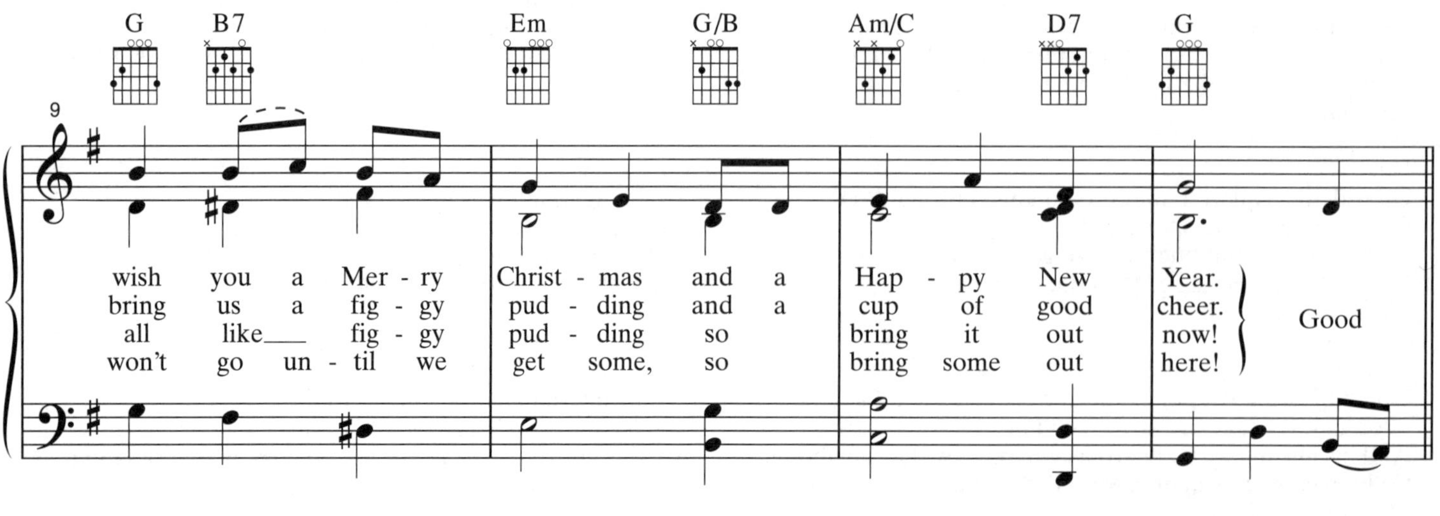
G
B7
Em
G/B
Am/C
D7
G
9
wish you a Mer - ry Christ - mas and a Hap - py New Year.
bring us a fig - gy pud - ding and a cup of good cheer.
all like___ fig - gy pud - ding so bring it out now!
won't go un - til we get some, so bring some out here!
Good

Chorus:
D Em A D G D Em7
13
tid - ings we bring to you and your kin, good tid - ings for
D G C D7 G G
1.–3. 4.
18
Christ - mas and a Hap - py New Year. 2. Oh, 3. We 4. We Year. 5. We
Verse 5:
G G/B C A/C♯ A7 D
22
wish you a Mer - ry Christ - mas, we wish you a Mer - ry Christ - mas, we
G B7 Em G/B Am/C D7 G
26
wish you a Mer - ry Christ - mas and a Hap - py New Year.
rit.

The Wheels on the Bus

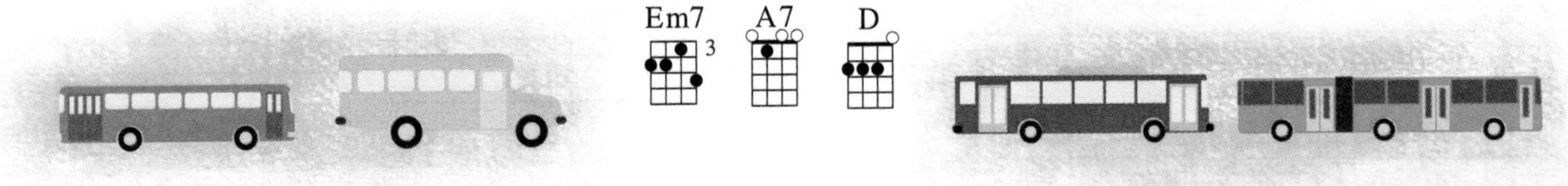
Em7
A7
D
3

By Thomas Arne

Moderately (𝅗𝅥 = 72)
Em7
A7
D
mf
1. The
wheels on the bus go
doors on the bus go
wipers on the bus go
4
A7
D
'round and 'round,
open and shut,
swish, swish, swish,
'round and 'round,
open and shut,
swish, swish, swish,
'round and 'round. The
open and shut. The
swish, swish, swish. The
wheels on the bus go
doors on the bus go
wipers on the bus go
8
Em7
A7
1.–3.
D
Em7
A7
'round and 'round
open and shut
swish, swish, swish
all through the
all through the
all through the
town.
town.
town.

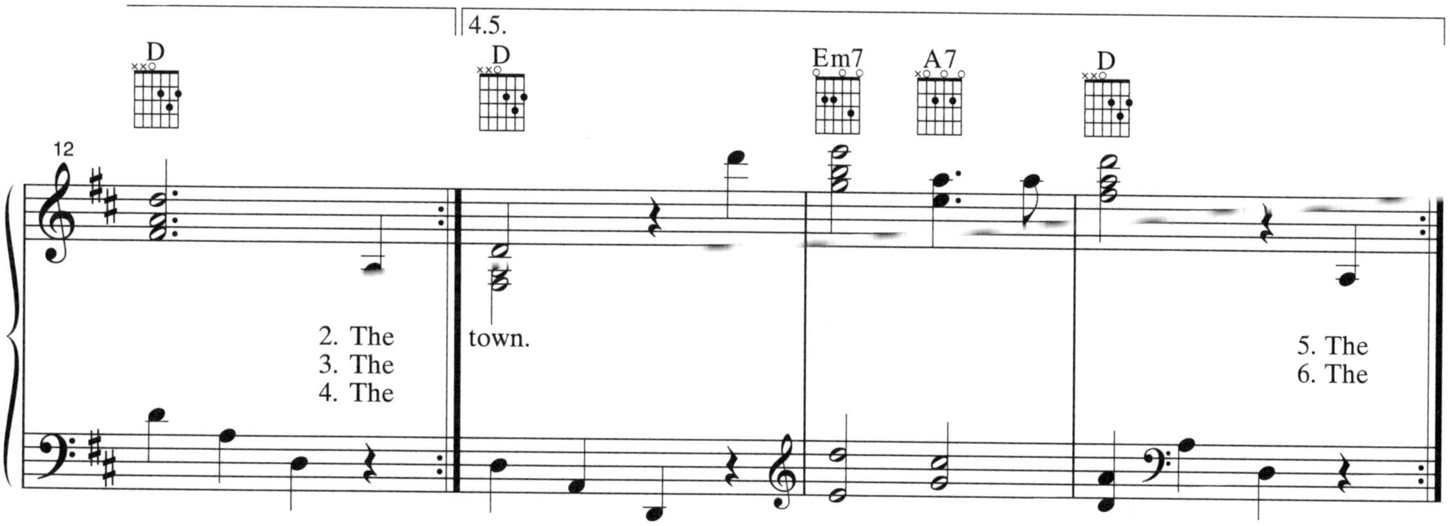
4.5.
D
D
Em7
A7
D
12
2. The
3. The
4. The
town.
5. The
6. The

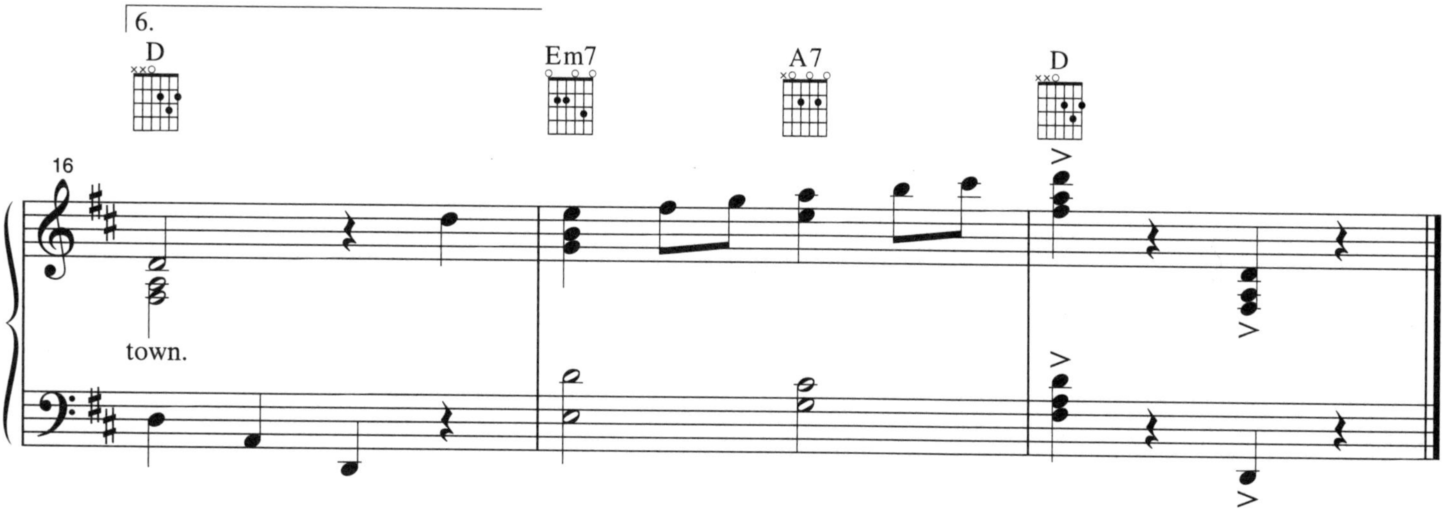
6.
D
Em7
A7
D
16
town.

Verse 4:
The horn on the bus goes beep, beep, beep,
Beep, beep, beep, beep, beep, beep.
The horn on the bus goes beep, beep, beep
All through the town.

Verse 5:
The windows on the bus go up and down,
Up and down, up and down,
The windows on the bus go up and down
All through the town.

Verse 6:
The driver on bus waves goodbye,
Waves goodbye, waves goodbye.
The driver on bus waves goodbye
All through the town.

When Johnny Comes Marching Home

Em B7 G
Moderate march (♩. = 84)
Traditional
Em B7 Em B7 Em B7 Em
mf
1. When
5
G
John - ny comes march - ing home a - gain, hur - rah! Hur -
old church bell will peal with joy, hur - ray! Hur -
3.4. See additional lyrics
8
Em
rah! We'll give him a heart - y wel - come then, hur -
rah! To wel - come home our dar - ling boy, hur -
11
G
rah! Hur - rah! Oh, the men will cheer and the
rah! Hur - rah! The vil - lage lads and

B7
Em
B7
14
boys will shout, the la - dies they will all turn out. And we'll
las - sies gay with ros - es they will strew the way, and we'll
Em
B7
Em
B7
Em
B7
17
all feel gay when John - ny comes march - ing
all feel gay when John - ny comes march - ing
Em
1.–3.
B7
Em
20
home.
home.
2. The
4.
B7
Em
B7
Em
B7
Em
23
rit.

Verse 3:
Get ready for a jubilee, hurrah! Hurrah!
We'll give the hero three times three, hurrah! Hurrah!
The laurel wreath is ready now to put in place on his loyal brow,
And we'll all feel gay when Johnny comes marching home.

Verse 4:
Let love and friendship on that day, hurrah! Hurrah!
Their choicest pleasures on display, hurrah! Hurrah!
And let each one perform some part, to fill with joy the warrior's heart,
And we'll all feel gay when Johnny comes marching home.

Yankee Doodle

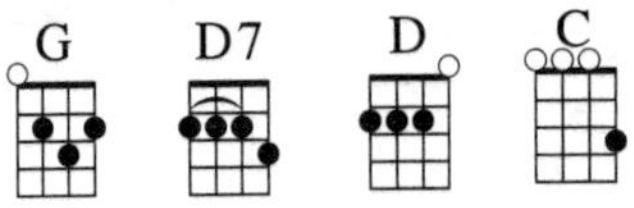
G
D7
D
C

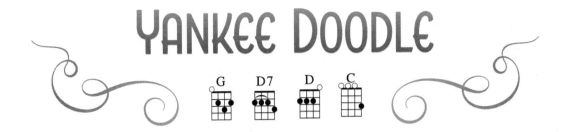

Traditional

Moderate march (♩ = 96)

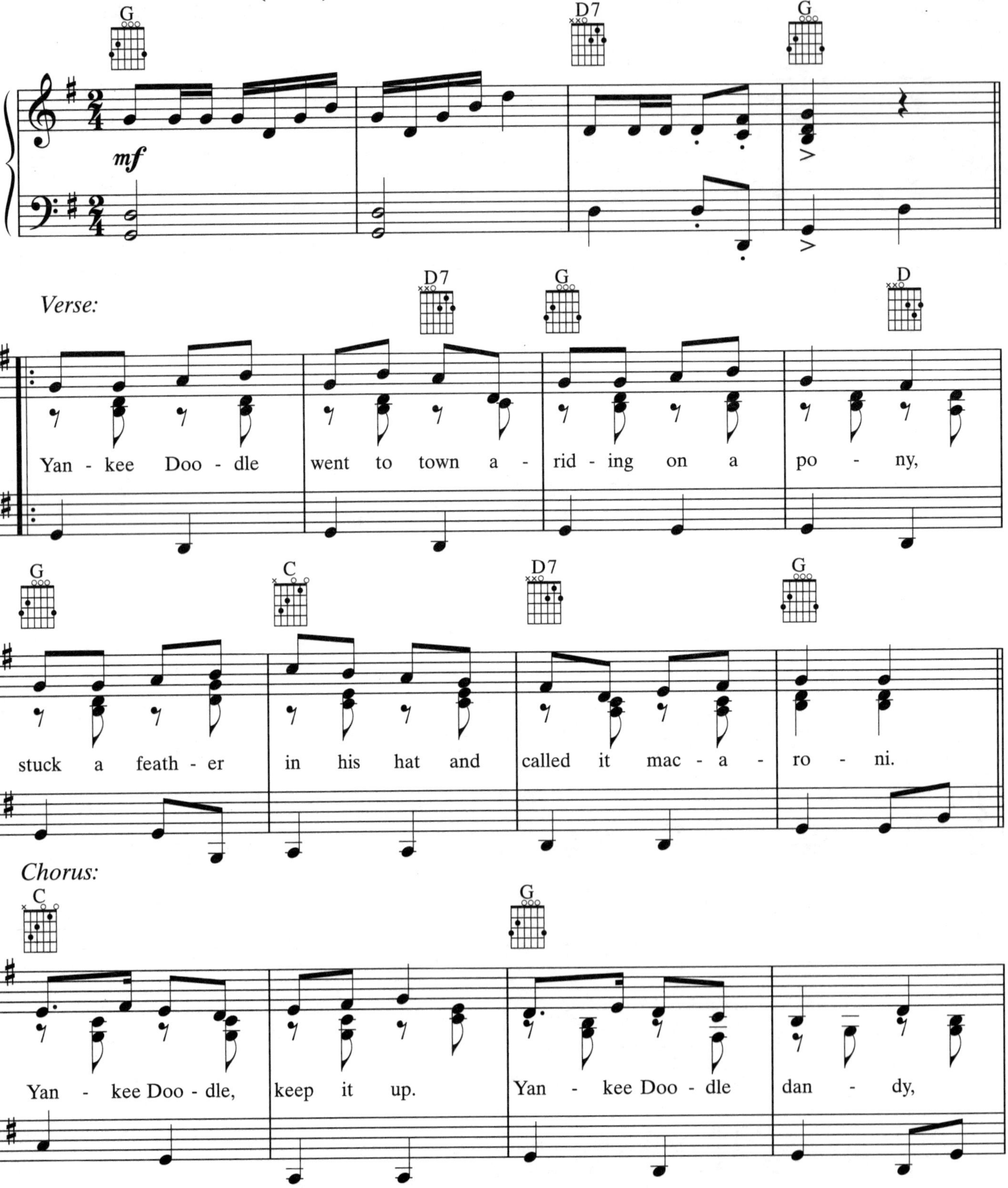
G
D7
G
mf
Verse:
D7
G
D
Yan - kee Doo - dle went to town a - rid - ing on a po - ny,
G
C
D7
G
stuck a feath - er in his hat and called it mac - a - ro - ni.
Chorus:
C
G
Yan - kee Doo - dle, keep it up. Yan - kee Doo - dle dan - dy,

1.
C
G
D7
G
17
mind the mu - sic and the step and with the girls be han - dy.
D7
G
21
2.
G
D7
G
25
han - dy.
f